GILL SHAW

CANAL BOAT LIVES

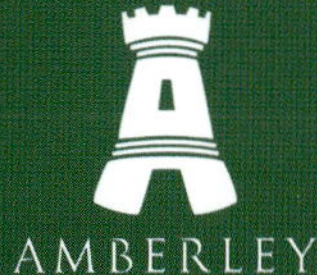

AMBERLEY

ACKNOWLEDGEMENTS

Thank you to my wonderful family and friends for their support creating this book. A special thank you to Judy Head without whom I would not have known where to start with *Canal Boat Lives*, Charlie Parker Oakenhurst Aircraft Services Ltd, Kevan Bishop Aeropeople Ltd, Jill Fountain at Digitalab Professional Photography Lab, James Gilbert at Fuji Professional, Andy Sands at Chiswick Camera Centre, Ray Lowe at MPA & RPS, Sr Liza Randall, Kevin Carr & James Pilgrim at Resolution Print & Design, Susan Bookbinder at Zamala, Mairi Hughes & Angela Linforth at *This England* magazine, Felicity Wilson at BEMER and all the girls at 'A Cut Above', Ealing.

And to everyone who was brave enough to have their photograph taken and allowed me to have a glimpse into their really interesting lives aboard a canal boat.

A special thank you to Gyles Brandreth for writing the foreword – Gyles thank you for your very special words.

First published 2023

Amberley Publishing
The Hill, Stroud
Gloucestershire, GL5 4EP

www.amberley-books.com

Copyright © Gill Shaw, 2023

The right of Gill Shaw to be identified as the Author of this work has been asserted in accordance with the Copyrights, Designs and Patents Act 1988.

ISBN 978 1 3981 2067 9 (print)
ISBN 978 1 3981 2068 6 (ebook)

All rights reserved. No part of this book may be reprinted or reproduced or utilised in any form or by any electronic, mechanical or other means, now known or hereafter invented, including photocopying and recording, or in any information storage or retrieval system, without the permission in writing from the Publishers.

British Library Cataloguing in Publication Data.
A catalogue record for this book is available from the British Library.

Typesetting by SJmagic DESIGN SERVICES, India.
Printed in the UK.

ABOUT THE PHOTOGRAPHER

Gill Shaw AMPA ARPS has been a celebrity and people photographer for over twenty-five years. She is in her element in all situations – at the Palace with the royals, at a church covering a wedding, or with the local people on a remote island in Africa. Gill has worked with royals, celebrities, presidents, prime ministers and of course mostly the general public, and she is very passionate about her work and loves putting her subjects at ease. She is an Associate of the Master Photographers Association and Royal Photographic Association. Examples of Gill's work can be seen here: http://www.gillshaw.co.uk/.

Although Gill is very committed to her work, she still finds time to use her talents to raise much-needed funds for charities. She is a trustee of WellFound, which works to bring clean water to remote communities in Africa. She is a patron of Help for Heroes, the leading Armed Forces and veterans' charity in the UK. She has also supported the Society of Stars, Mane Chance Sanctuary, the Caron Keating Foundation and Support for Africa to name but a few. Her two books so far have raised hundreds of thousands of pounds to help children with cerebral palsy and our wonderful inspirational wounded soldiers.

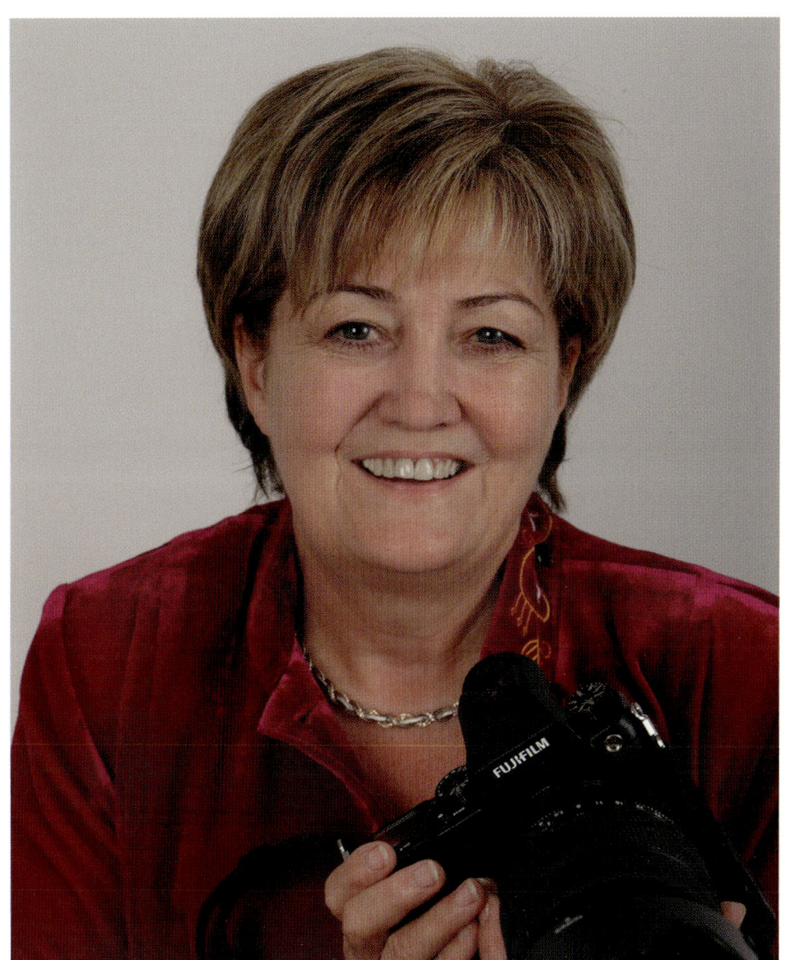

FOREWORD BY GYLES BRANDRETH

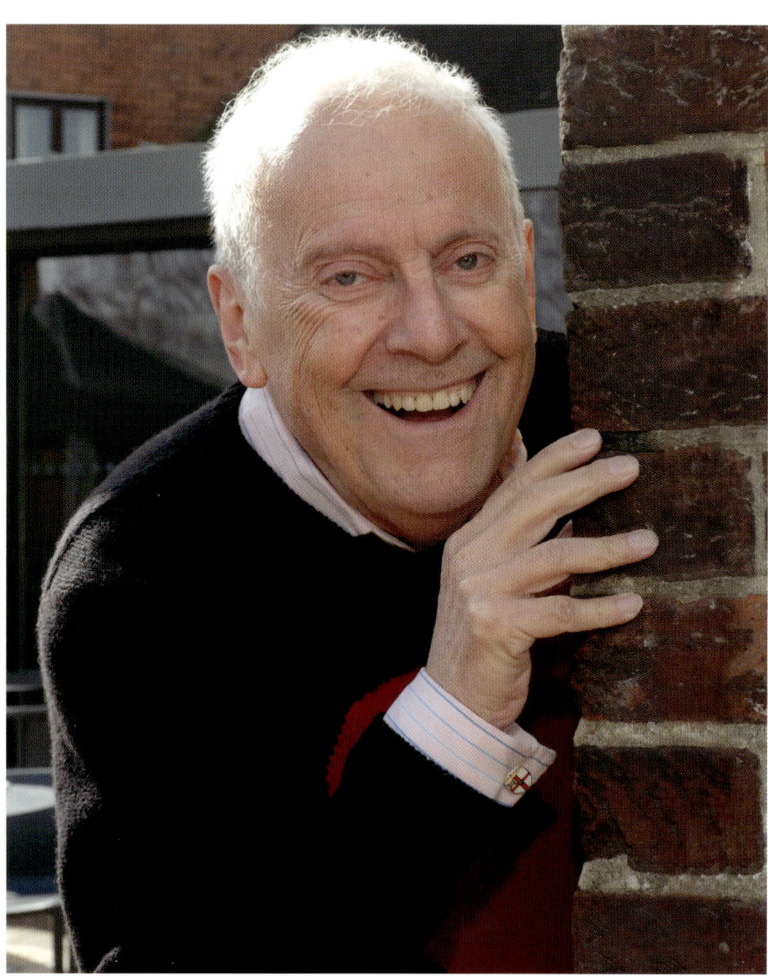

They say a picture is worth a thousand words. That's certainly true when it comes to this little foreword to Gill Shaw's magnificent book *Canal Boat Lives*. It is a photographic portrait of our wonderful canals and the people who live on them.

I cannot pretend to know a great deal about canal life, but I can tell you that some of my happiest days have been spent on British canals, travelling them with my friend, the great actress Dame Sheila Hancock. We made two series of *Great Canal Journeys* for Channel 4 and through the programmes I discovered there is no better way to explore your own country than by canal. I revelled in the life of our inland waterways – and realised that Dame Sheila was a rather more effective canal-boat captain than I was as her shipmate. She was a brilliant navigator and I at least managed to open and close a few of the locks!

What is wonderful about Gill Shaw's work is that she has the talent to find unusual, quirky yet natural-looking images. She is already recognised for her skill and ability, photographing portraits of celebrities, members of the royal family and sporting heroes, so travelling the canal network of England and capturing these wonderful images and the diversity of people living on our canals was a new venture for her – and a special treat for us.

I do recommend this book, a perfect accompaniment to Gill's exhibition. That's enough words from me; turn the page and enjoy the photographs. They tell the real story.

INTRODUCTION

Canal Boat Lives came out of a commission from *This England* magazine, who asked Gill to photograph ten people to feature in their beautiful summer magazine and show the alternative lifestyles of the narrowboat community.

The project took on a life of its own as she followed some of her new boating friends as they cruised around our canals. Some had projects and combined the creative challenges with adventures in their boats, whilst others travelled extensively round the world for work and used their boat as their base – a place of solace and peace amongst a unique community that understands the pressure of being part of an international, multi-time-zoned workforce. The result is a set of stunning photographs showing the characters and lifestyles of this community of people living amongst us on our canals.

Canal Boat Lives is in conjunction with a National Touring Exhibition, featuring photographs of wonderful people who live or work on a canal boat.

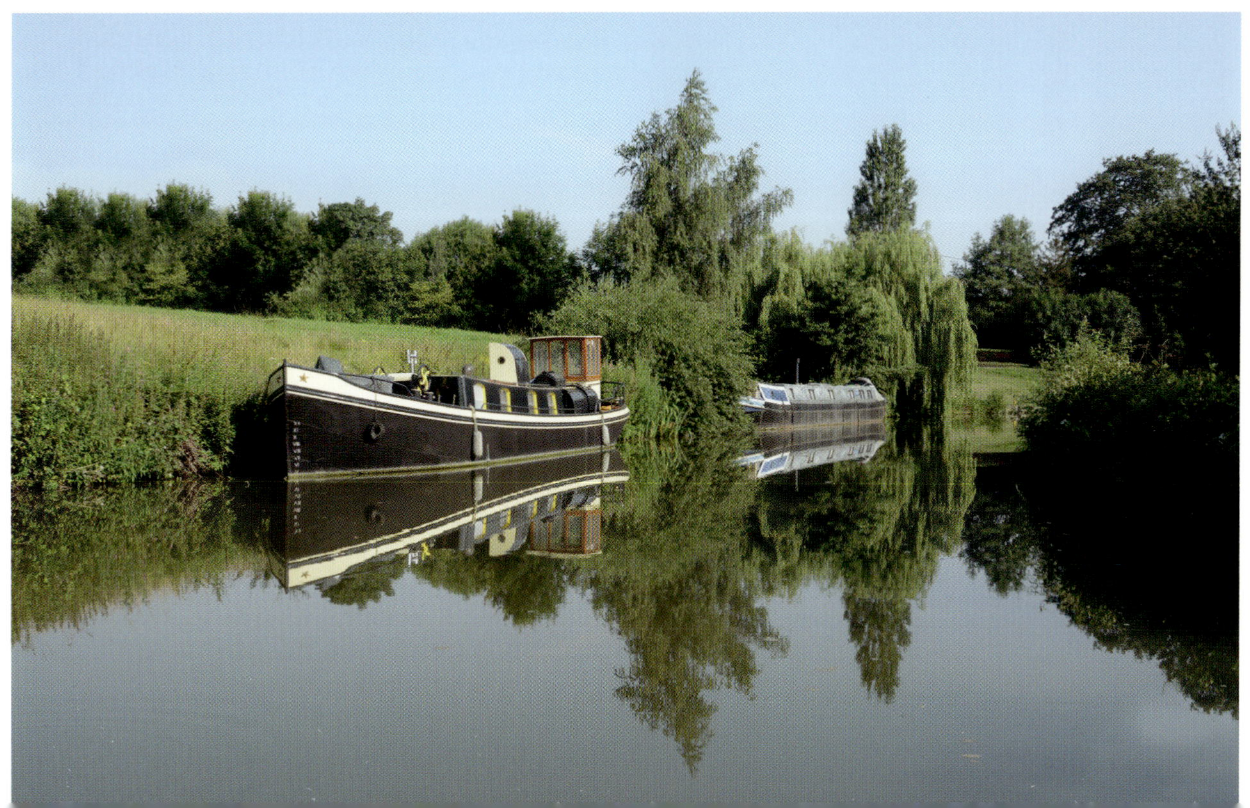

Abi Beane

Clinician Researcher

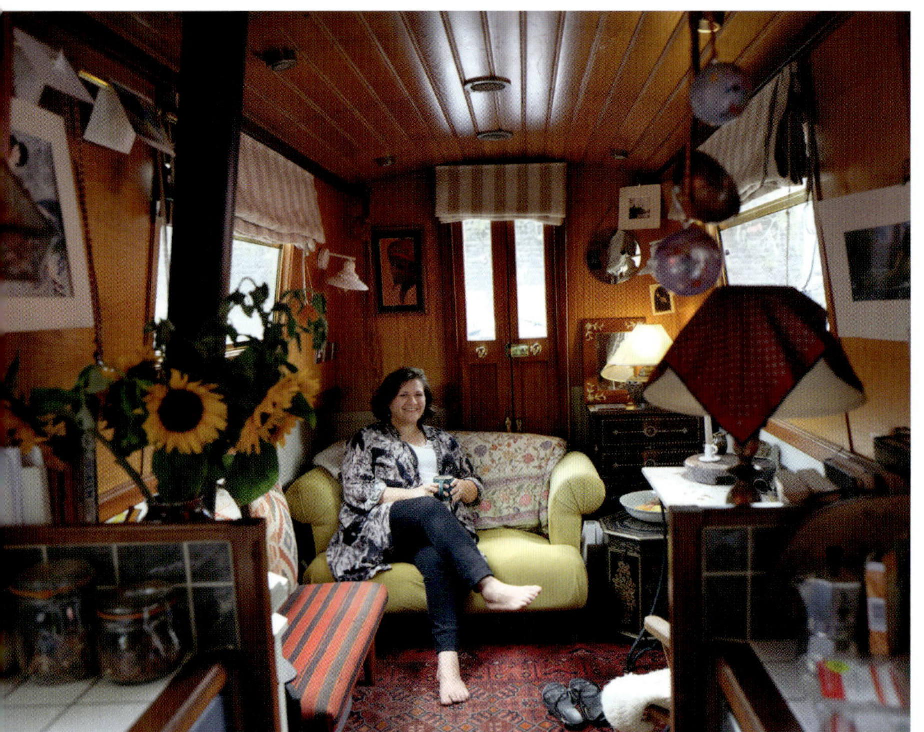

Living on a traditional narrowboat in the centre of London is both a dream come true and a humbling way to learn about one's own priorities and resilience. Warm summers spent idling by the canal, with the convenience of shoreline amenities. The joy of lighting the stove as the cool autumn nights draw in; all just a stroll from St John's Wood. It is a truly unique way to live as part of a community and nature in the heart of London.

The simplicity of canal life for me, like many boaters in our towpath community, is in being able to preserve the traditional constants of a more analogue way of life whilst incorporating the best of the ever-evolving newness of the city. Whether it is a novel idea for compact storage or better ways to use renewable energy, it's the perfect tonic to a busy, multi-time-zone work schedule that applies a constant digital pressure.

Canal living has taught me to have awareness of my neighbours and my own surroundings, and to embrace compromise and adaptation, whether to the changing community or the visitors who share the canal side. The impact of the warming climate on the boat's steel hull, or our own less than steely ability to tolerate the winter chill!

Mostly, living on a narrowboat teaches one to be both self-reliant and a community member, to use resources wisely and to slow down and listen to the rhythm of life. The rewards make all the compromises worthwhile.

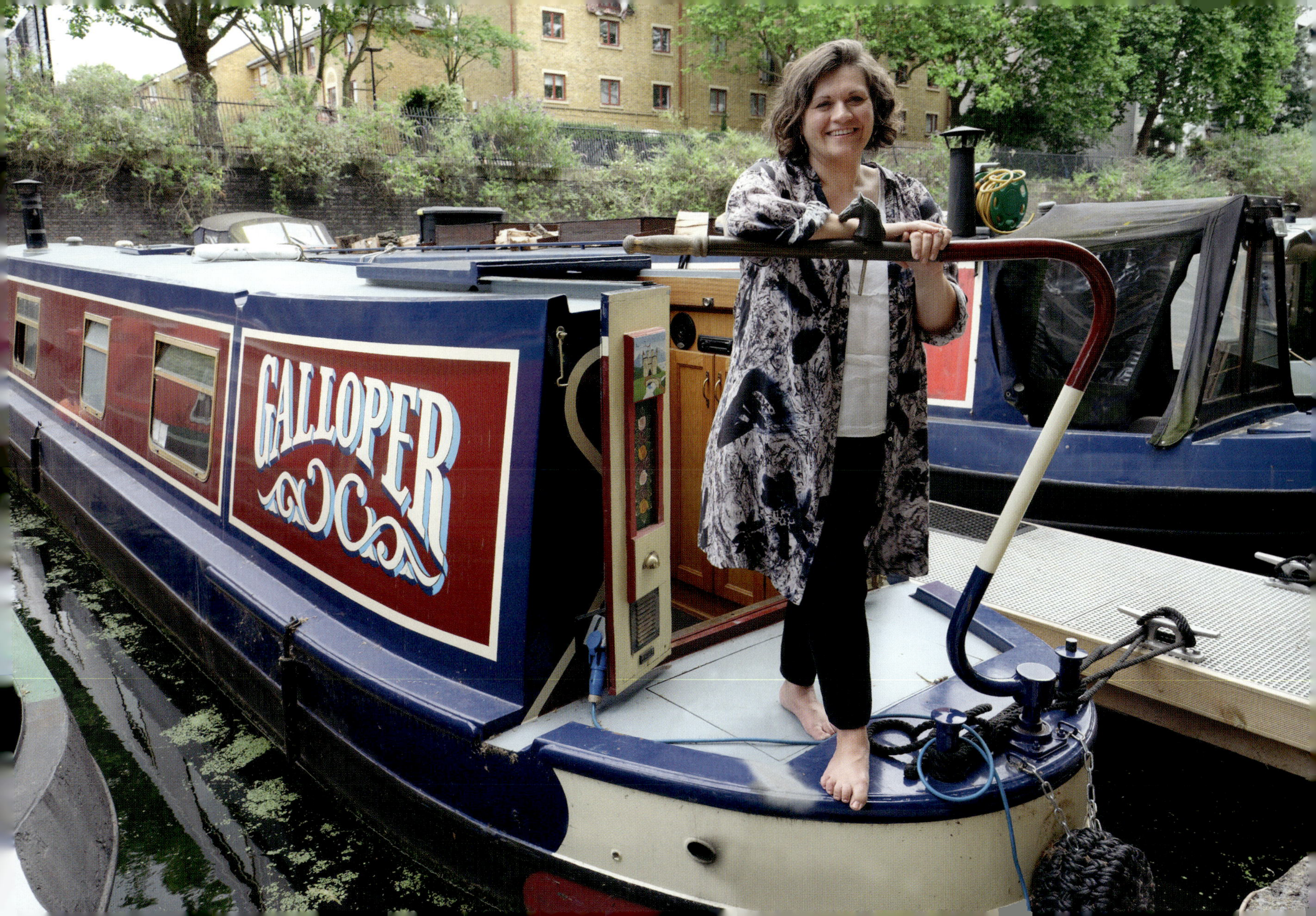

GALLOPER

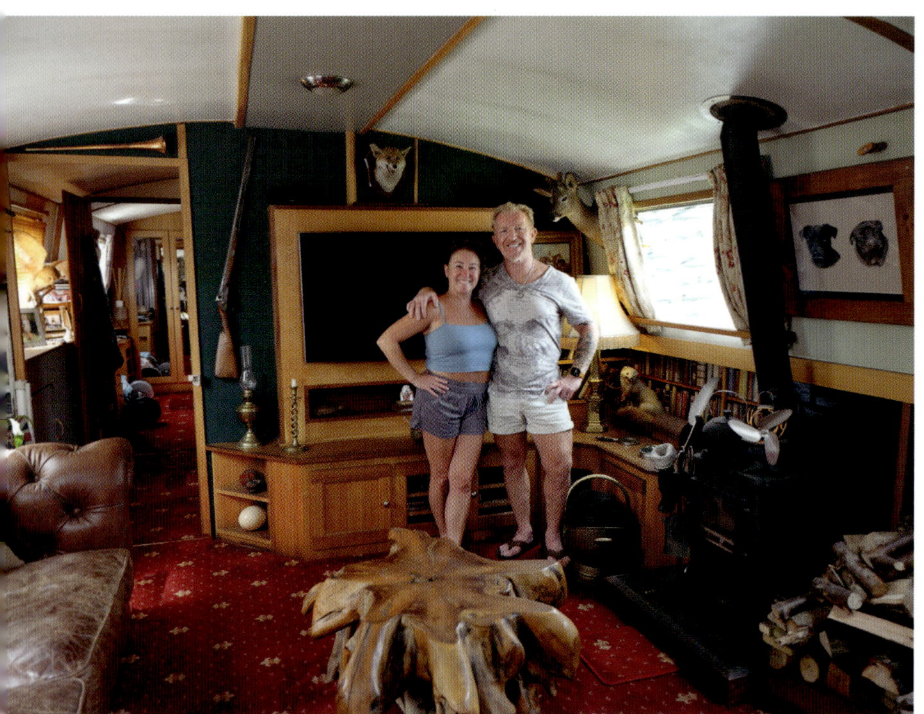

Adam & Jools Smith

I have lived on this boat now for eleven years. It is pretty much equivalent to a deluxe floating apartment, which is fabulous. I would never want to go back to living on land and most people who live aboard seem to have the same opinion. I have lived in five different marinas and in that time all you have to do to move is find another mooring, untie the ropes and off you jolly well go! The freedom is brilliant, and you are not tied to anywhere for any length of time. Whereas if I owned a property on land, I would have to find an estate agent, put it up for sale, get solicitors involved and it would take at least three months and a lot of stress to move.

The big plus is that you are living in the countryside pretty much wherever you go on our wonderful canals in Britian. It is really sociable and I am always meeting different people along the towpath – walkers, cyclists, dog walkers, etc.

Jools and I have been together now for the past two years. When she first moved aboard, she really loved the freedom and the laid-back lifestyle. Like me, she absolutely loves it and has never looked back … And long may it last!

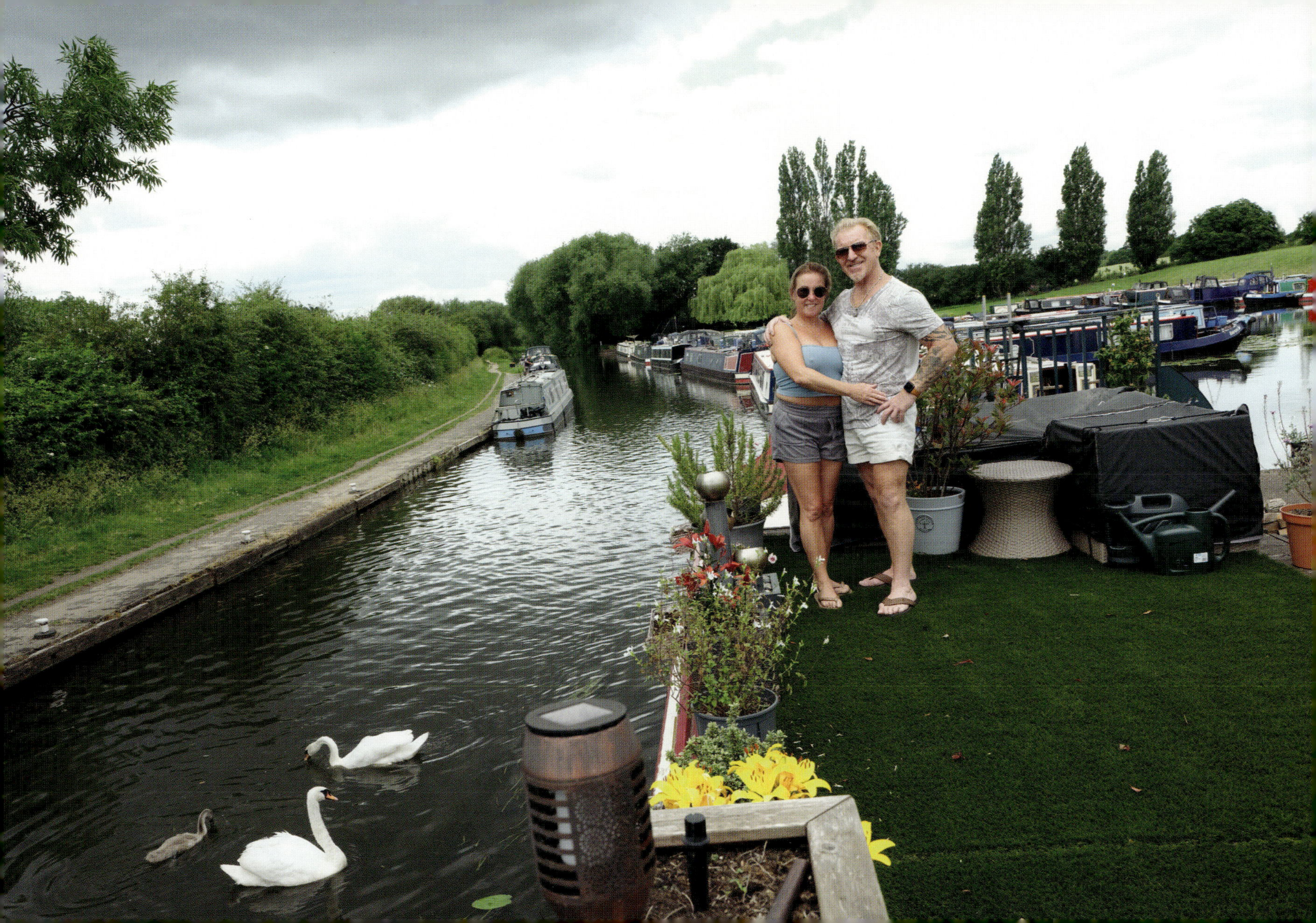

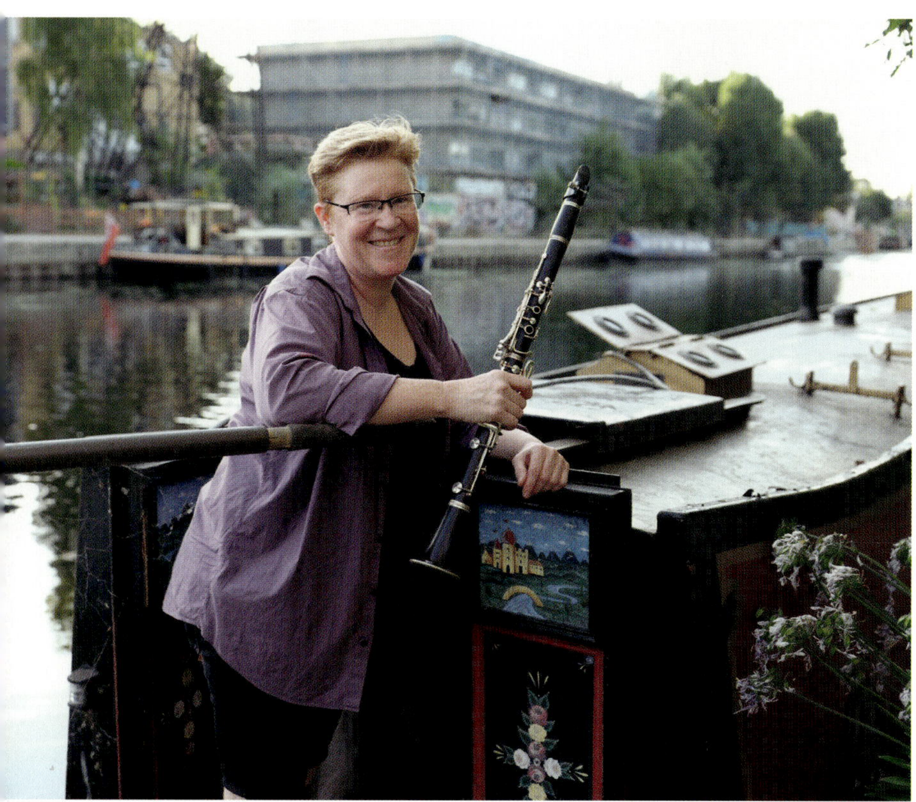

It happens like that with boats. Some people hear about them and have little or no interest. Some people are curious and find themselves wanting to know more. And some people just find themselves living on a boat because it seems like the next logical step in their life. I was definitely one of those people.

I don't think I really stopped to think of it as a particularly different way of life at the time. I fell into a relationship with someone who lived on a boat. It was obvious that was the preference when compared to the flat share.

I emigrated from Australia to London at the age of thirty. Within eighteen months I moved onto a boat. My biggest issue was that I'd never lived without a piano, and it took me a few months to admit that I didn't know what to do about it. 'Oh', said my partner, 'You need to meet Justine!' Within a week I had met this Justine character – who lived in the same marina – and saw how a piano fitted on her boat. I was told the size and height of the doors, together with the size of piano I should consider buying, and it would fit just fine! And it did.

Justine and I got on pretty well. We always booked the piano tuner for the same day to save him coming to the marina twice.

After several years I moved off the boat, for reasons unrelated to the boat, but completely related to personal life. The change was loud. The creature comforts of the landlubber were much appreciated, but the marina community, the peace of living on water and all the birds were hugely missed.

And I missed the quiet. I missed the sound of not much at all. I think that's actually why playing music on a boat is so good. You can hear. We did have other places to rehearse, but we always ended up on Justine's boat. It's just best that way.

There is no doubt that living on a boat requires more work. But the lifestyle is just somehow very real. There's no pretending and there's no politeness. It's just real and kind, honest and good. I'm not at all surprised to find myself back living on a boat in recent months, soaking up the community, the quiet – and the birds.

Now I am just measuring up to see how to fit the piano in again!

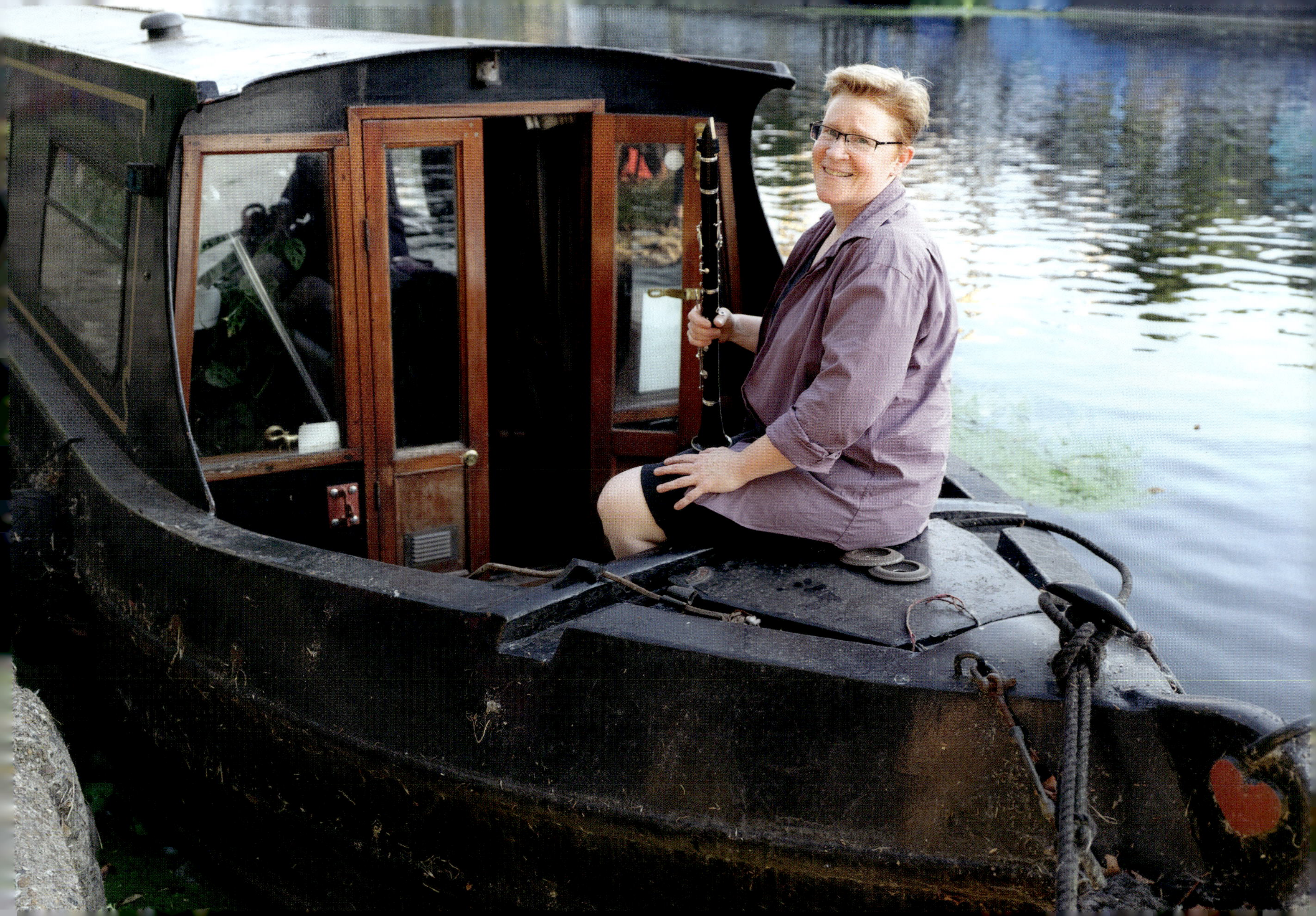

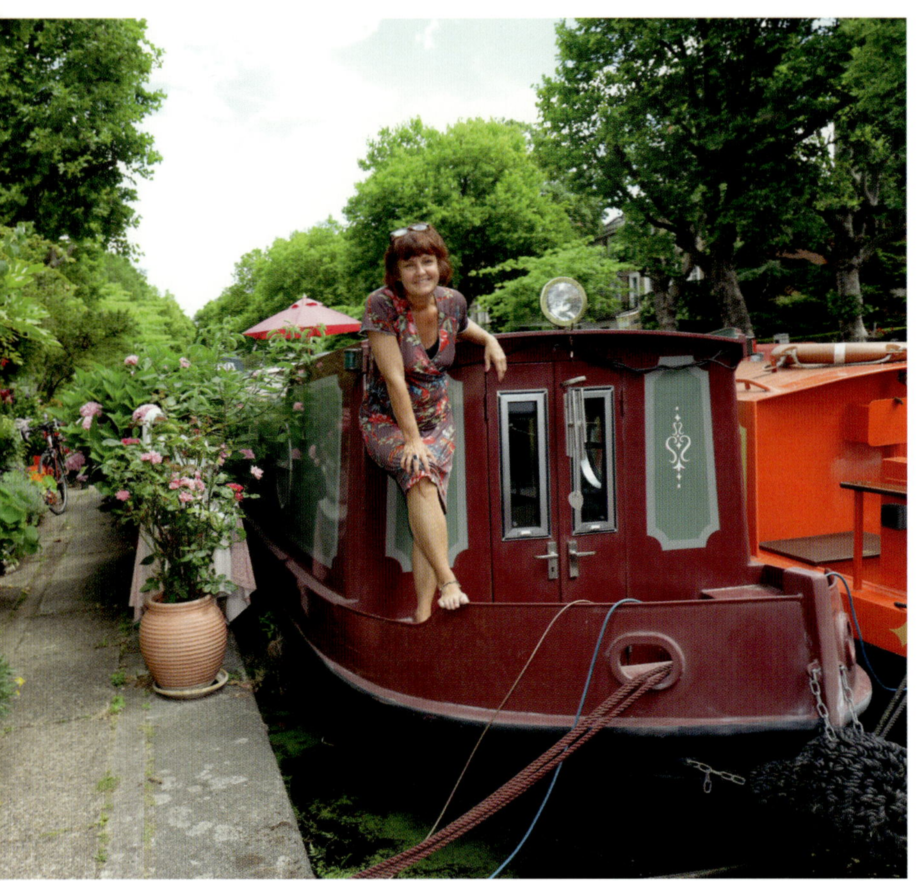

I came to work in London for ARD, a German TV company, in 2008 as their foreign correspondent. ARD is the public broadcaster in Germany, comparable to the BBC here in the UK.

The first person I met was Owen Davies, a QC at the time, and he introduced me to the wonderful world of canal boats in England. I was then asked by ARD to make a documentary on something picturesque around England for German TV. So immediately I thought why not make a longer documentary on canal boats, starting in Manchester and finishing in London's Little Venice.

It was here in Little Venice that I found an old boat called *Emily*, which I loved. I sold her in 2014 to have a newer one built to my own specifications. After some searching around, I chose Colecraft Boats in Warwickshire to build her, and they did a wonderful job. The new one now is called *Emilia* – so a sort of grown-up version of Emily! She has double-glazed windows and very good insulation. I am so very happy with everything and love spending time in her; I couldn't have imagined a more professional and kinder man than Gary from Colecraft Boats to build her.

One of the nicest things about our moorings in Little Venice, where *Emilia* is moored, are the little gardens we boaters have established over many years. I spend a lot of time and money to make mine look as pretty and colourful as possible throughout the year. It's very rewarding. Not only do we enjoy the fruits of our labours, but the people who pass by take notice and enjoy them as well.

It is my haven and a beautiful quiet place to work and relax.

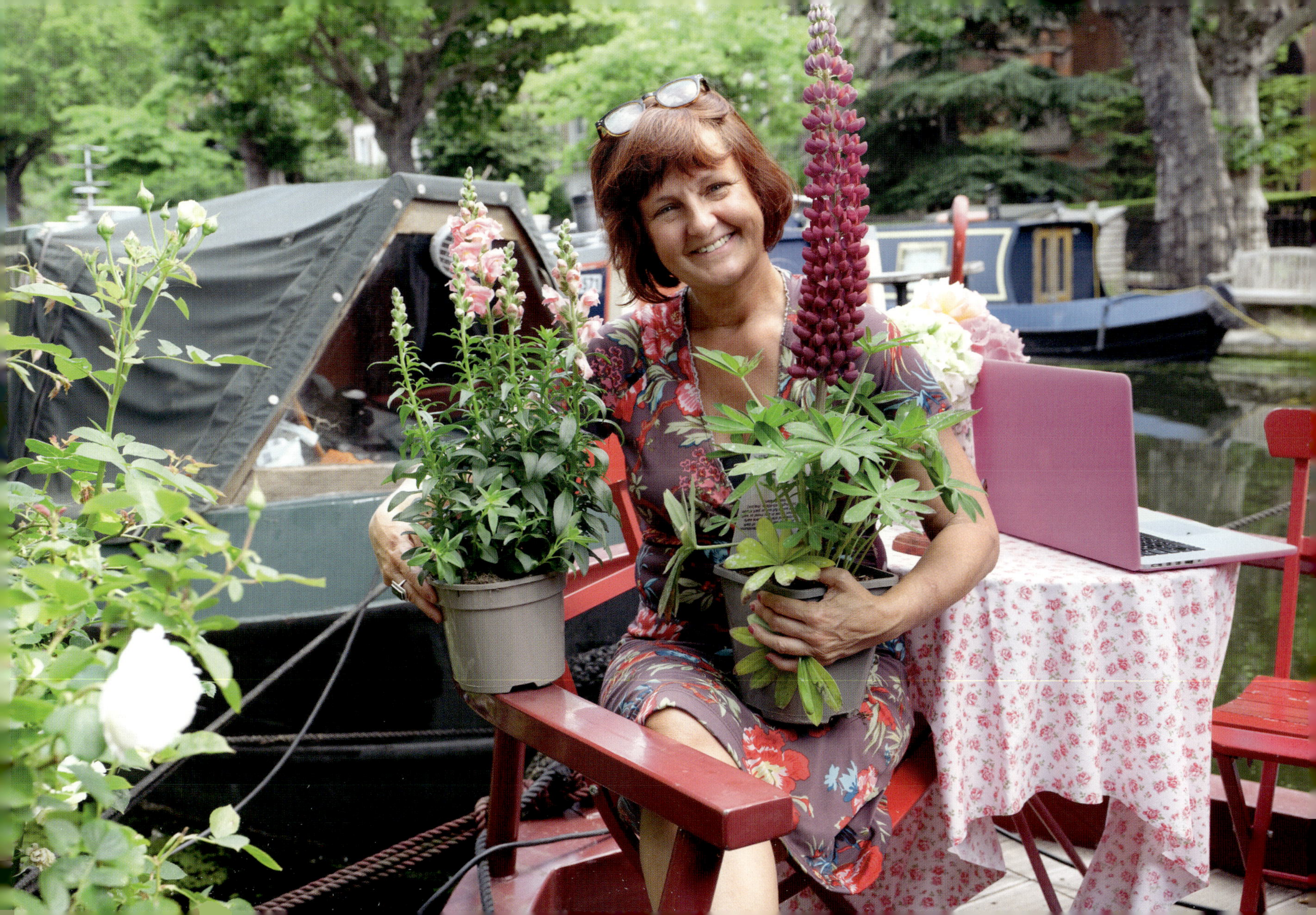

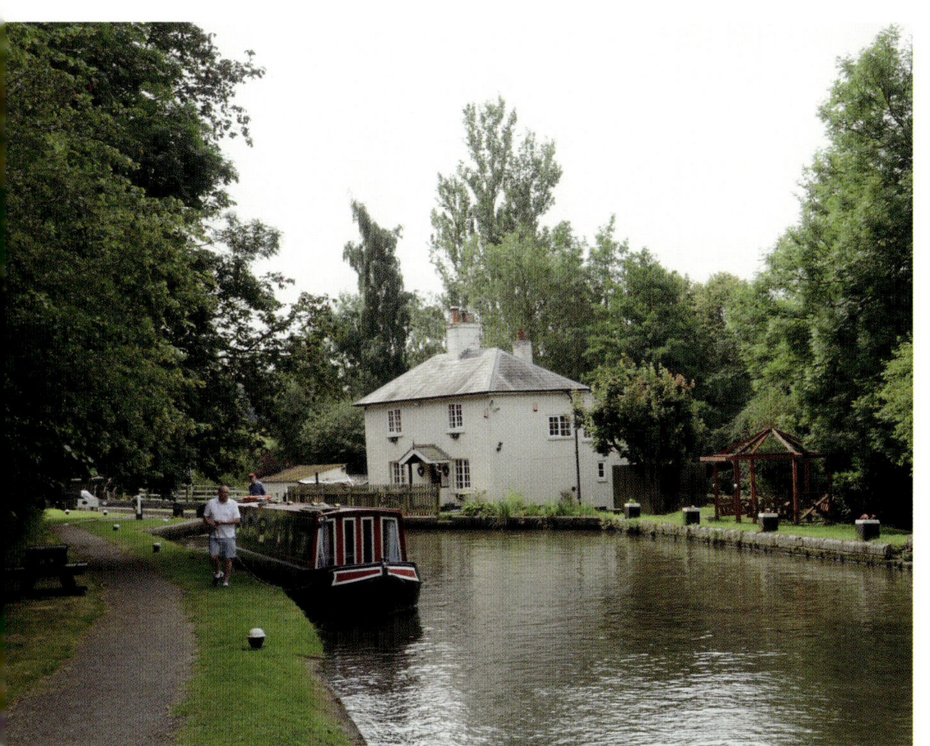

A magical narrowboat holiday! It is really lovely and can make you very lazy but if you want to make it more physical you could get off the boat, walk to the next lock and prepare it for your boat.

It's really nice to think about our journey, to plan where we are going to eat, drink and moor up for the night. We plan our leisurely progress via the different pubs and restaurants along the canal. I always thought that if you can spot a church in the distance, there would be a pub nearby. But that is not always the case, is it?

It can be challenging. We come to a junction and sometimes we are not sure which way to go. But it is hard to get lost! And it's all so very tranquil – and memorable.

Our favourite time is around 4.30–5 p.m. when we moor up and relax with a gin and tonic. We watch the world as it continues slowly cruising past us.

The locks provide us with the means of travelling up and down stream. I seem to be always armed with the windlass. This is the handle that we carry with us on our journey to wind the paddles on the lock gates up and down to control the flow of water. But it requires a lot of energy and some well-honed muscles to crank up those paddles! When the water level inside the lock matches that on the outgoing side, the gates can be swung open – but that too can be hard work! They can get stuck!

Most of the locks were designed and built in the nineteenth and early part of the twentieth century, so replacement lock gates have to be made to measure.

The lock system is simply a brilliant method of moving boats up and down steep inclines. They were first designed for use in China in the tenth century for use on the Grand Canal. There are over 1,500 in England and Wales and some steep hills require a 'staircase' of locks such as Foxton Locks – a flight of ten, built during the nineteenth century.

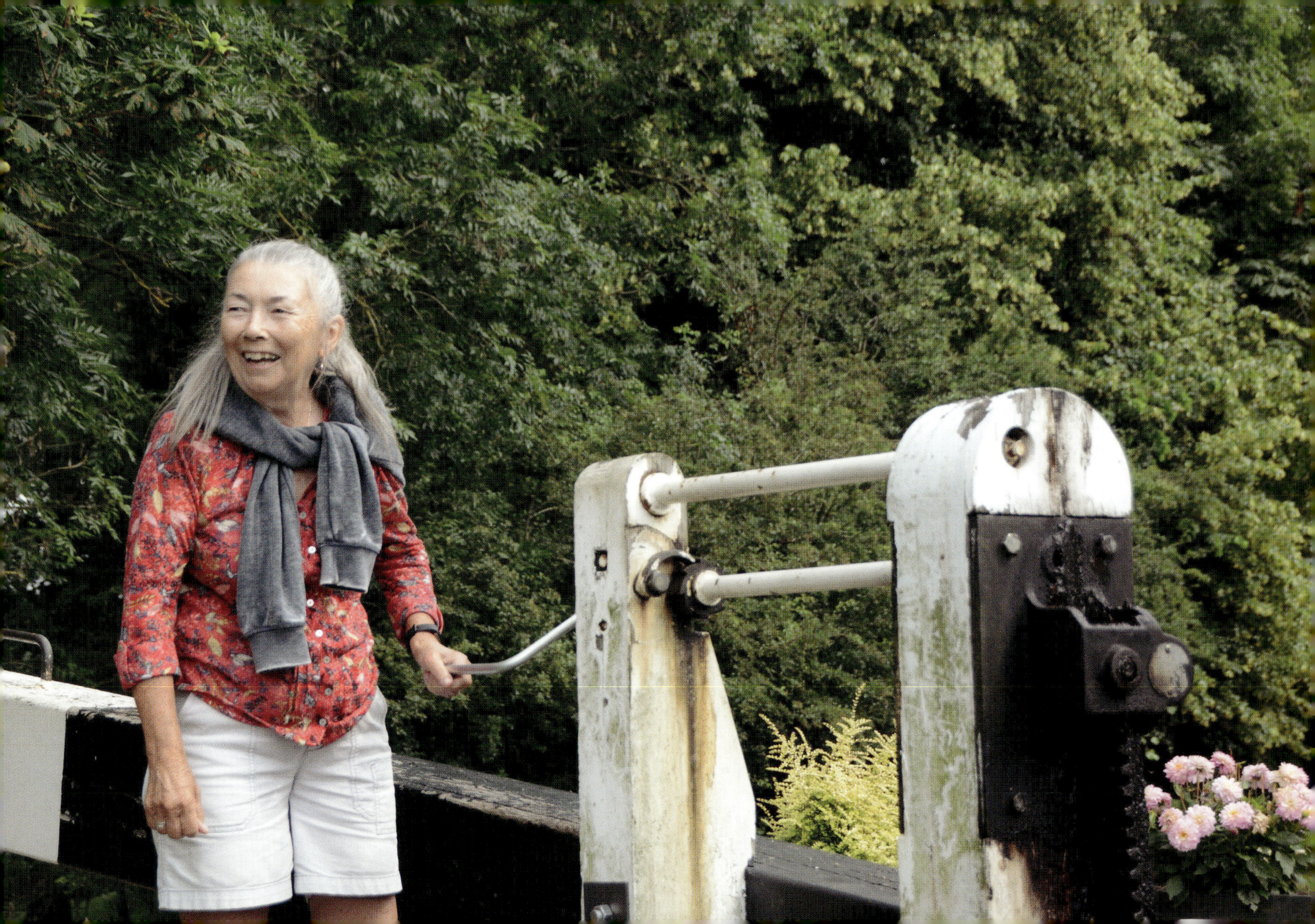

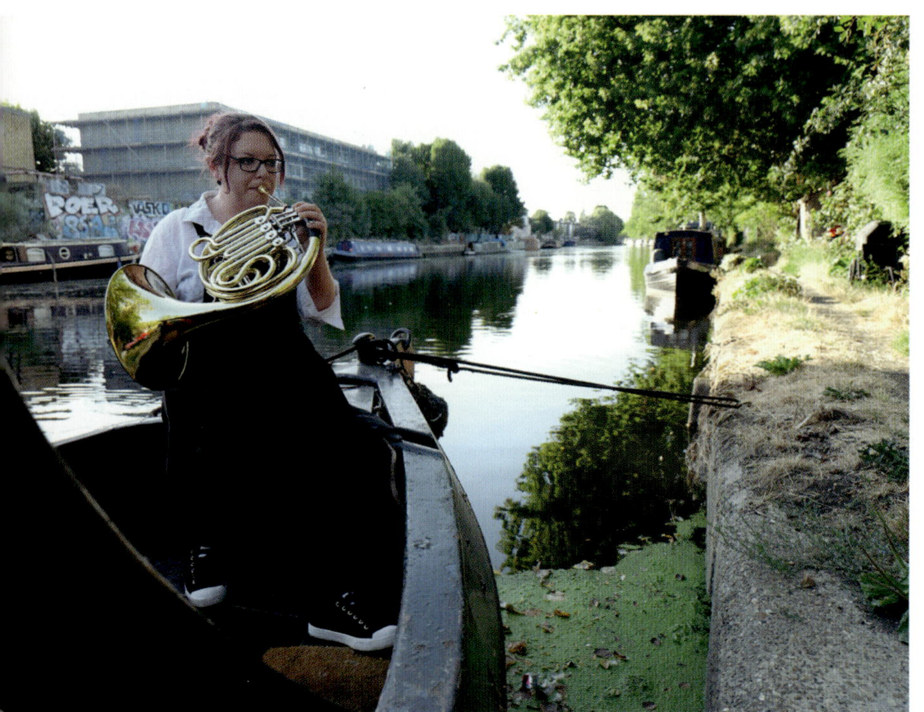

I never imagined that a narrowboat could be a home until I met the people who would end up becoming my musical family. The first time I stepped on board Justine's boat, I was terrified I would fall in!

I came to a crossroads where it was evident that I could not afford to rent in London, so it was suggested that I get a personal loan and buy a boat of my own. So that is what I did. The first journey into London was quite hairy. I had a friend helping me move it. The first time I was left to steer on my own, I ended up crashing into a huge wide beam – whoops!

When we got the piano, that was an interesting day. We bought it from Camden Piano Rescue and they told us to moor up at the loading bay by Camden market. We had quite an audience – it was inched this way and that to try to slide it through the front door without damage to either the boat or the piano!

I can't believe that we have been aboard seven and a half years now. We used to move around every couple of weeks, which was fun, and we met some really interesting people along the way. But it is tricky to commute to work from different places every couple of weeks. What can also happen is that I head for home, exhausted after a long day at work, only to find my boat is no longer where I thought she was. I sometimes totally forget that I have moved her the day before!

We are pleased to now have a mooring and a bit of security, although singing opera as loud as I could when travelling through the Islington tunnel for the amazing acoustics is an experience that I really miss! Playing the Romanza from Mozart's *4th Horn Concerto* from the bow of a narrowboat, listening to myself echo across the valley, will have to do for now – and the Canadian geese don't mind when I split a note!

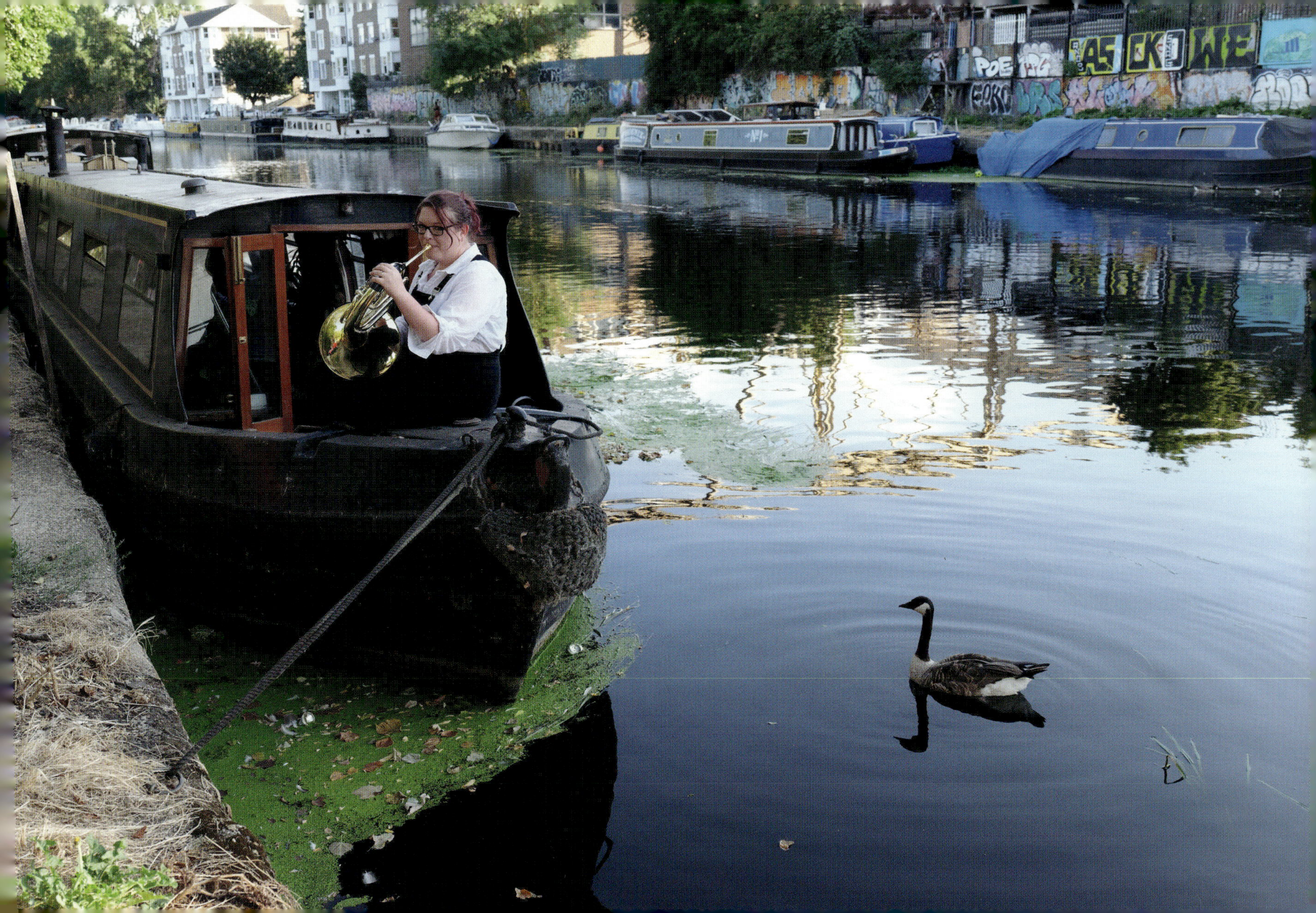

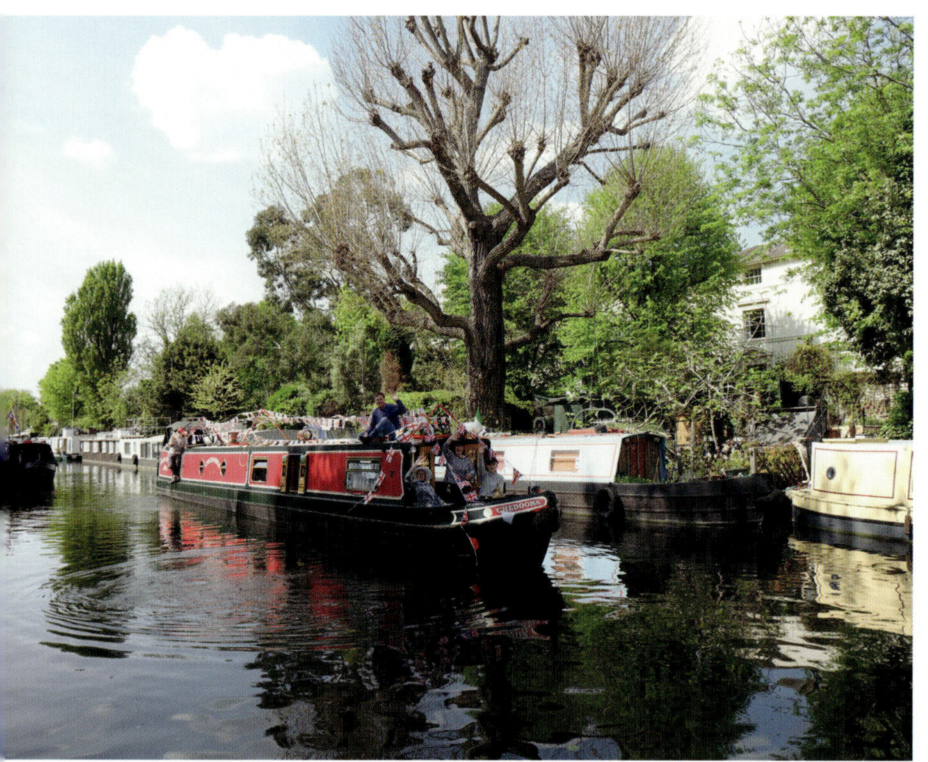

We started off hiring boats for a few years and after we retired, we had *Chedoona* built to our own design twelve years ago by Colecraft Boats in Warwickshire. For the first few years we spent the whole summer on it. Now, we attend festivals such as Canal Cavalcade at Little Venice and the Water Festival at Rickmansworth – a round-trip cruise lasting about six weeks. We make a few short outings during the summer but then do one of the 'ring canal routes' in September/October for another six or seven weeks. As shown in the photo, we usually have family and friends join us at various times, especially at festivals. We can overnight two guests.

It is such a beautiful, relaxed lifestyle, travelling beautiful countryside and villages, as well as passing through towns and cities and seeing a very different side to them.

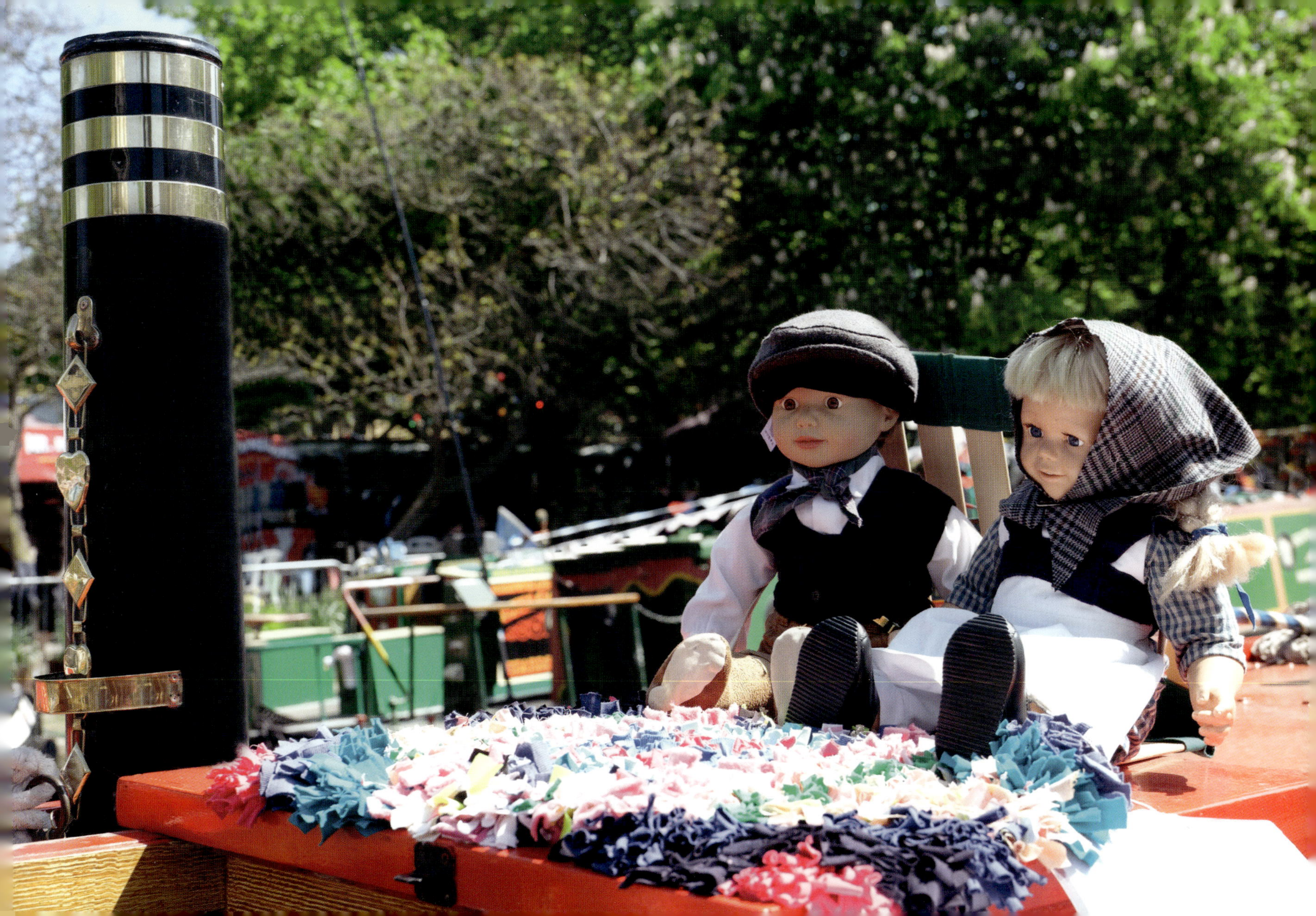

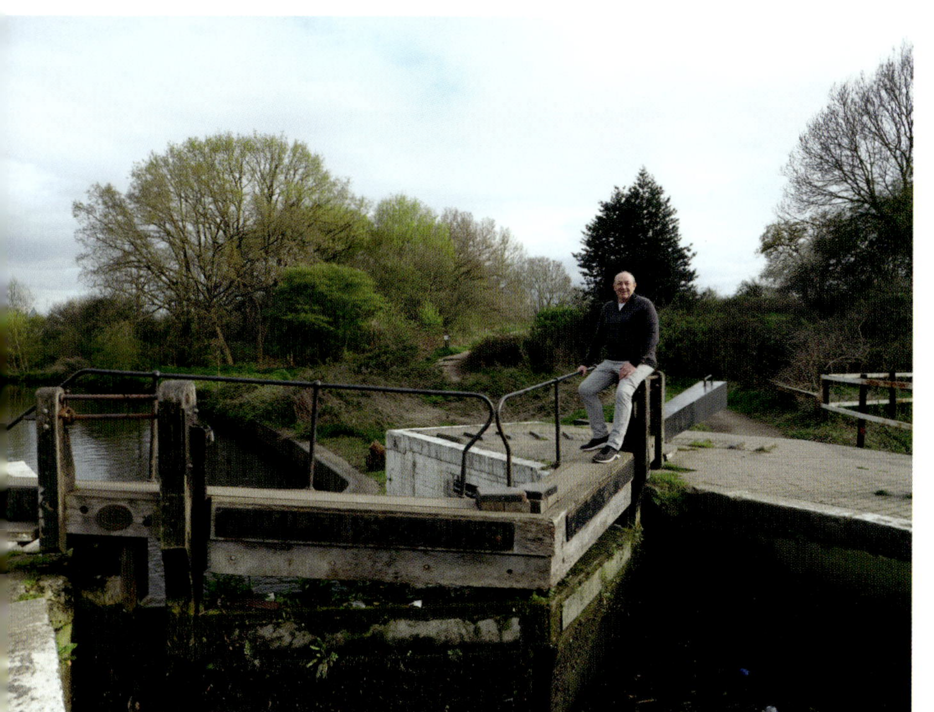

Having grown up very close to the Trent and Mersey Canal just outside Derby, I have deep-rooted happy memories of canals. A lot of my early teenage years were spent by the canal, enjoying the varied wildlife that inhabit these inland waterways whilst spending a lot of time fishing, hoping to pull out a roach or perch, with varied success.

When Gill Shaw told me about her current project, I was more than happy to get involved personally and with Oakenhurst.

I agreed to personally sponsor and support the exhibition that preceded this book; any project that raises awareness of our canals and contributes to the future and safeguarding of this wonderful habitat gets my vote.

I have found that travelling on our wonderful canals is extremely relaxing. The slow, sedate progress through the water makes me feel calm and reflective. One thing that I have found fascinating is that as I travelled through the centre of some very busy towns, amongst all the hustle and bustle of daily life, I still feel very relaxed and at peace with the world.

I now live in London very close to the River Brent and the Grand Union Canal. It does seem that wherever I live there is a canal nearby, maybe because many years ago the canals were the transportation lifeline to the whole of England and spread across the country in a complex and comprehensive network. As I get older and look for a more sedate lifestyle, the canals near my home seem to provide that, and just as I did as a child, I use this unique environment for both relaxing and exercising. Long may we all be able to use these magnificent waterways.

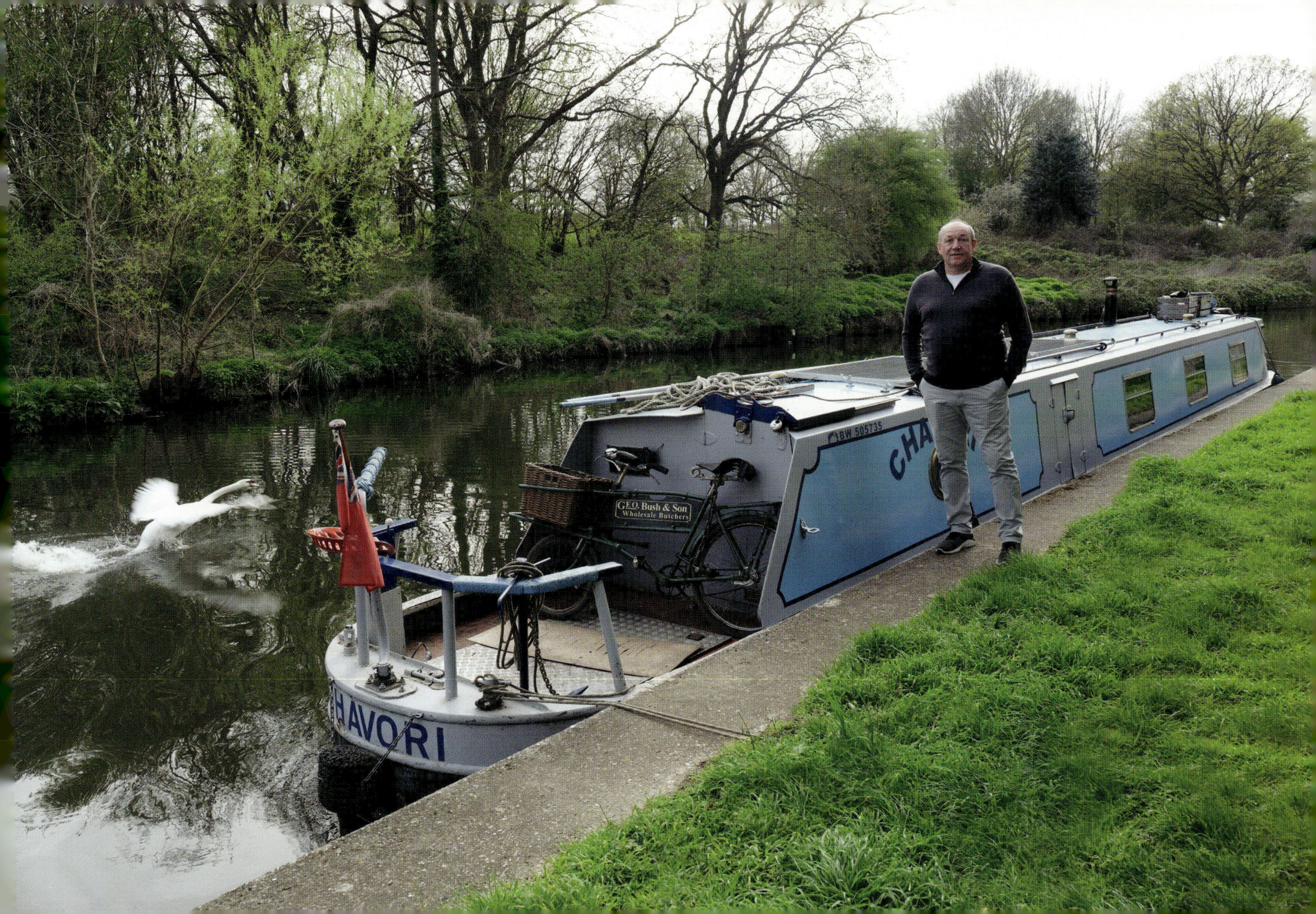
BW 505735
CHA
G.E.O. Bush & Son
Wholesale Butchers
HAVORI

Chris Lehmann

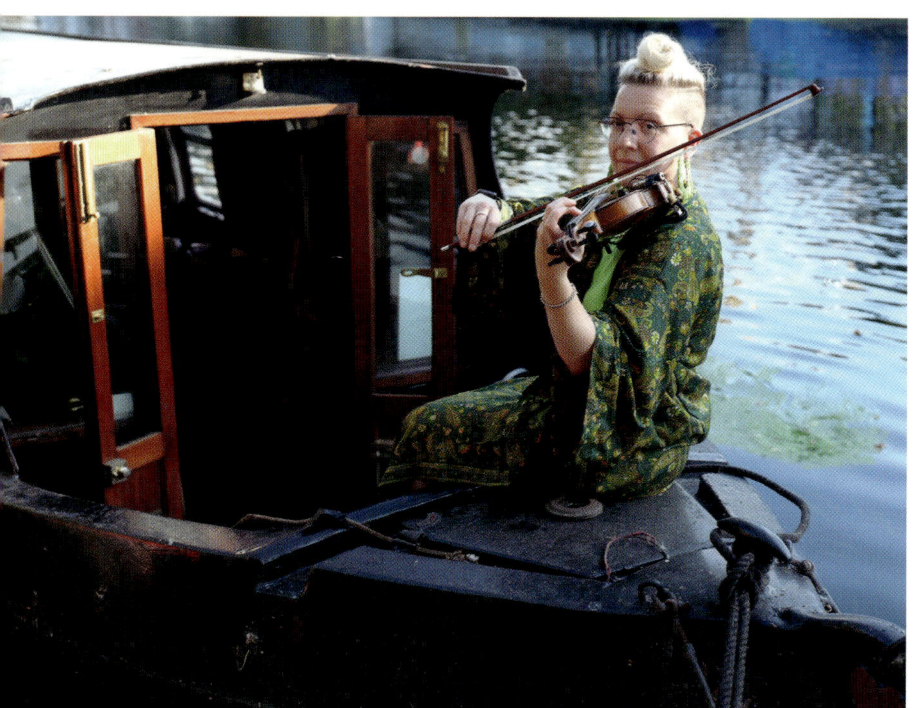

I have always felt a real affinity with water. I was born in Hawaii, grew up south of Boston on the Atlantic and then after a short stint on the Maine coast, found myself living by San Francisco Bay. When I made my way to London in the early 2000s, I was suddenly land-locked. I found myself searching for places that gave me the comfort I was used to. Walking along the Thames was amazing, but it was so full of noise and tourists. The ponds in Hampstead were lovely, but too still and full of people I couldn't relate to. When I finally discovered canals, it was like I had come home. I spent my spare time going for walks along the canals, admiring the pace of life, the birds, natural spaces and diverse communities that lived there.

My wife and I met soon after I moved to London, and although we have been together for nearly two decades and have a fair few holidays under our belts, our favourite was our honeymoon. We took a canal boat trip through Shropshire and it was the most incredible experience. It made me fall in love with canals even more.

When I returned to London from our canal-boat adventures, I picked up my violin again after many years of taking a break from music. It is truly amazing to me that I ended up meeting inspiring musicians who live on boats, people who have encouraged me to enjoy collaborating and playing violin outside of my comfort zone. A magical world of friendship, music, water and narrowboats opened up for me. It was like I had finally found where I truly belong.

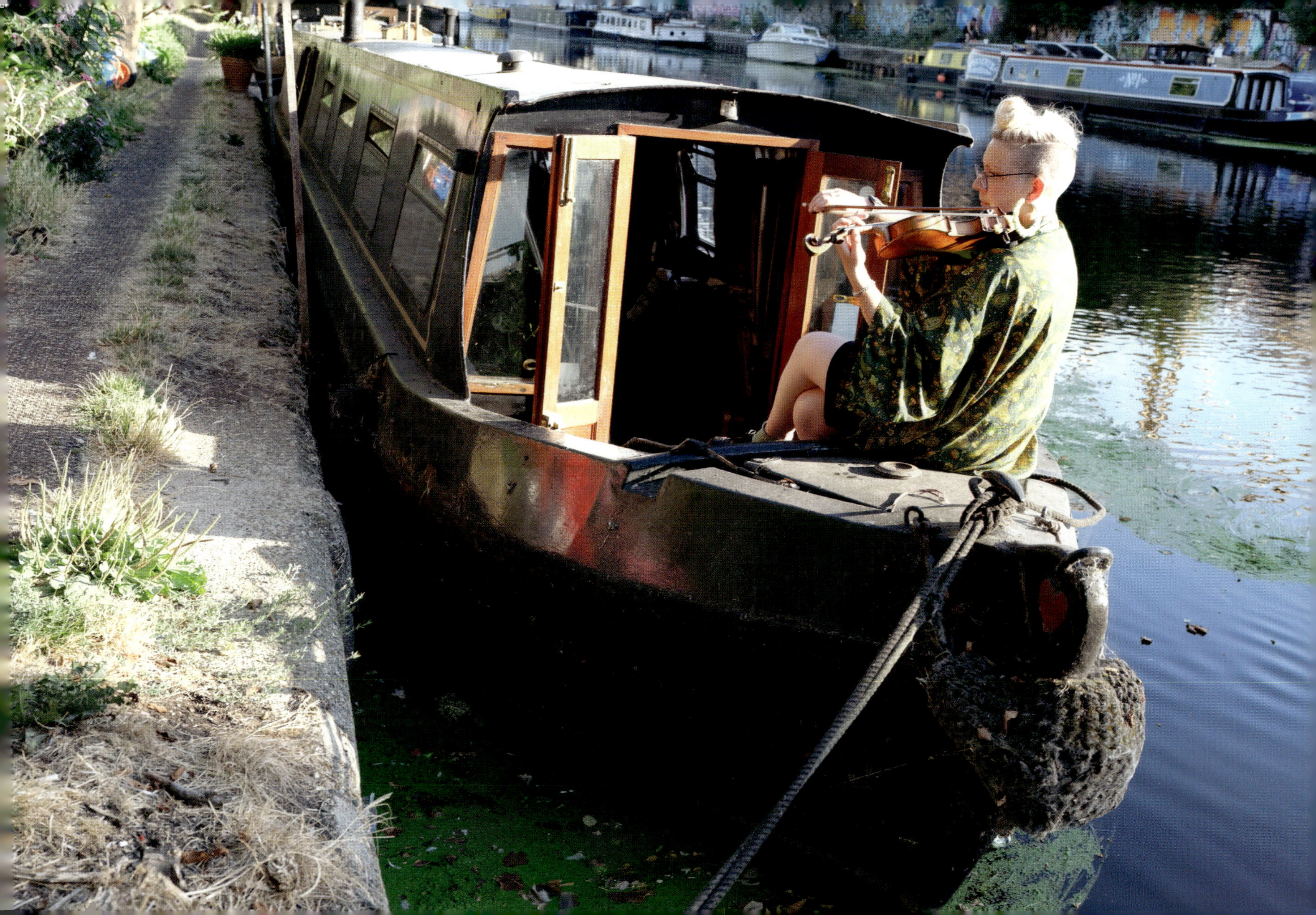

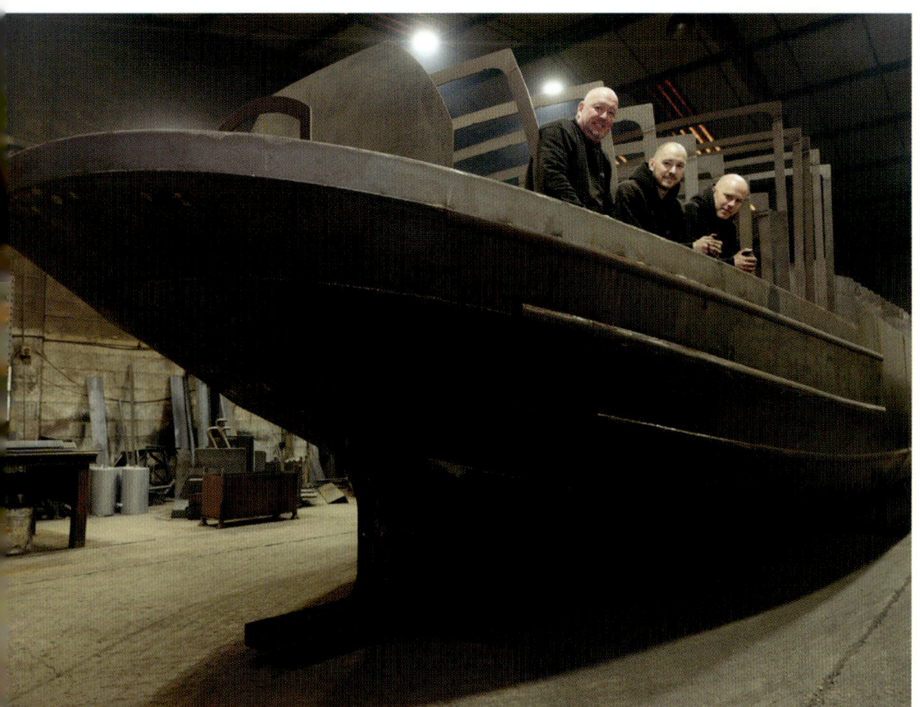

Colecraft was established in 1974 and is currently enjoying its forty-ninth year of successful boatbuilding. They are based in Long Itchington, Warwickshire, just a few miles from the Grand Union Canal. It is a family-run business, headed up by Gary Cole. Gary joined his father in the business in 1977 and enjoyed many years working alongside him. Gary is joined by his two sons, Luke and Josh, who you can see in the photo, who have been very much involved in the business for over eighteen years.

Colecraft are best known for the superb quality of their shells and fit-out and are possibly the largest supplier of steel shells to hire fleets and other boatbuilders. They specialise in sailaway options for private customers to any stage of completion and bespoke luxury fully fitted boats. All of their steel is certified, and they are constantly improving and updating their machinery and equipment.

Overleaf you can see Paul Reading working on the hull stiffeners of a new boat.

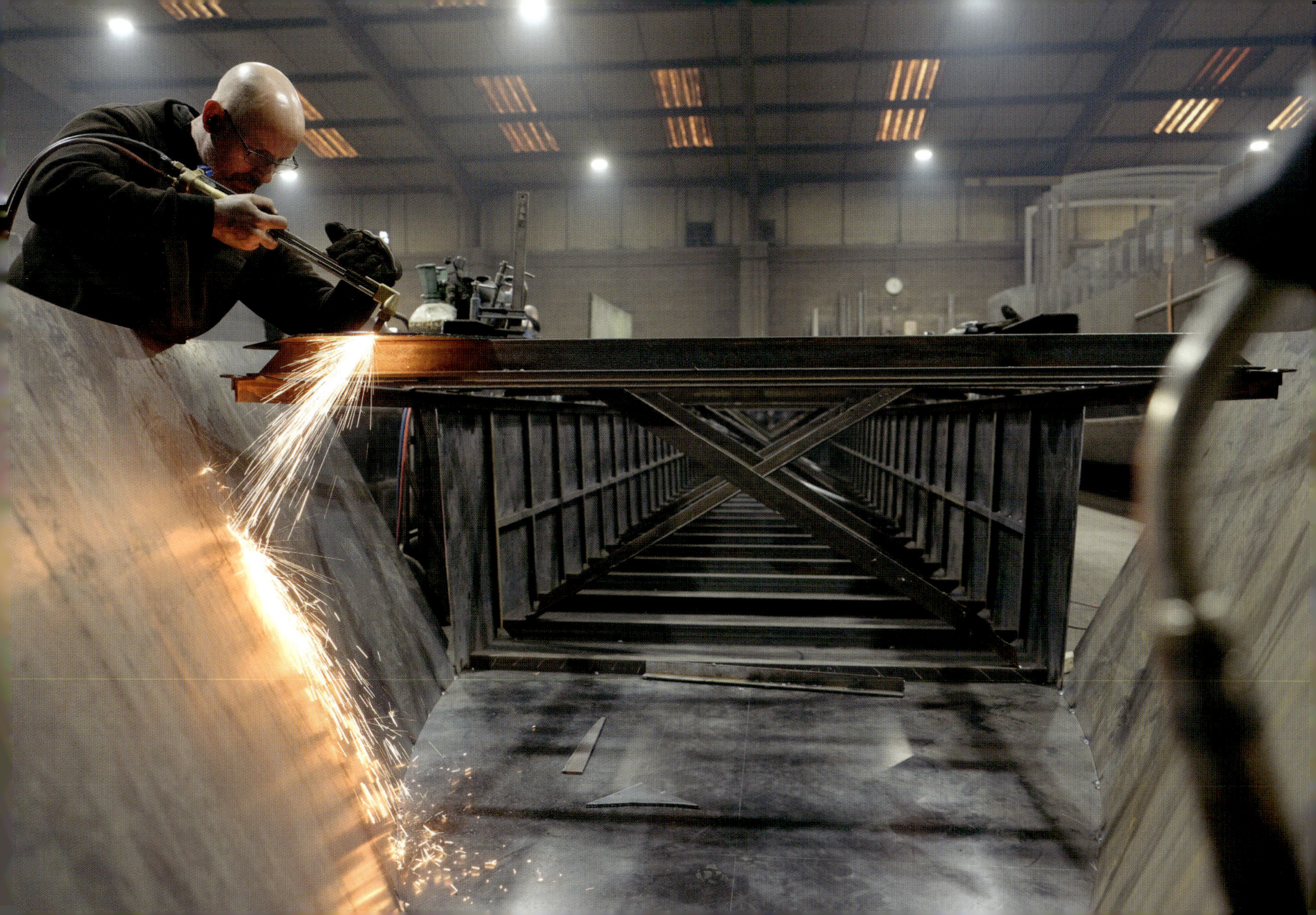

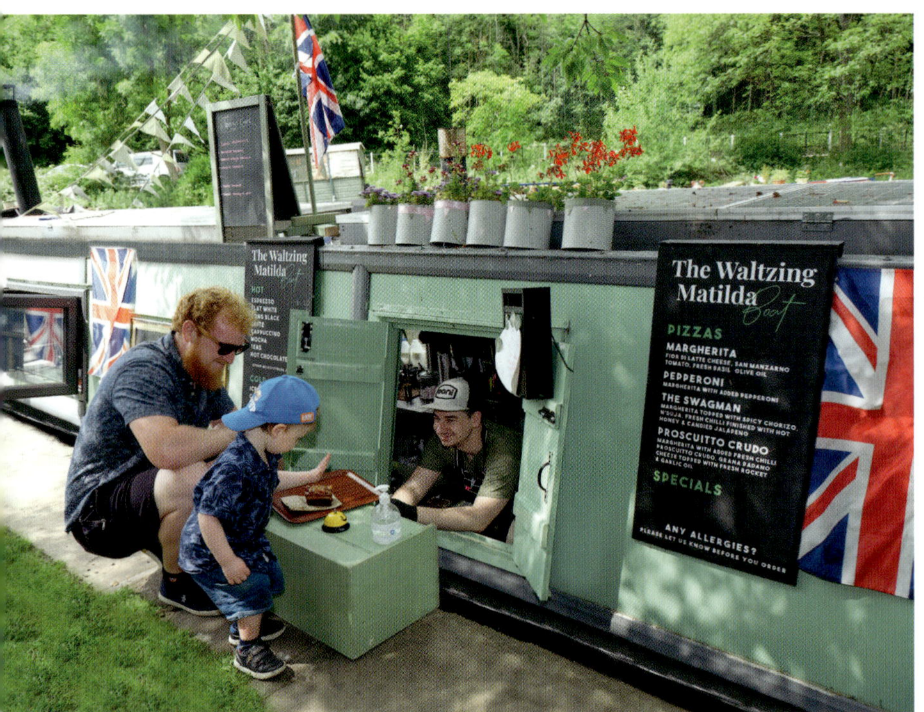

The history of the canal is fascinating and we are very fortunate to live near Whaley Bridge where we go for a walk as a family along the canal and feed the ducks most weekends.

Elijah and I like to share a pizza for lunch. They are handmade and delicious – we buy them from the floating pizzeria, The Waltzing Matilda. There are never any leftovers with Elijah about and he is always very excited when he gets to ring the bell.

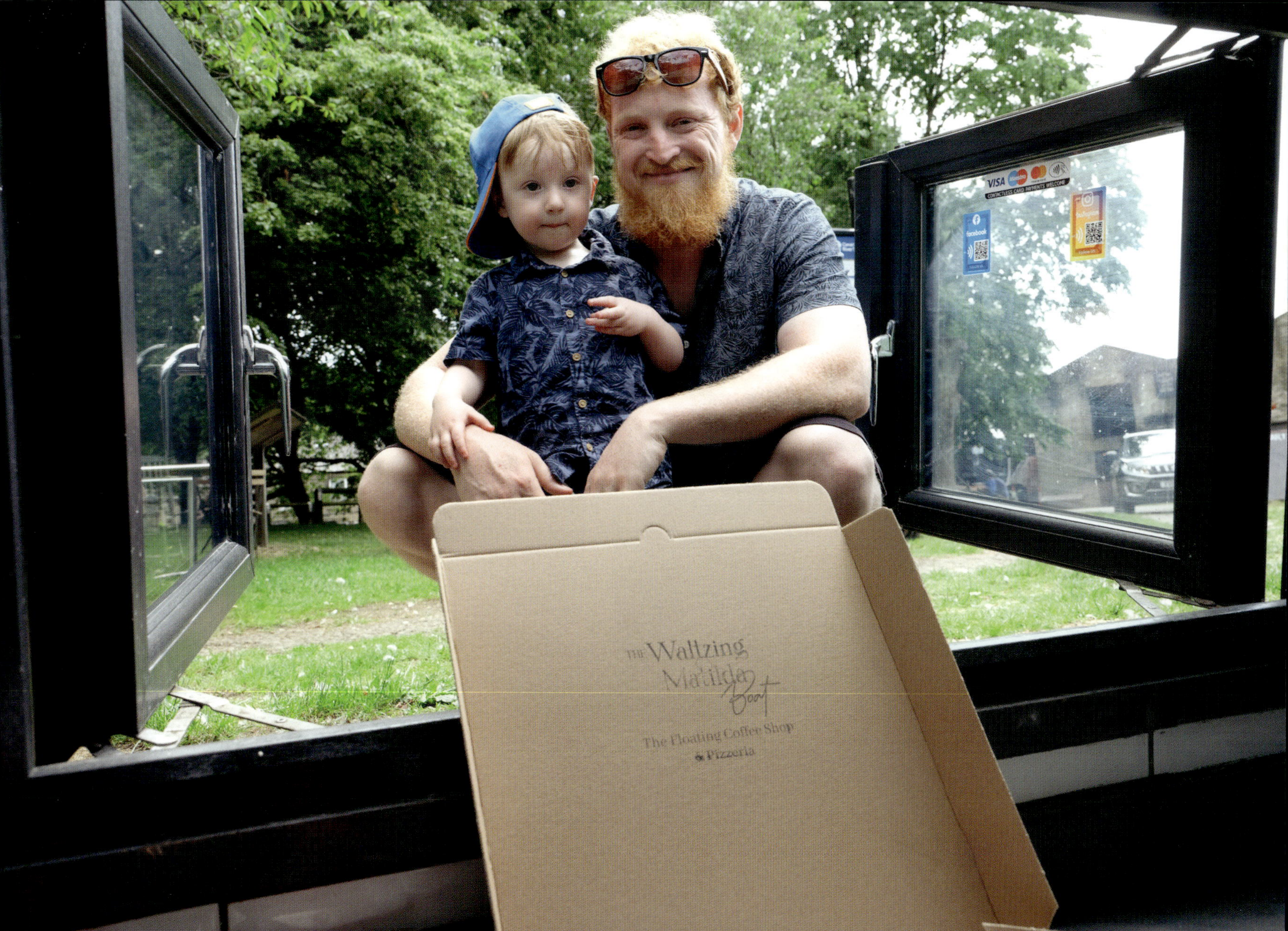

The Waltzing Matilda Boat
The Floating Coffee Shop
& Pizzeria
VISA
CONTACTLESS CARD PAYMENTS WELCOME
facebook

David Cooper

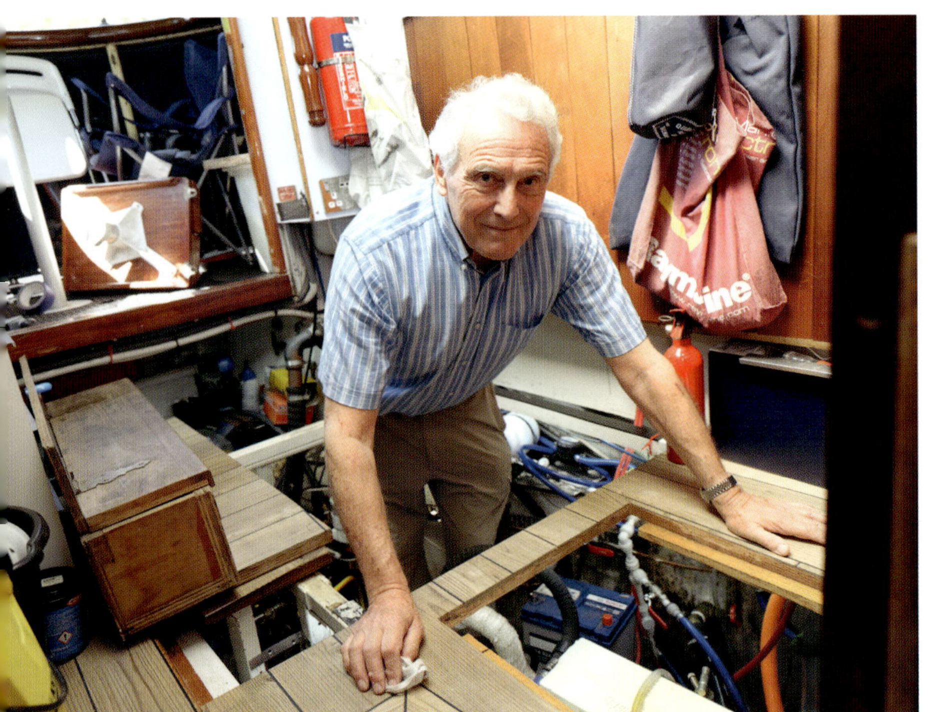

It's a great help to be mechanically minded to keep a canal boat. This applies anywhere, but particularly in London, as the area is not well supplied with engineers or boatyards, compared with – say – Braunston or the Midlands.

In the forty-five years since my boat was built, it has had two engines and five central heating systems in addition to sundry bulge pumps, water pumps, toilet systems, etc. Doing it yourself not only saves money (usually!) but also time and the stress of searching for someone to do it. It's a bonus if the engine is inside the boat. On my boat, it is under the wheelhouse floor, rather than under the stern decking where it is often cold and wet.

Much has changed in the Little Venice/Maida Vale area since the late 1970s when I first moved my boat onto this mooring. There are three times as many boats moored there now and a great increase in trip boats and floating restaurants, all of which add to the vitality of the area.

The large and very beautiful nineteenth-century houses with their white façades have been refurbished from the, often run-down, multi-occupancy properties they had become during the 1950s and 1960s. The elegant wide streets, lined with London plane trees that surround the canal, continue to provide a shady and graceful environment.

My boat looks set for many more years on the canal, thanks mainly to the engineers and specialists I have been lucky enough to meet and learn from. So this glass is raised to thank them for their help (and tolerance!) over many years.

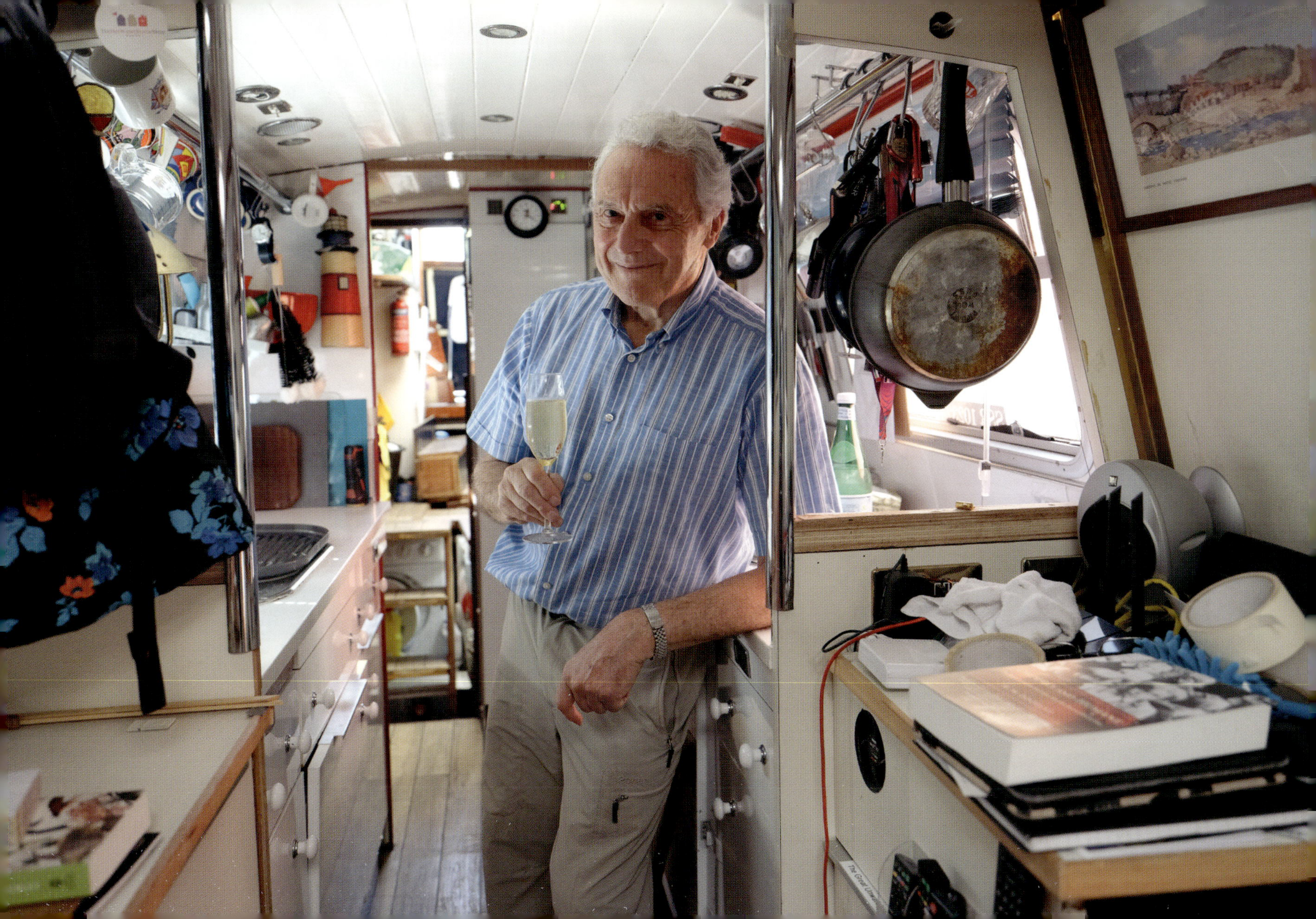

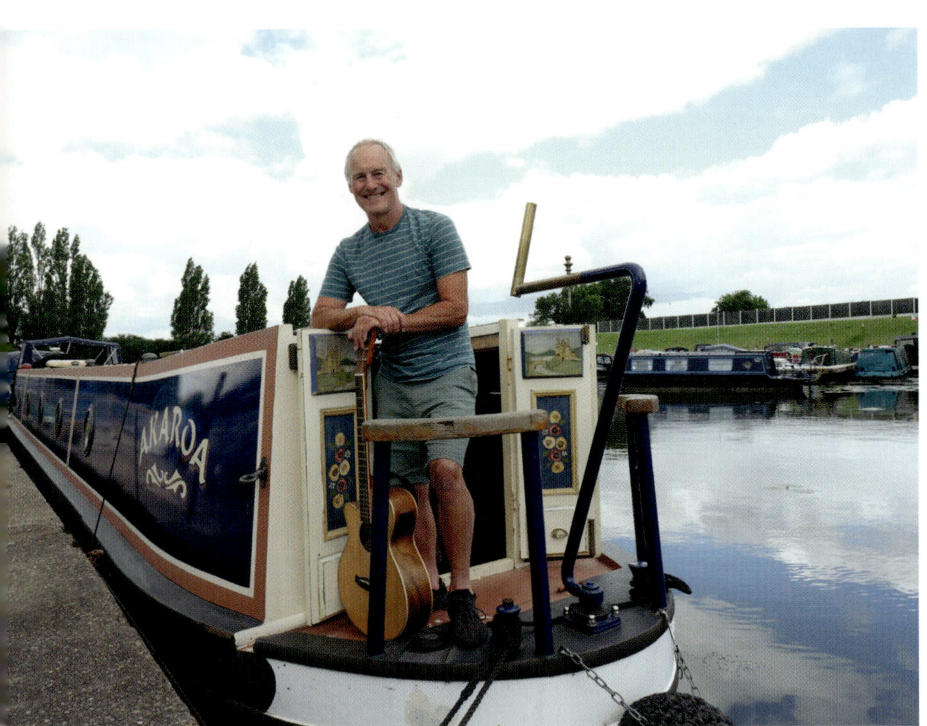

Concerning my purchase of the narrowboat *Akaroa*, I have to backtrack twelve months prior to my becoming a narrowboat owner. I was on a sabbatical from work, hiking in New Zealand. Upon flying into Christchurch I picked out the little-known resort of Akaroa as my first base. Upon exploring the hills around the town, I came across the ruins of 'Worsley's House'. Information in the local museum informed me that this was the family home of Akaroa's most famous son, Frank Worsley. Frank Worsley was the navigator of Ernest Shackleton's ill-fated expedition to the South Pole. The crew were forced to abandon ship when their vessel was crushed by pack ice. There followed an epic and heroic rescue mission by four of the crew. In just a humble rowing boat, Worsley navigated over 1,100 miles of the Southern Ocean to reach South Georgia and launch the rescue mission to try to save the remaining crew!

Roll forward twelve months when seeking a lifestyle change, I decided to buy a narrowboat that I came across – a 54-foot boat which I fell in love with other than I disliked its name. The paperwork recorded that it was built on the Bridgewater Canal at Worsley.

I cast my mind back to my first experience of the magical land that is New Zealand, recalled Frank Worsley and knew then what the new name of my boat would be: *Akaroa*.

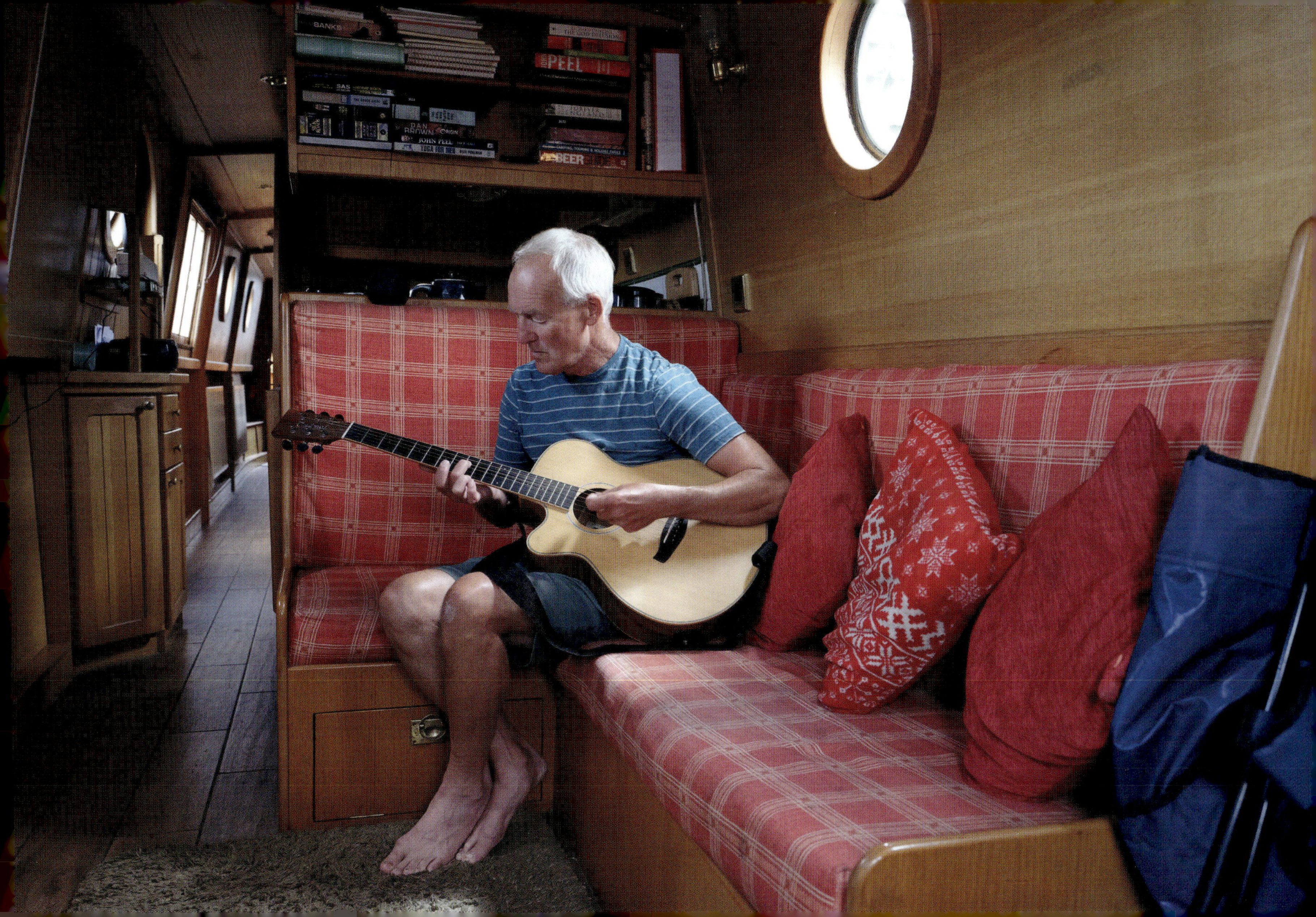

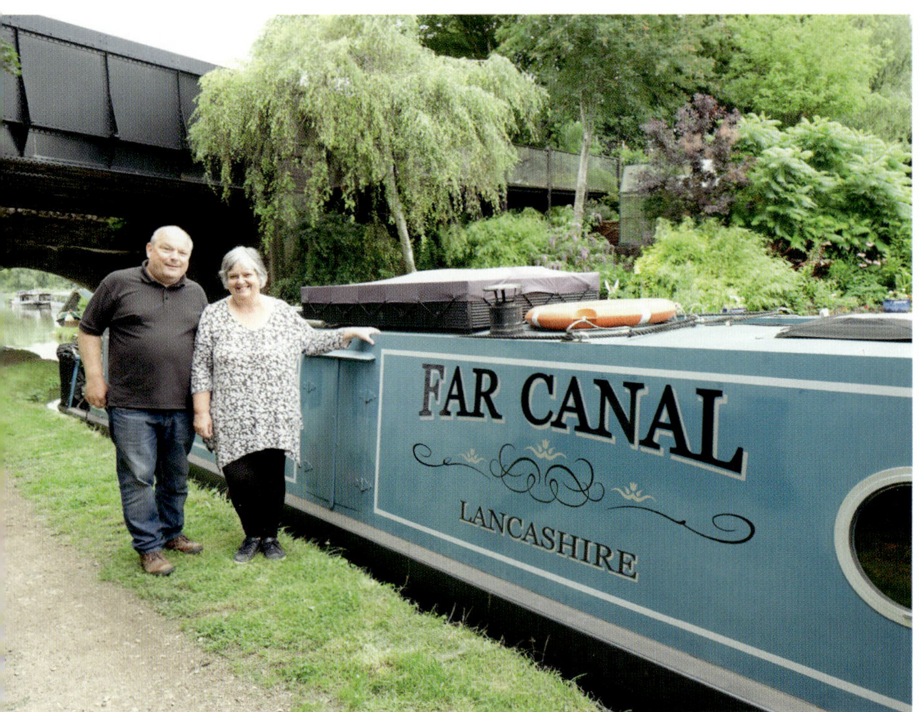

I was born in Australia. My parents were £10 Poms and emigrated for fourteen years. They returned to England in 1972 because they were homesick.

I trained as a nurse in Blackpool before moving to my first job in Preston. I met Steve in 1984. He had just completed his apprenticeship as an auto electrician when I met him and we married in 1988.

Steve set up his own business and I worked as a nurse, fitting my job around our two daughters. As our careers developed so did the stress – and then Steve had a heart attack. In 2019, we took stock of our lives and decided to quit our jobs, take my pension early, sell up and live on a narrowboat.

We loved boats but had never actually sailed one! So it was difficult to begin with but three years on we have adapted our lives to a 57-foot boat and love it! It can be hard work at times – the cold and the mud in winter, walking miles for shopping. But being close to nature and its treasures has a massive impact on well-being. We live frugally, foraging for wood or elder flowers to make wine.

We have applied for a roving trader's licence so that we can trade from the boat and I have set up a vlog of our journey on YouTube so we can reminisce!

It was a big step but definitely the best decision we have ever made. We feel lucky to be able to choose this lifestyle.

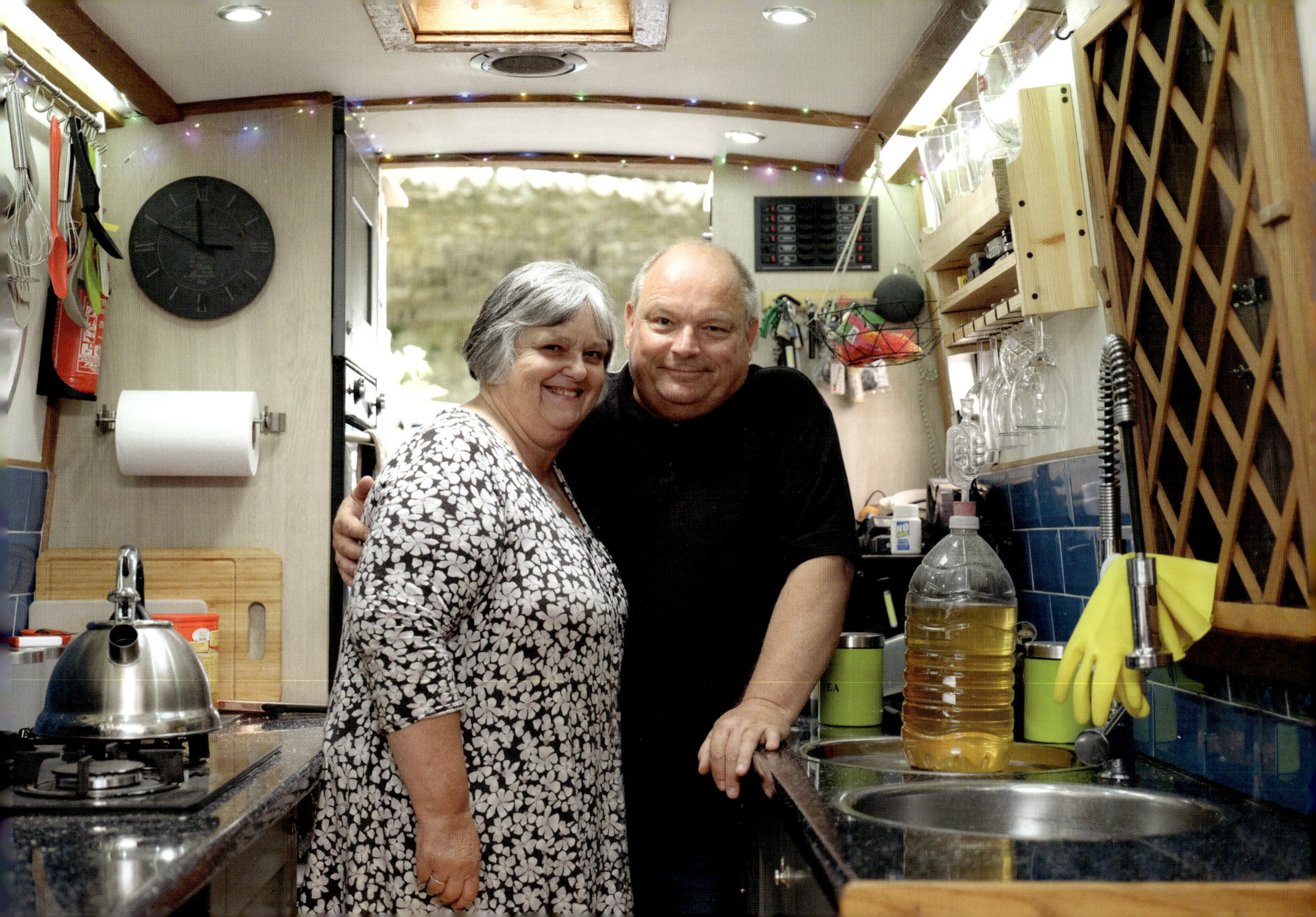

Ele Gower & Jake Thorold

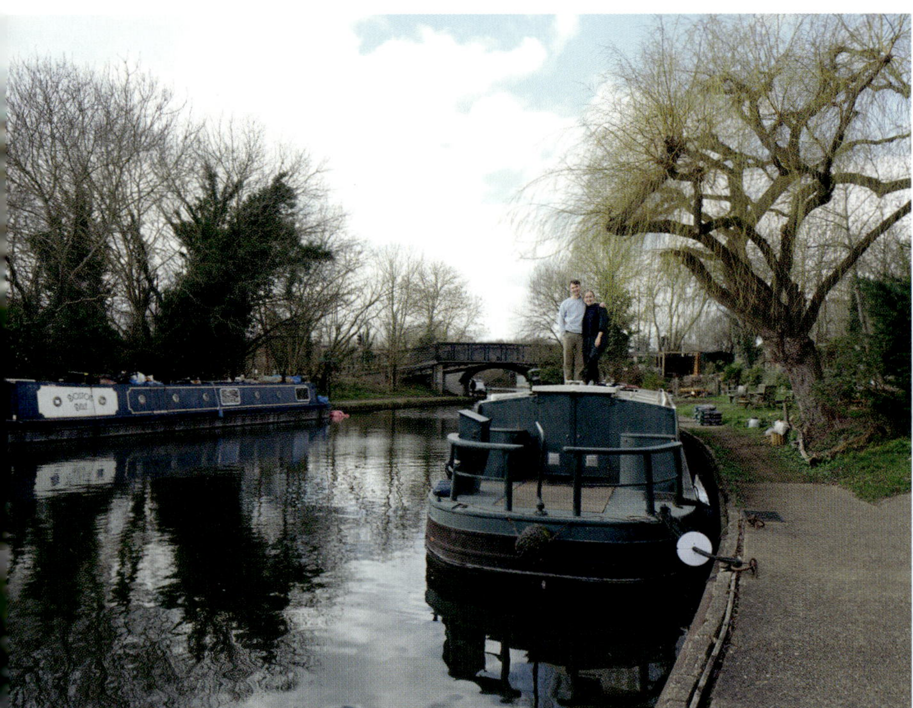

Here we are on top of our boat in our glorious rural location. Behind us is our garden, which is part of our moorings at Horsenden Hill and our 2023 project.

We have lived on a boat for the last two years, moving to Horsenden Hill moorings in 2021. For our first home together, we decided to move to a boat; almost certainly inspired by the fact Jake's granny had lived on a barge, and later his parents had bought their own boat too. We love the community of people here – both on the moorings, and then all those involved in the activities that centre on Horsenden Farm. Within reach of our boat is a brewery, a bakery and a community-run library.

We are trying to find time for more instrument practice. Seen here is Ele on the bassoon and Jake on the guitar.

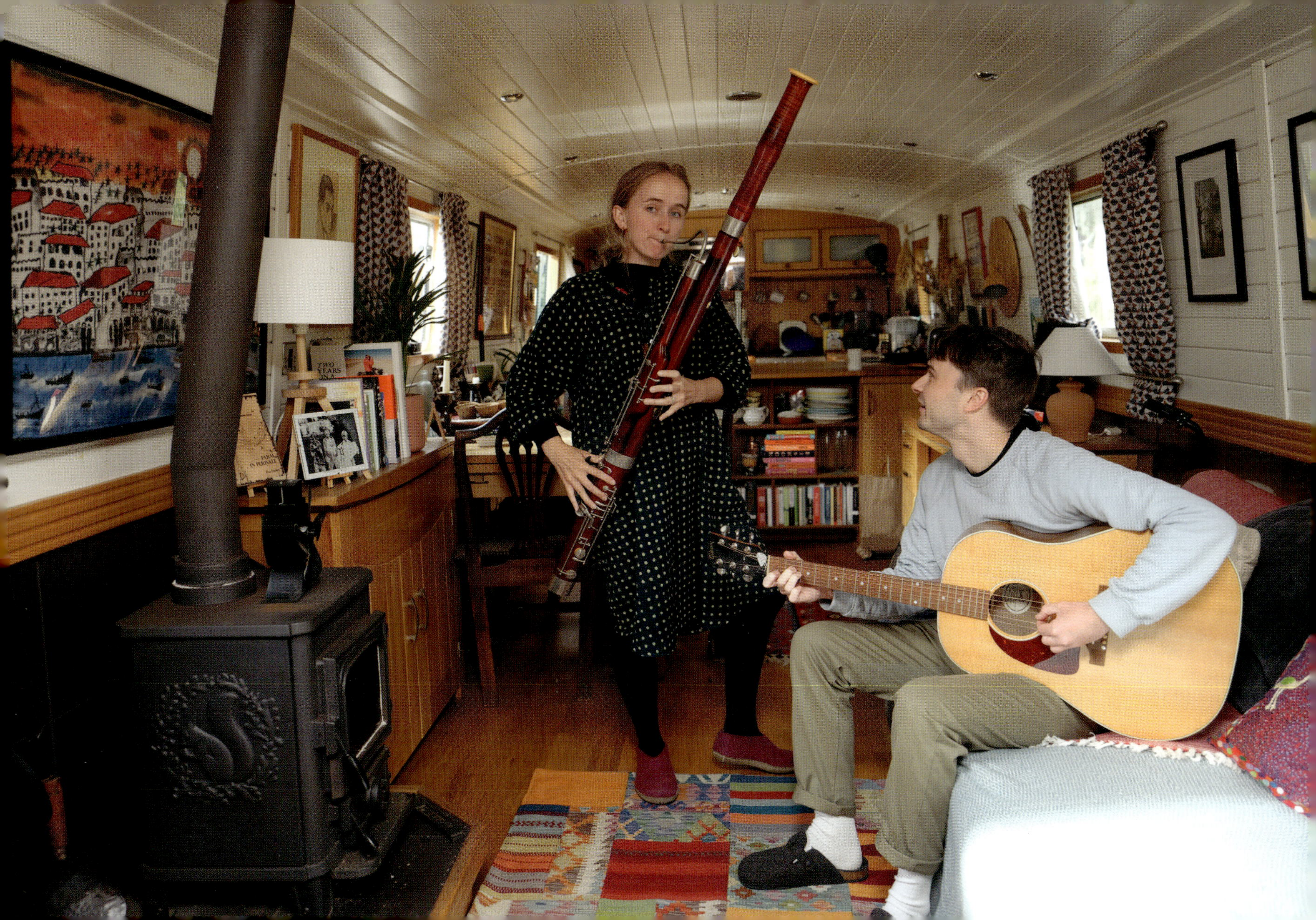

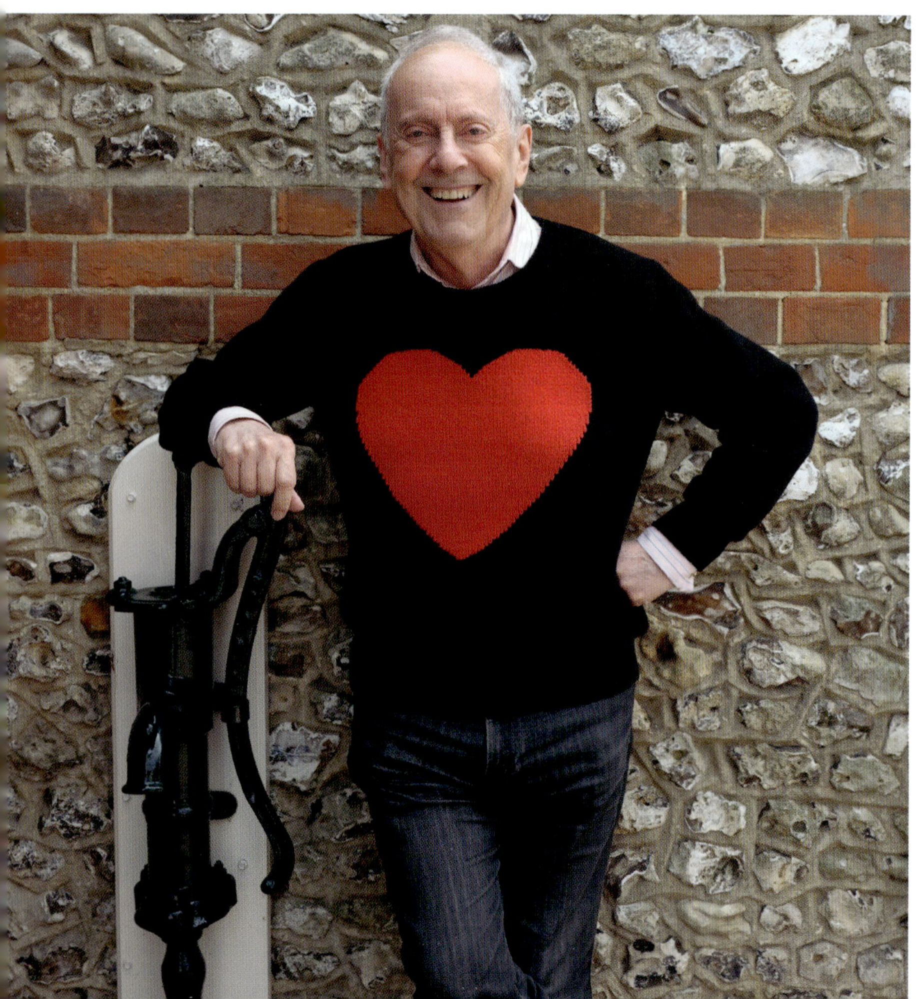

I first saw Sheila Hancock on stage in 1959. We first appeared together on the radio in *Just A Minute* in the early 1980s, but it wasn't until late 2010 that we began to appear together regularly on TV – first in *Celebrity Gogglebox* (where we had a lot of fun) and then in two series where we travelled together along Britain's canals.

We had fun then, too, but we learnt a lot as well. I learnt more than Sheila because she taught me so much – not only about steering a canal boat, but also about life. She is a wise and wonderful person. She is fierce, feisty and full of life – and heart! That's why I am wearing this jumper in her honour.

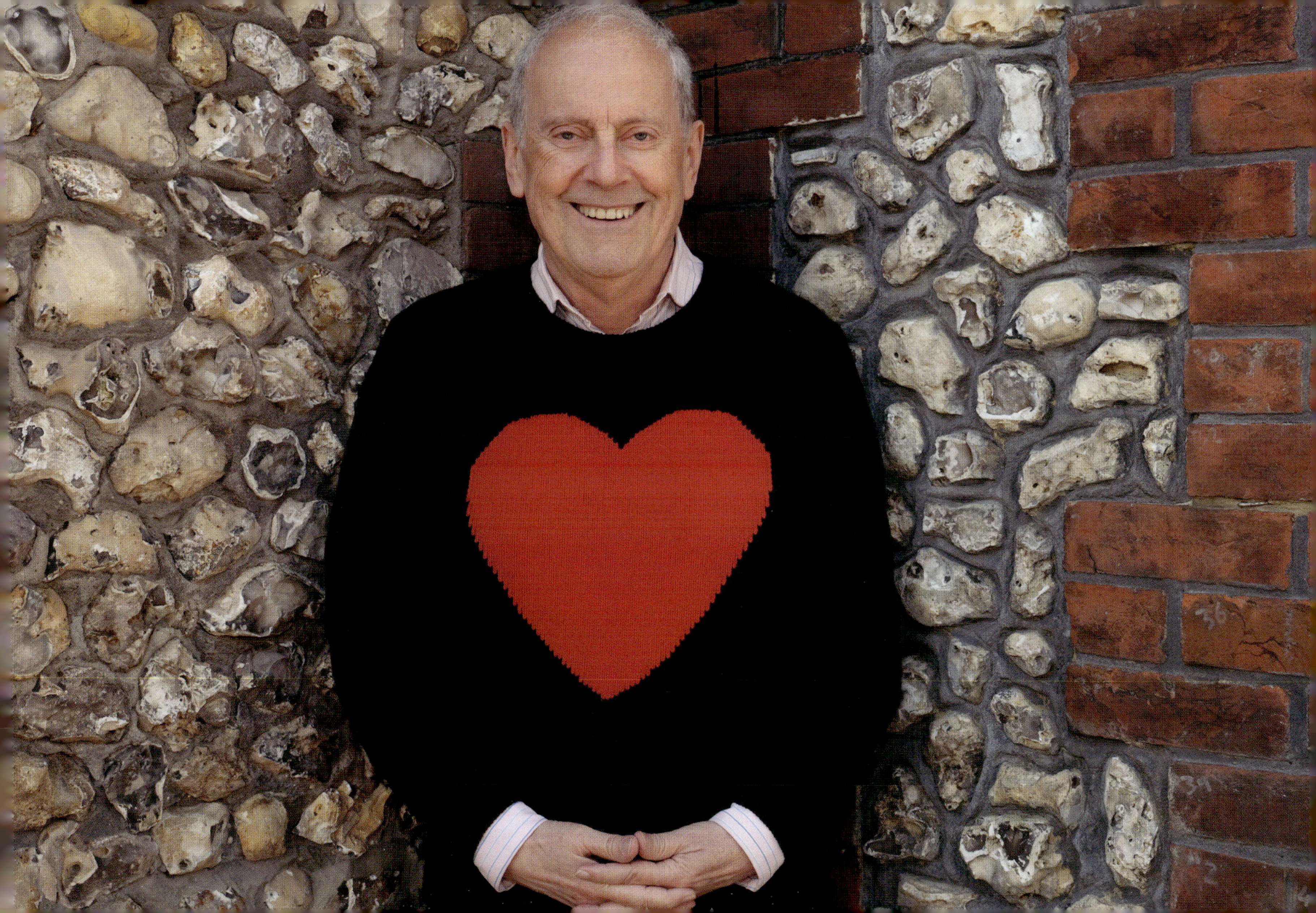

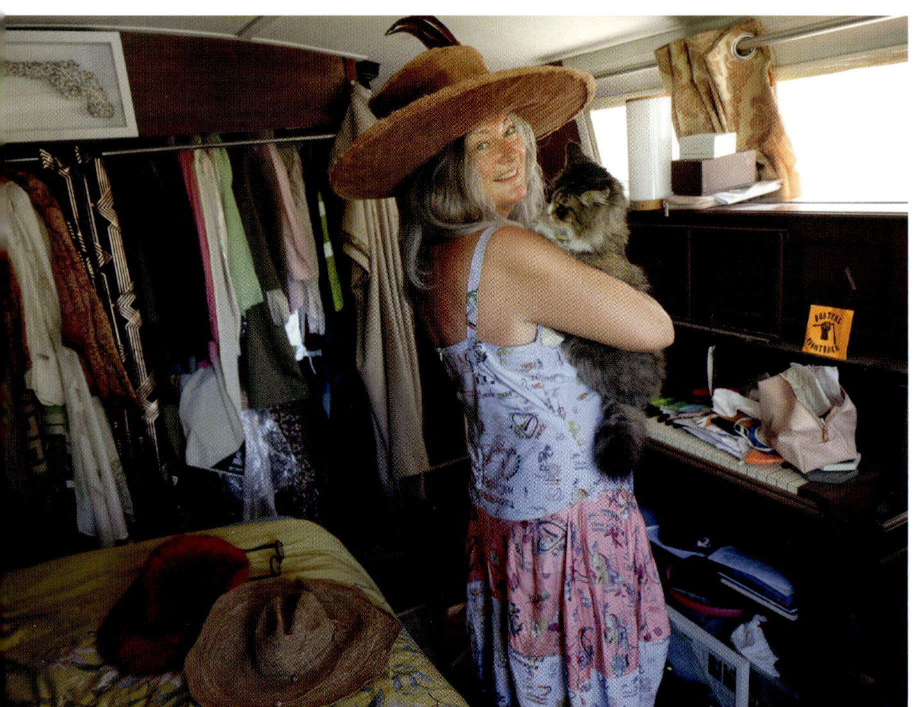

Nothing shipshape about this vessel!

I'm Helen and I'm a psychotherapist working at my private practice in Piccadilly. This is our boat – and I am in the tidy bit! She is called *The Wife of Bath* and is a wide beam, home to me, husband Tim, and cats Fe (pictured) and Pt. We've no home mooring, so we have to move our boat at least every fourteen days. I gave up my Soho flat fifteen years ago and had the boat built instead.

Living aboard as we have done for over thirteen years is complicated, unconventional and often times are very hard. In the photograph, you can see my 'yacht piano'. It rests on a console table, and doesn't have any pedals. It is desperately hard to keep in tune, since the strings are so short. I hardly play at all these days, but I do love singing in choirs and am partial to a bit of karaoke.

I love Vivienne Westwood (RIP), but I have desperately inadequate wardrobe space! Living on board is like living in an old car – everything's 12 volt, connections and wiring tend to vibrate loose as we cruise to our next mooring.

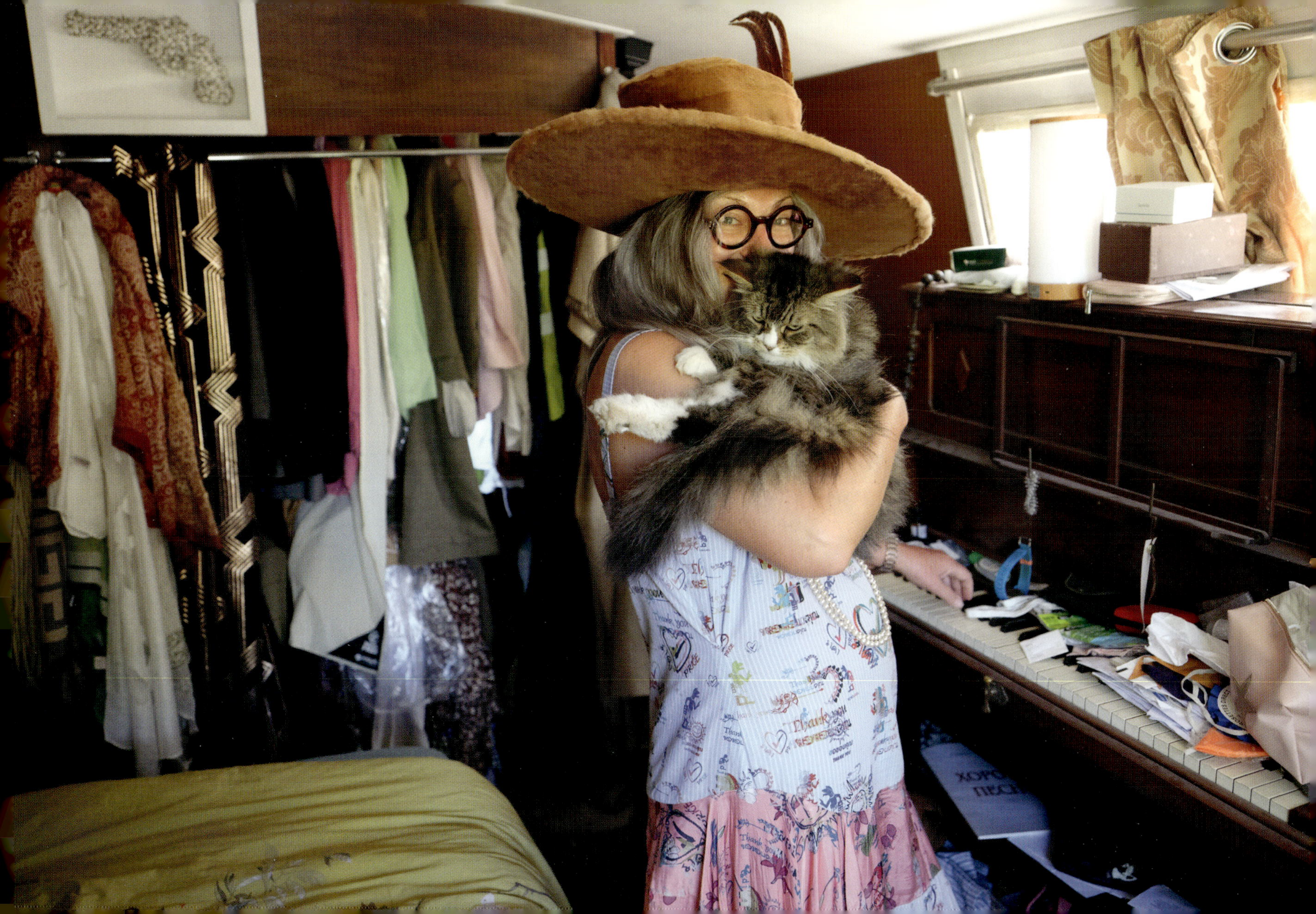

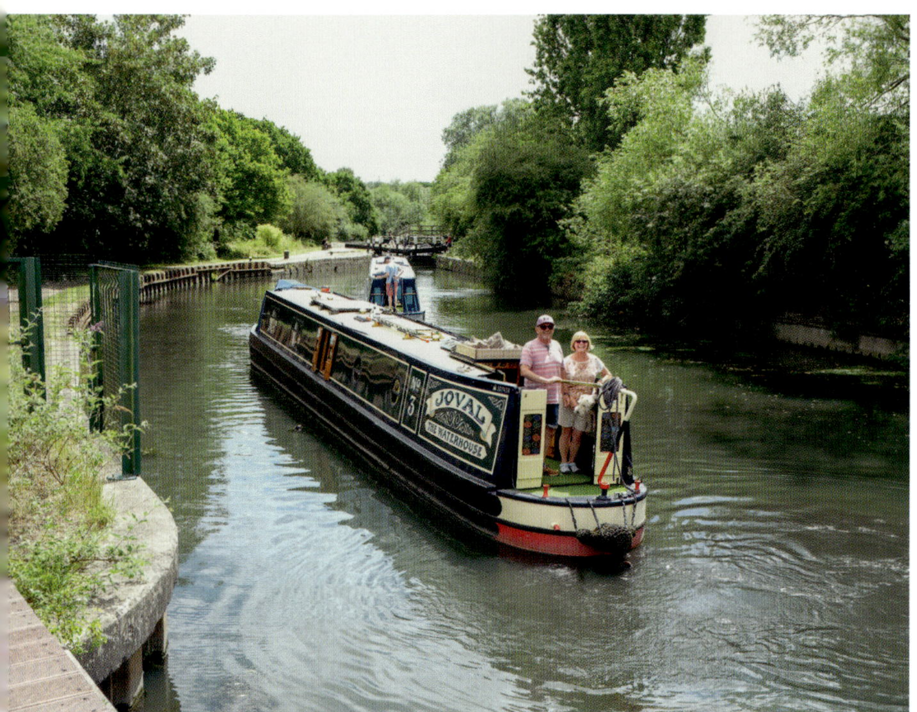

We live in Daventry and moor our boat at a marina a few miles away. We decided this year to have a five-week grand tour with our friends, travelling from Daventry all the way down to the Thames and then back up the Grand Union Canal to home. Unfortunately, it turned into a six-week trip because when we arrived at Banbury, the lock was closed off for eight days because of damage. Loads of people were stranded and we decided to turn and go back the other way and do the trip in reverse: so, a week later we were back where we started. Then another eleven days took us to the end goal, which was Islington on the Regent's Canal where we stayed on a pre-bookable eco mooring. Well worth the long slog to get there.

These photographs were taken on our way to the Thames lock coming into Brentford.

Who knows what the next two weeks will bring. Every day is an adventure and every day has some kind of incident that is either minor or major. When you are on a boat you need to be versatile, resourceful and resilient!

We wouldn't change it for the world; we do love our boat and every trip is memorable.

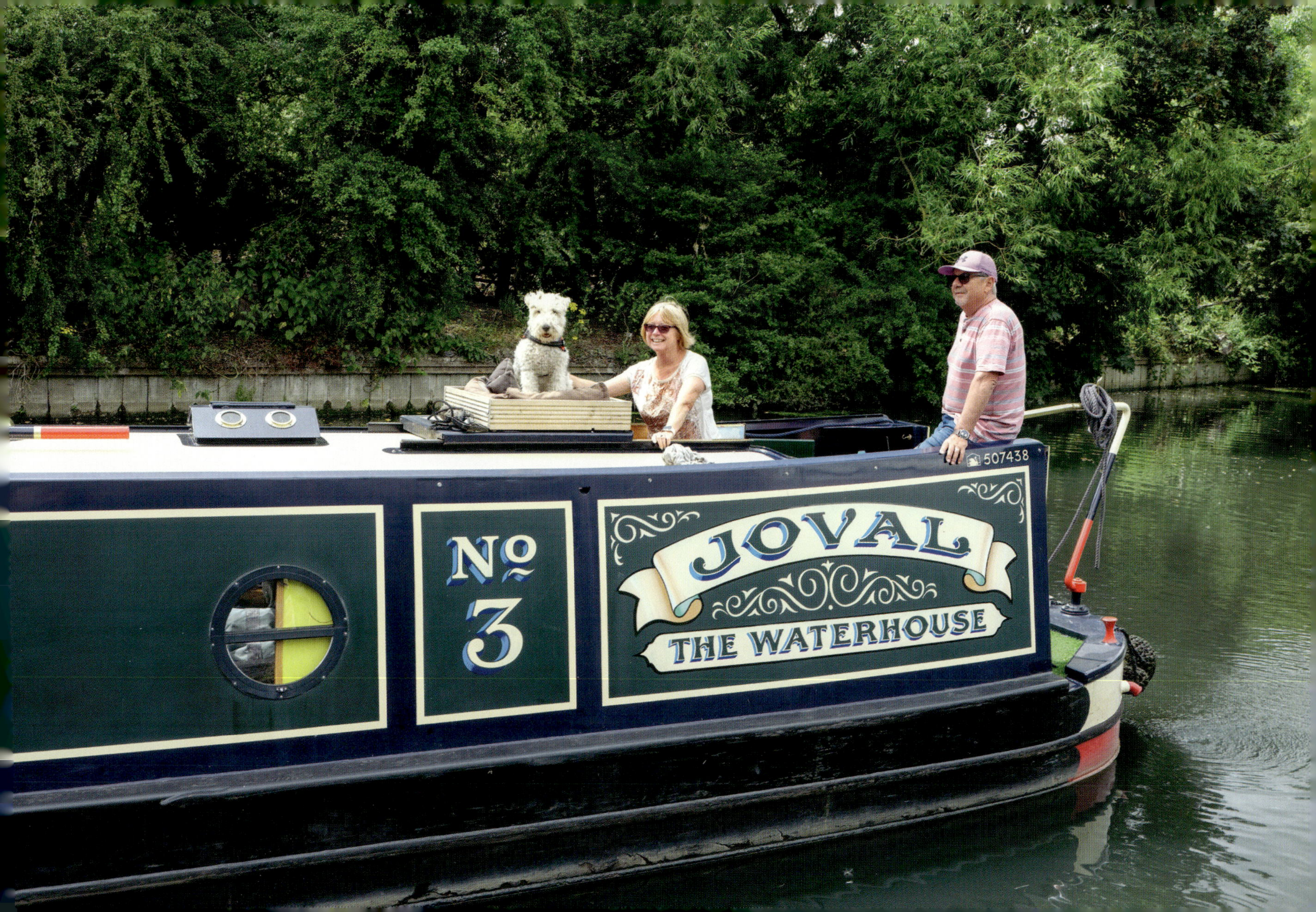

No 3
JOVAL
THE WATERHOUSE
507438

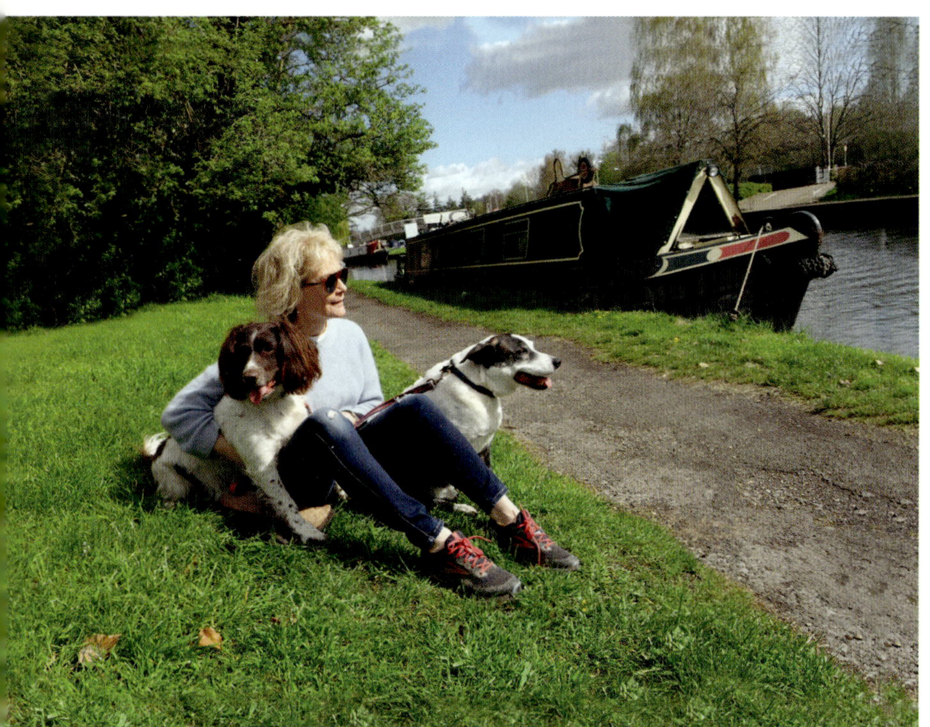

Canals and me: I lived alongside the canal in Little Venice, London, for many, many years and used to love walking my dogs along its banks. One way led to Regent's Park, Camden and beyond. It has a very different character to the other direction, which meandered out past the gasworks towards Brentford. I do believe that if I had kept walking, I would have ended up in Birmingham!

There were so many communities alongside the canal, not only of immaculately kept and much-loved houseboats, but also community gardens like Meanwhile Gardens and others, lovingly tended to by locals. People on the floating homes seem to live their lives at a different pace – they are always ready for a chat with each other, or a passing dog walker like me.

Canals stand for community, something that is fast disappearing in our rapidly moving, technologically 'enhanced' world. Something that should be cherished.

Meanwhile Gardens was established in the 1970s by Jamie McCollough, a local engineer, artist and visionary. It can be found in Kensal Road, North Paddington.

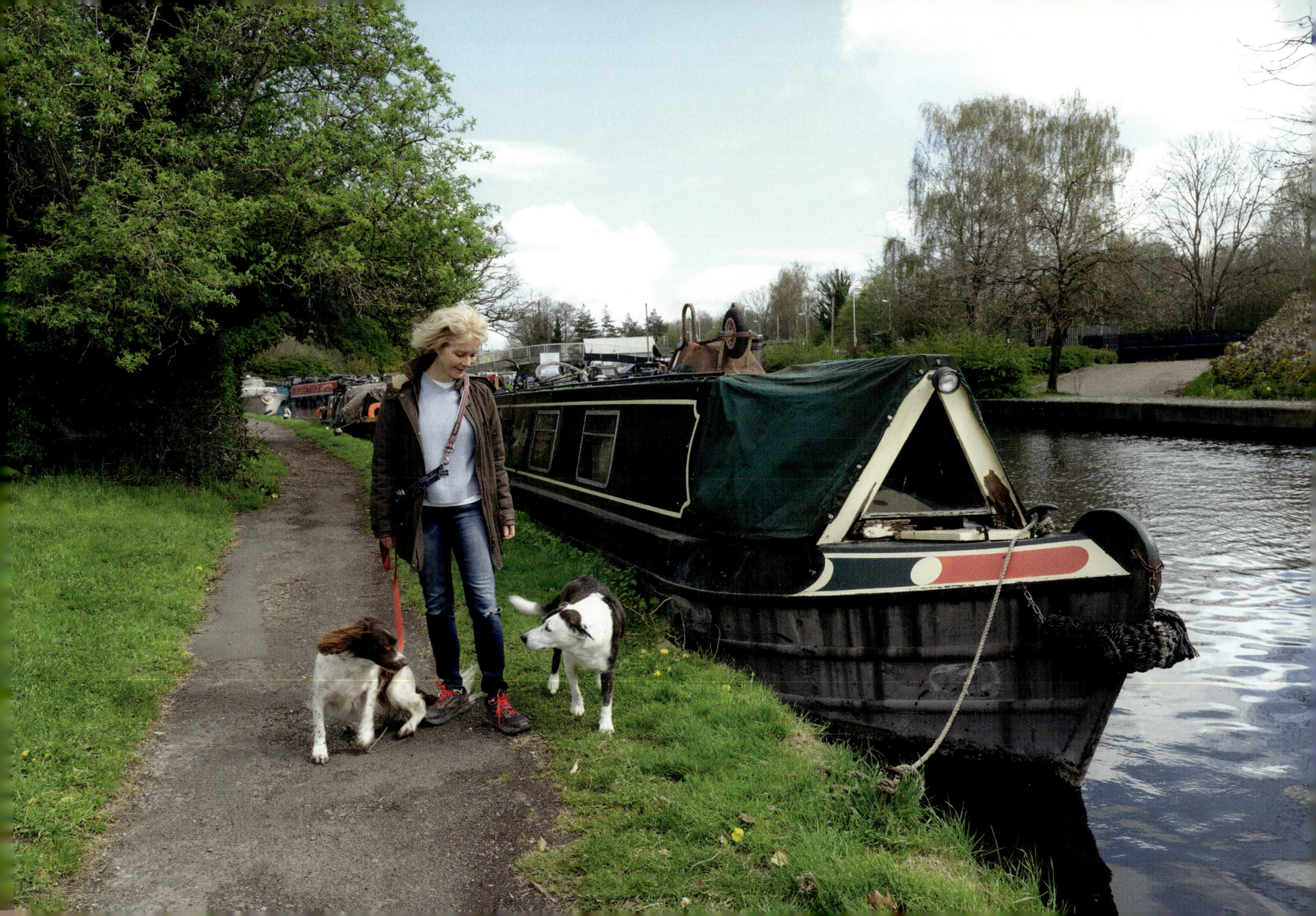

Joe Boyle

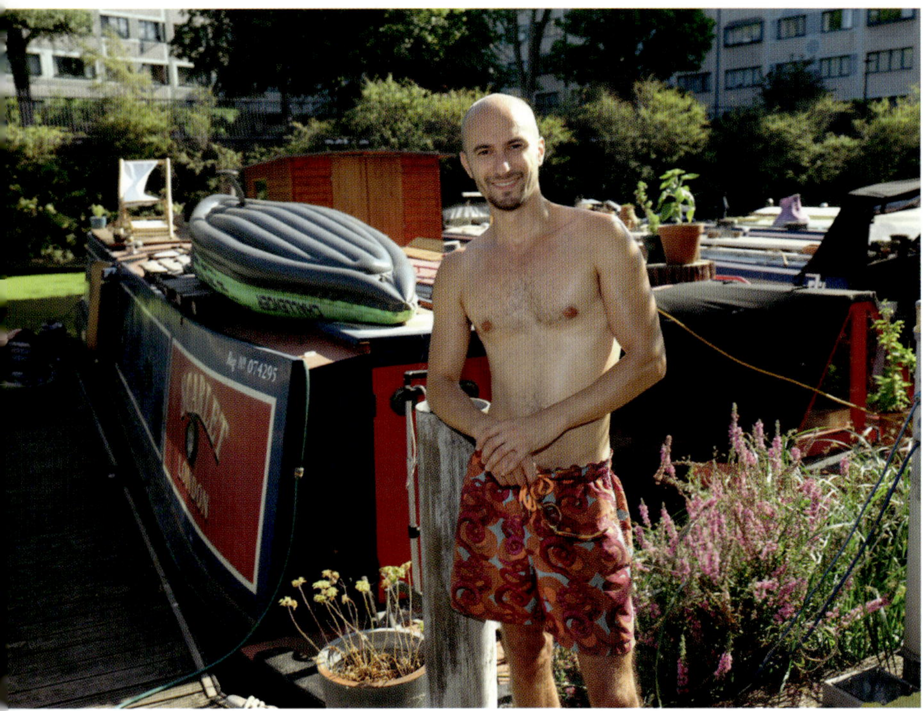

I never imagined I would end up living on a boat in Central London. Life tripped me up and I landed here on the canal next to Regent's Park and for that I'm grateful. It's a wonderful place to live amongst friends and nature and away from the asphalt jungle.

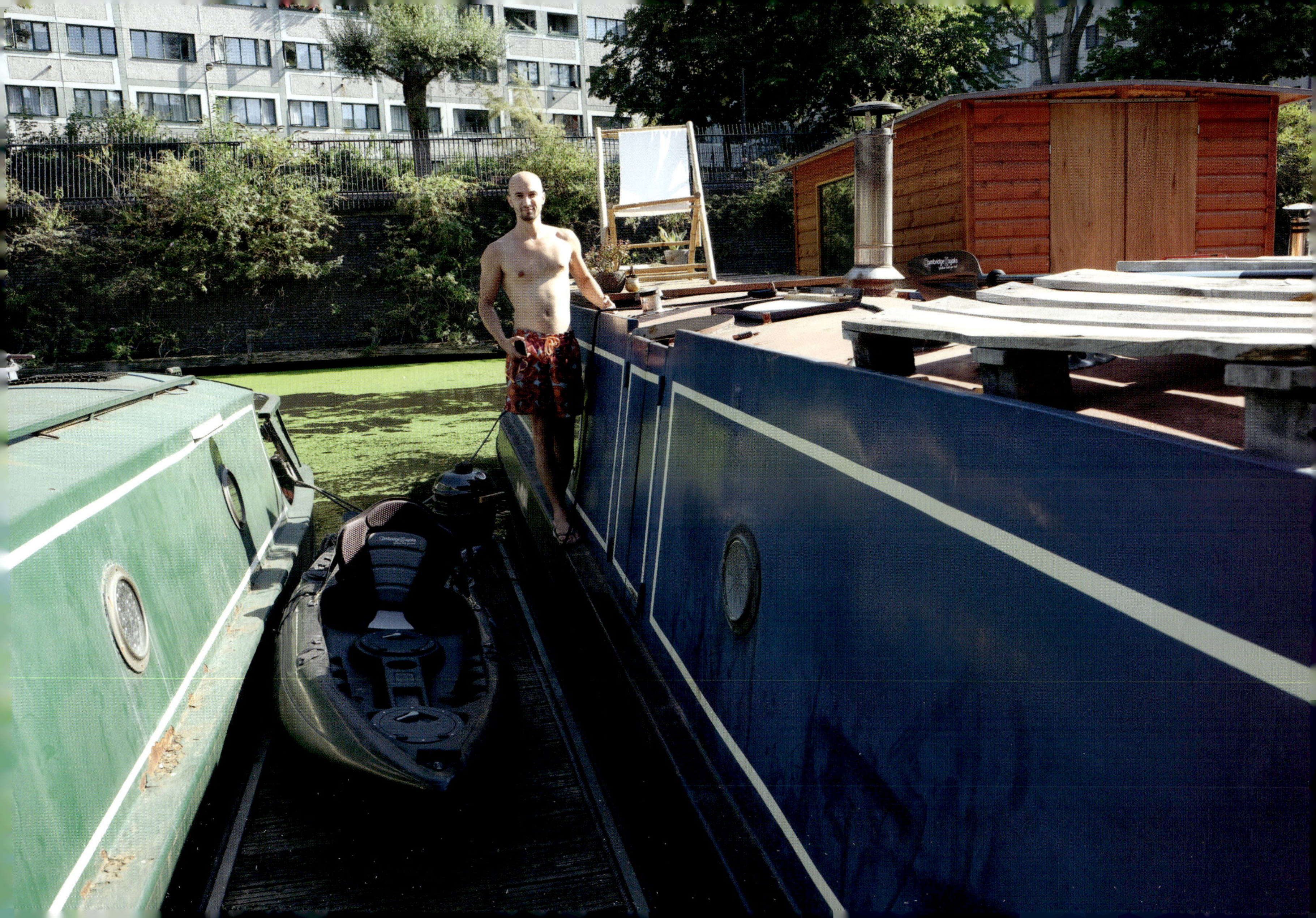

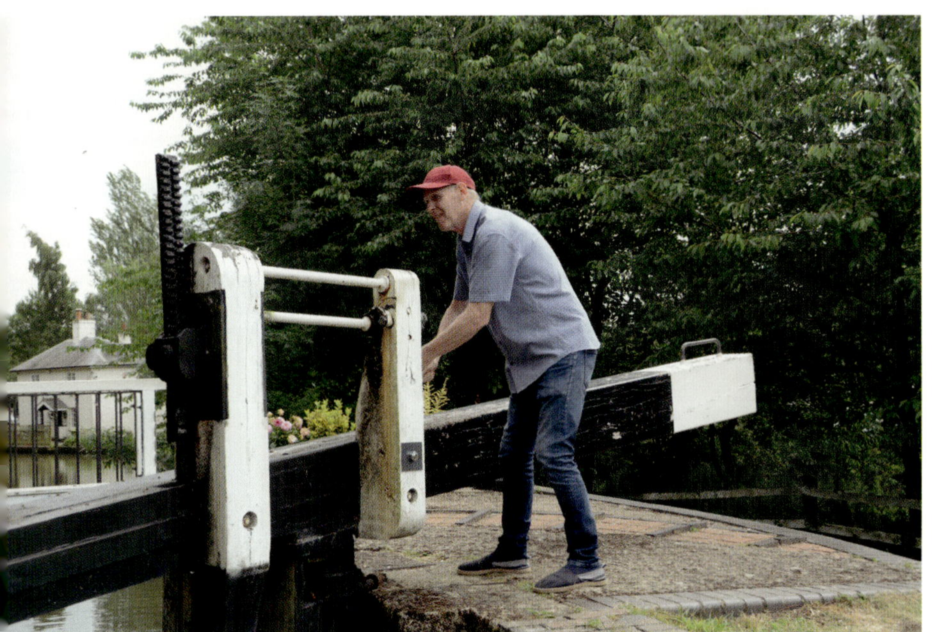

Steering the boat: It took me a while to get used to steering a boat but once I did it was not hard. The narrowboat is much easier to control by using a tiller rather than a steering wheel. The tiller is attached directly to the rudder, so to steer I had to push the tiller the opposite way to the direction in which I wanted to go. It is counter-intuitive, but ultimately it makes the boat far more responsive.

However, reversing can be tricky. I have to think about doing everything the opposite way round. It is a bit disconcerting to begin with. Most boats drift to one side or the other and that has to be corrected. Also, our slab-sided, live-aboard boats are very vulnerable to the wind, so that an unexpected blow can knock the boat off course or even send her into a spin!

On the inland waterways, everything happens very slowly. Boats tend to pass each other with what seems like just a few millimetres to spare! Conversations happen as we pass! We all like to hog the centre of the canal where the water is deepest, moving gently to the right if another boat appears ahead.

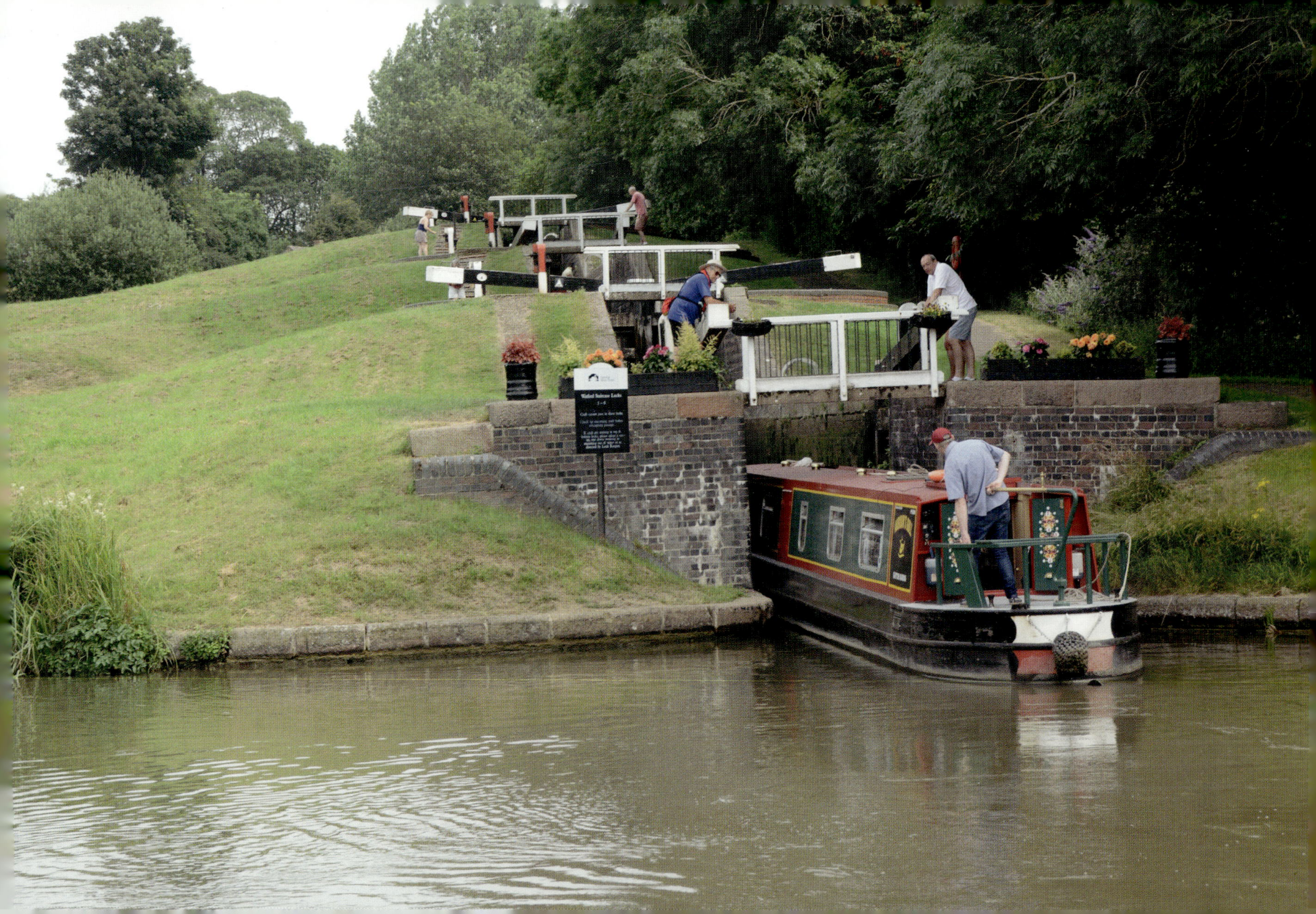

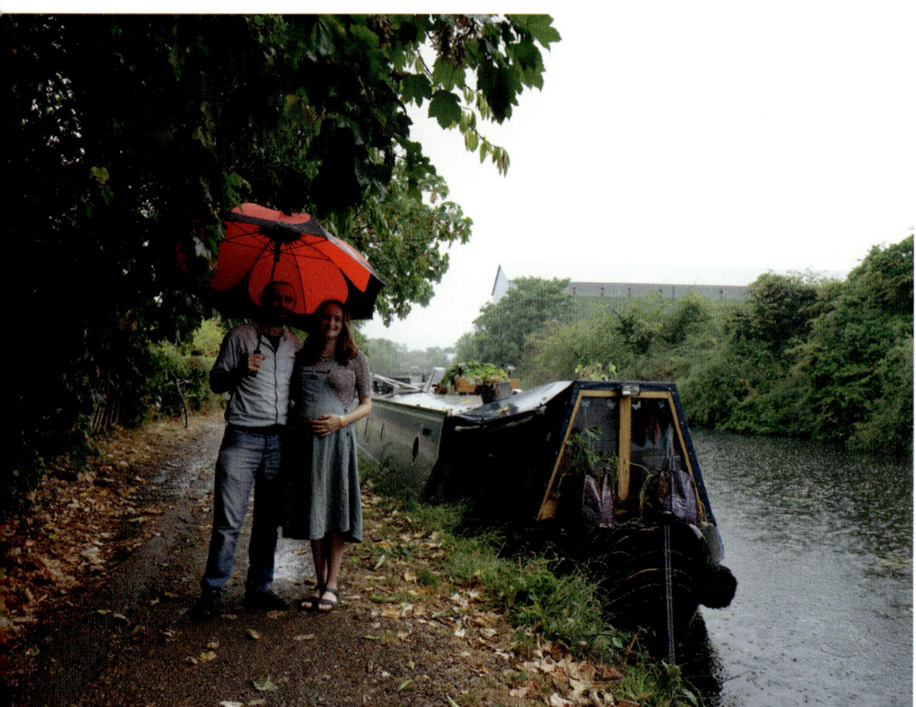

We have lived on the *Diana Grey* for the last eighteen months, cruising around the south-east of England. Previously land-based in a flat in Hackney, we had an epiphany while walking along the Regent's Canal there, deciding to buy a boat and move aboard.

'Juliet is nearing the end of her pregnancy seen in this photograph, as the summer rain falls, giving the vegetables growing on top of the boat a good watering.'

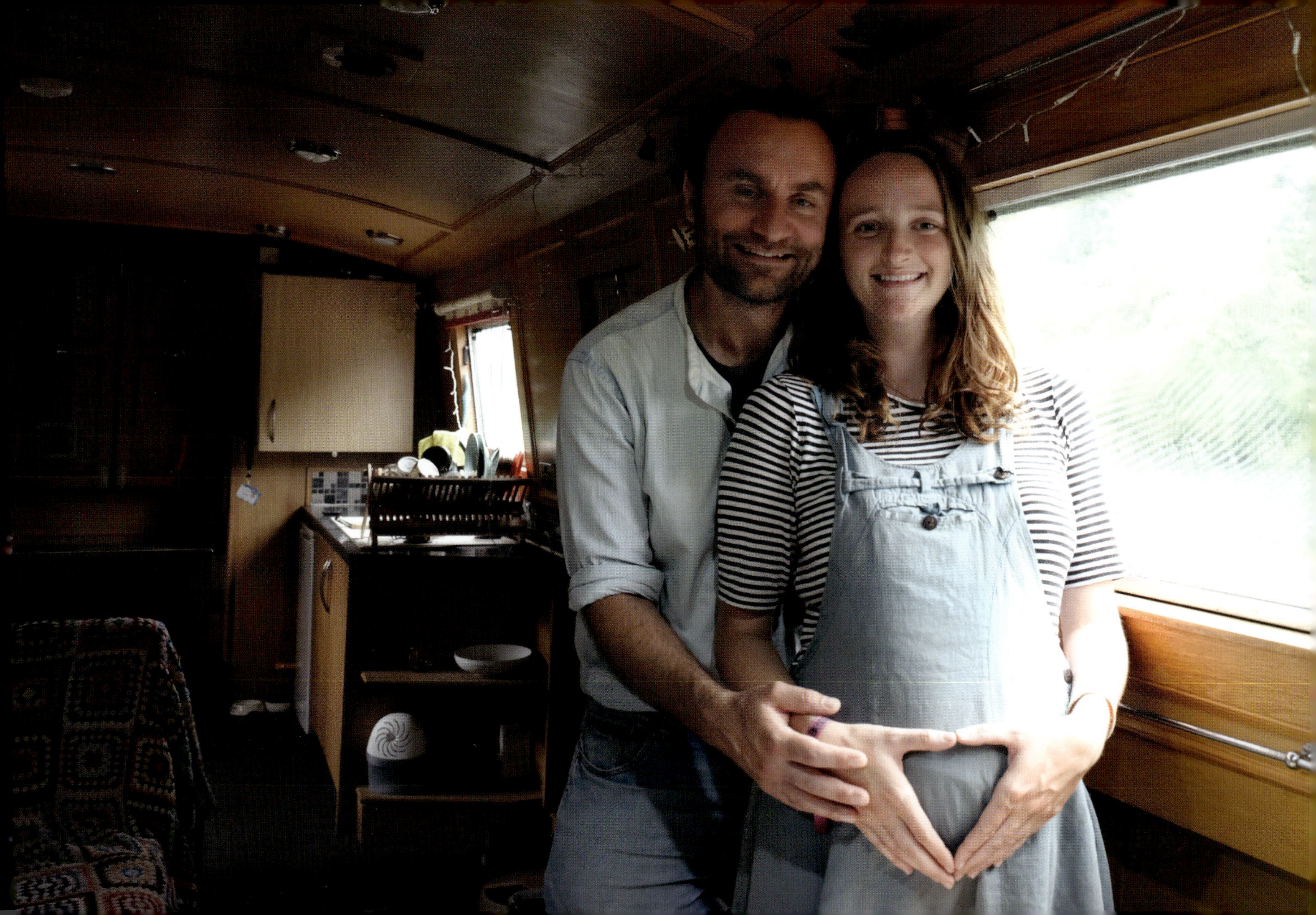

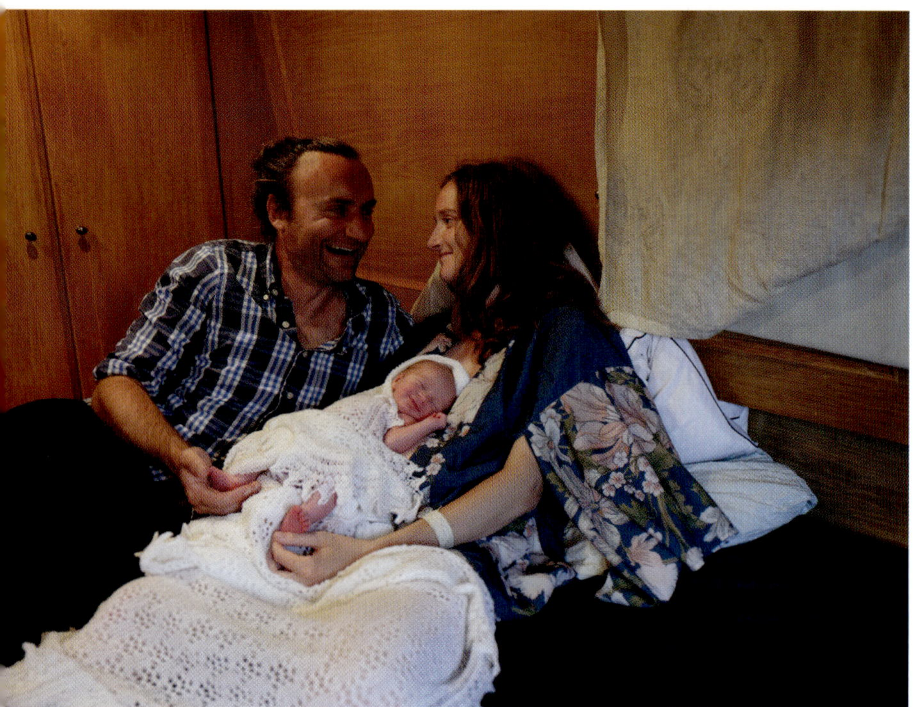

Our son Rupert was born on the boat last August and is around three hours old in these photos.

We were moored up near The Fox pub in Hanwell. Rupert became the fifth member of the crew as our two very fluffy Ragdoll cats, Albus and Akala, also live aboard. Of the five of us, only Joe and Akala have fallen overboard so far! We spent last winter in Kings Langley and then planned to head towards Milton Keynes and beyond.

Juliet told me that she has no regrets about giving birth on the boat. The two midwives were fantastic despite it being their first boat birth and one of them feeling a little seasick. Juliet said she felt very safe in our bedroom cabin almost like she was in a womb herself.

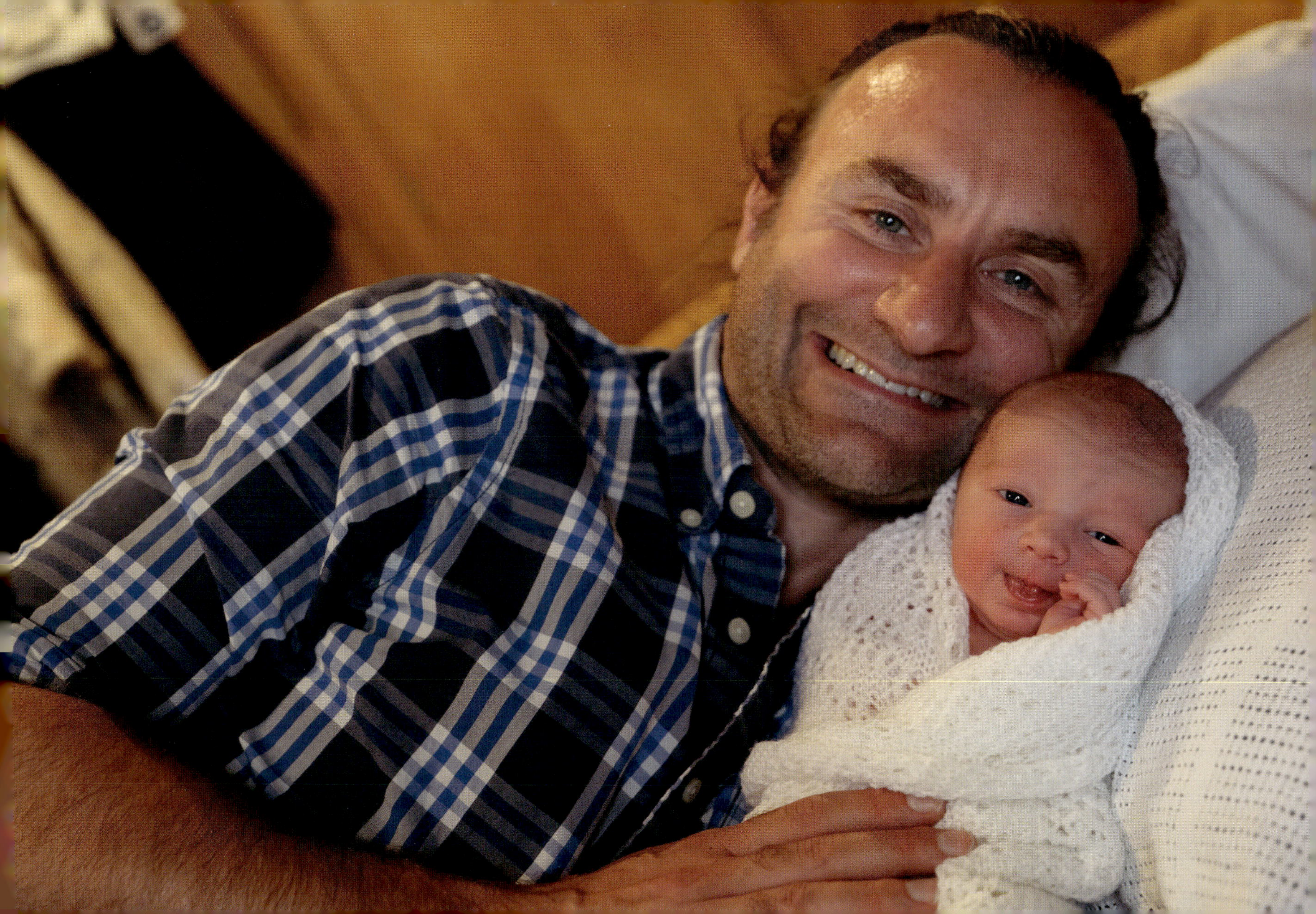

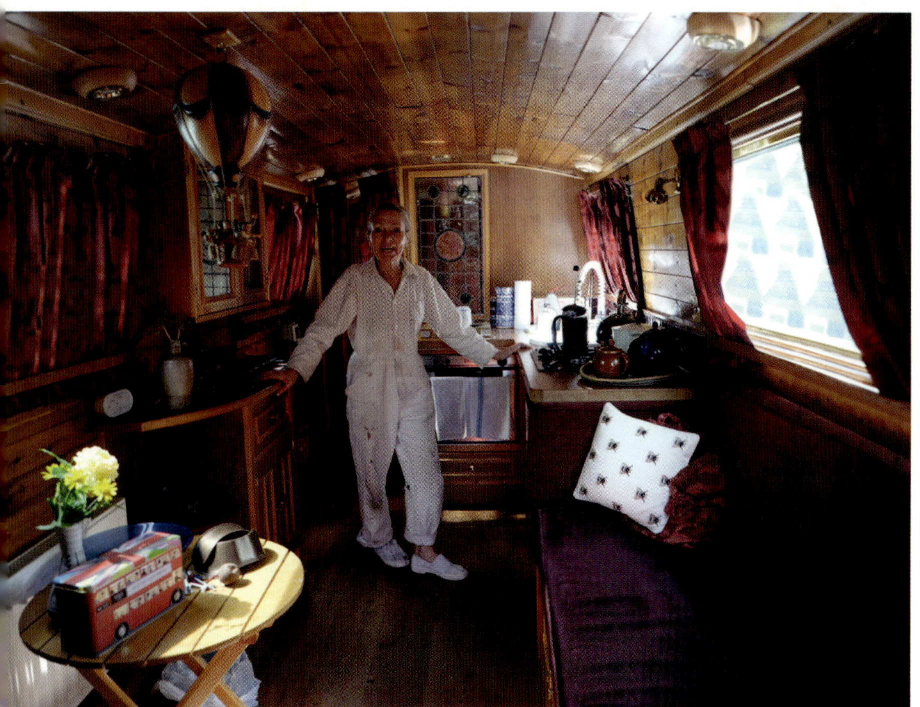

I bought my beloved 40-foot Springer narrowboat to escape from flat dwelling – and the hothouse environment of international corporate life. I did not think that she and I would still be together after thirty-two years, but the twists and turns of life make us all value what we have and reflect on what we have lost. It's a lesson in gratitude. The health of our waterways and the wildlife that shares our waterways are all-consuming topics of conversation.

About twelve years ago, I finally gathered the resources to redesign and rebuild of the interior of the boat to make her more comfortable for cruising. I changed my pump-out toilet for a Swedish compost loo. I have learnt to love and care for my stove – a lesson learned from a professional steerer on the waterbus who told me that my relationship with my stove would be more important that my relationship with my lover. He was right! I have a Franco-Belge and I love it!

I now have a tiller that does not wobble or squirt water all over me whenever I put on some power. A boat needs to be maintained constantly – keeping them afloat is a project. And I have spent many hours delving into the murky depths of my engine compartment or scrambling around a dry dock cleaning or painting her hull. That is when you really know your boat.

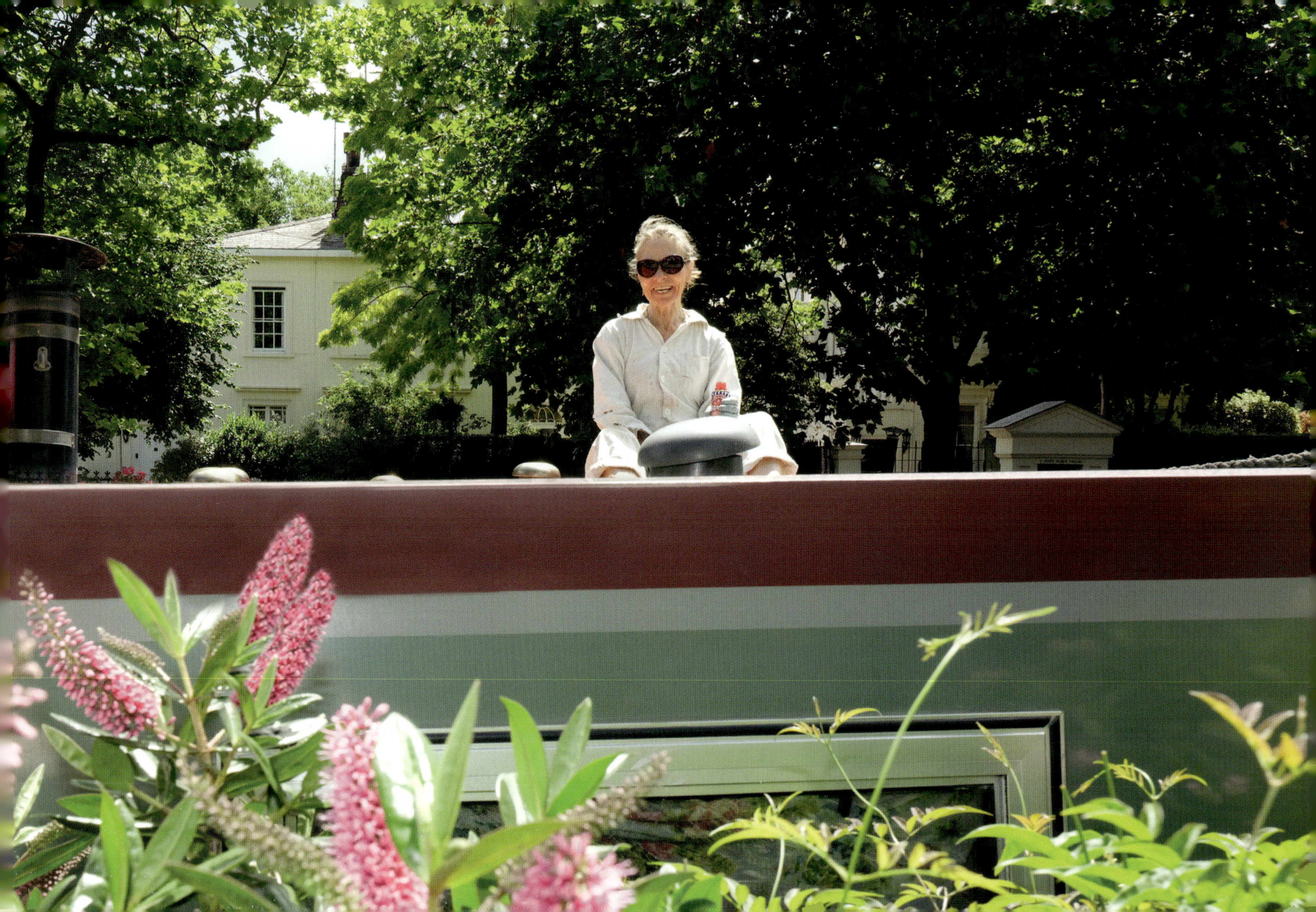

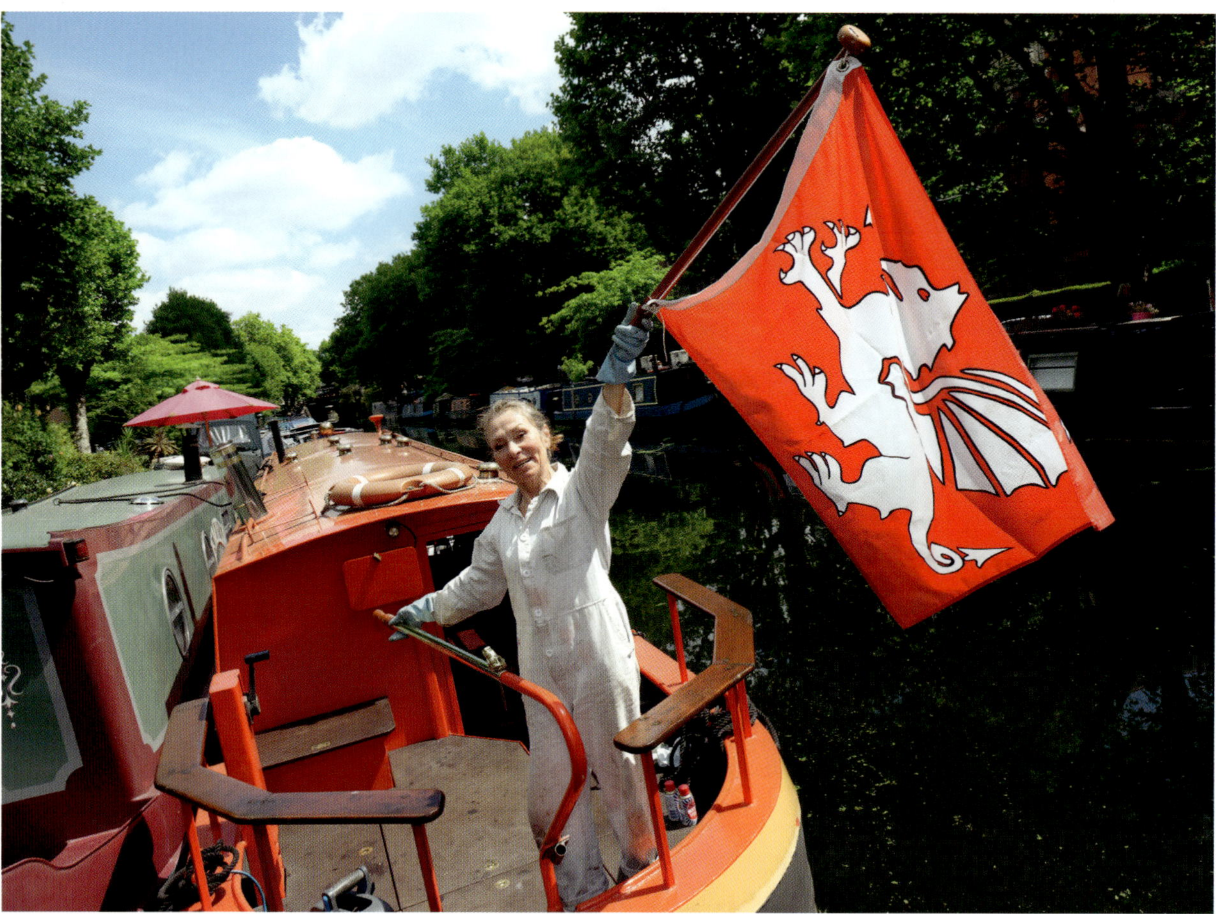

To celebrate my post-renovation relaunch, I purchased a flag. It has an orange background with a white dragon and it was the original flag of the Angles in the fifth century – later adopted as Oliver Cromwell's battle standard! That says quite a lot about my life, doesn't it?

My boat and my towpath garden in Little Venice are still places of solace, comfort and the space for calm reflection. A slow cruise early on a summer's morning has a meditative quality about it.

In Little Venice, we all know we are blessed.

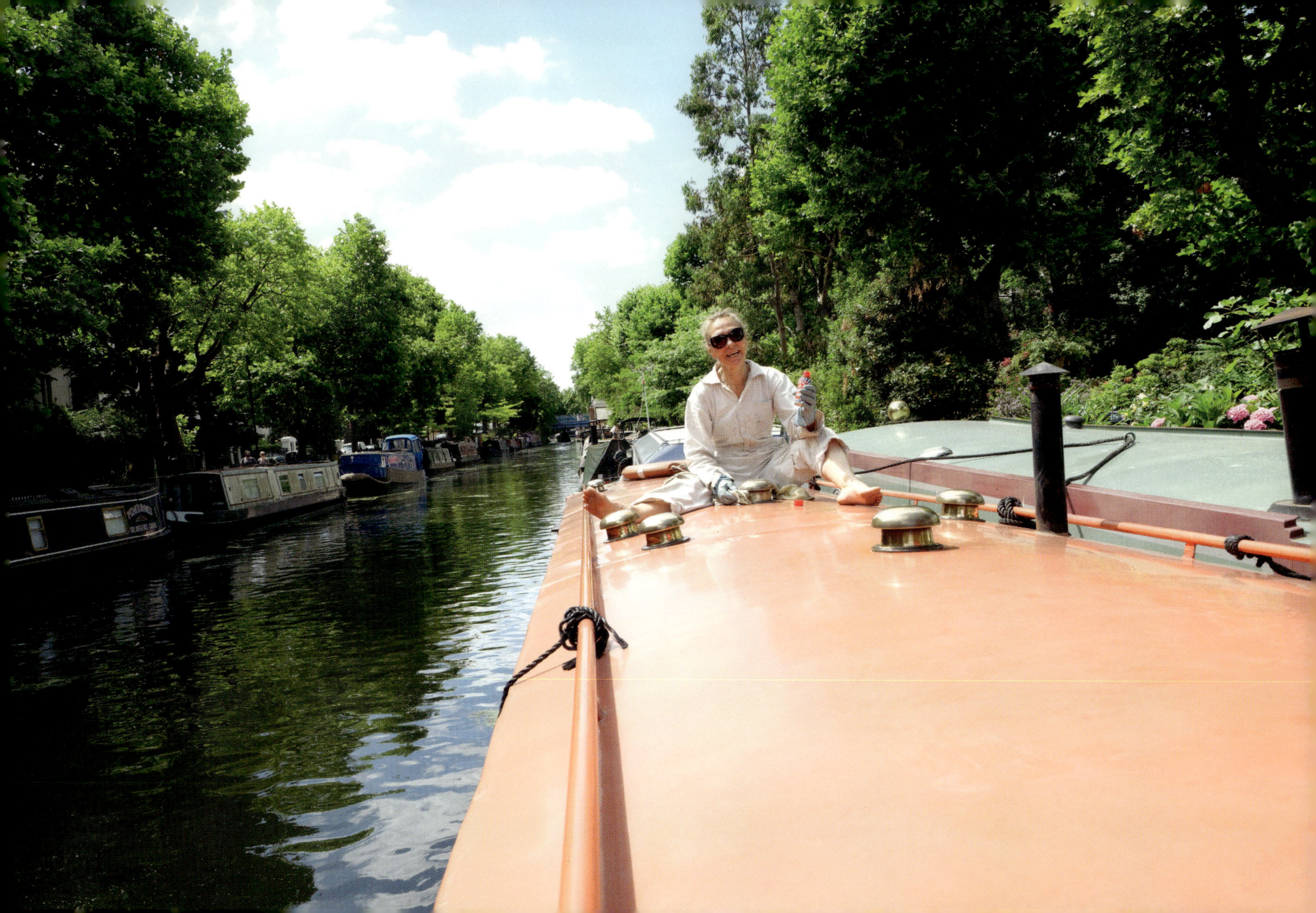

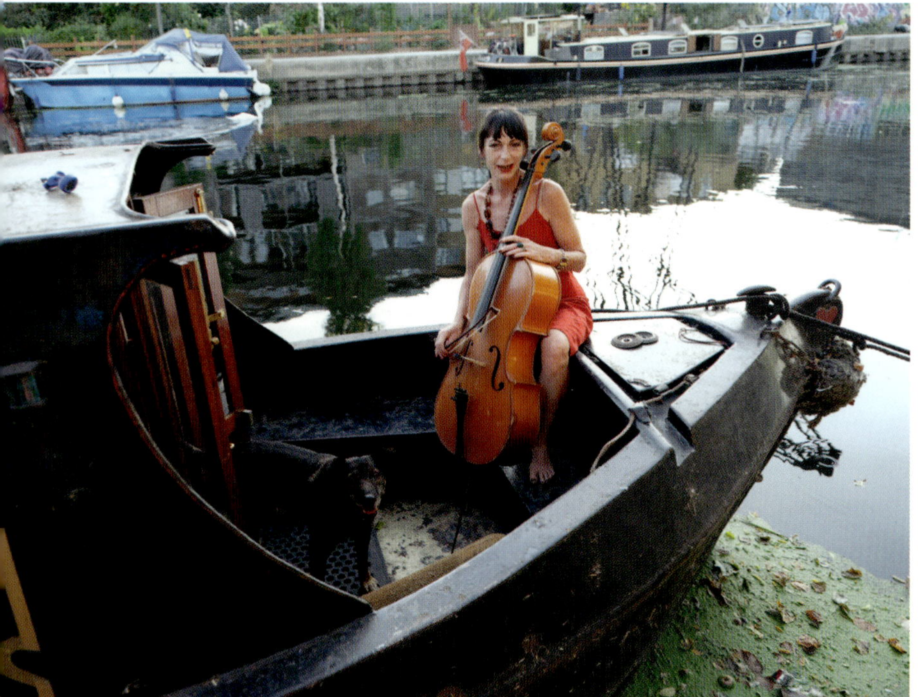

I moved onto my narrowboat several years ago as I was a nightmare neighbour and also had a hankering to see the moon.

I taught piano lessons in a tiny flat all day and wrote music on the piano through the night. I thought about moving to the country but I also worked with several bands based in London, so the boat was the perfect solution. Now, if I'm driving my neighbour's crazy, I just move the boat, although I have found boaters much more understanding and even appreciative than flat dwellers.

There is a strong sense of community amongst the boaters so you never have to be alone, and yet there is a sense of space and freedom that I need to be able to write.

And now I just look out of my window to see the moon.

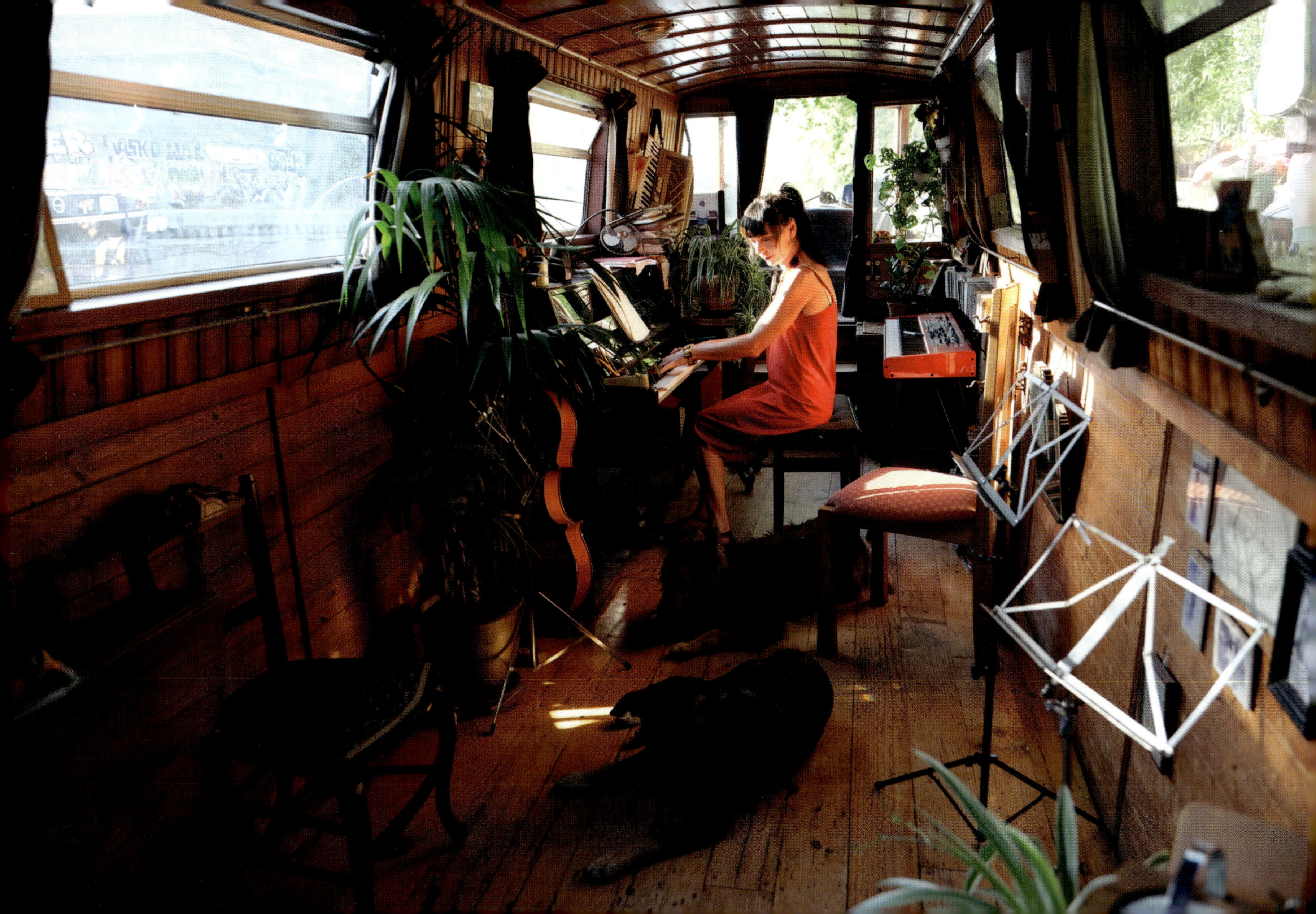

Karen Cook

Major in the British Army and Registered Nurse in the
Queen Alexandra's Royal Army Nursing Corps

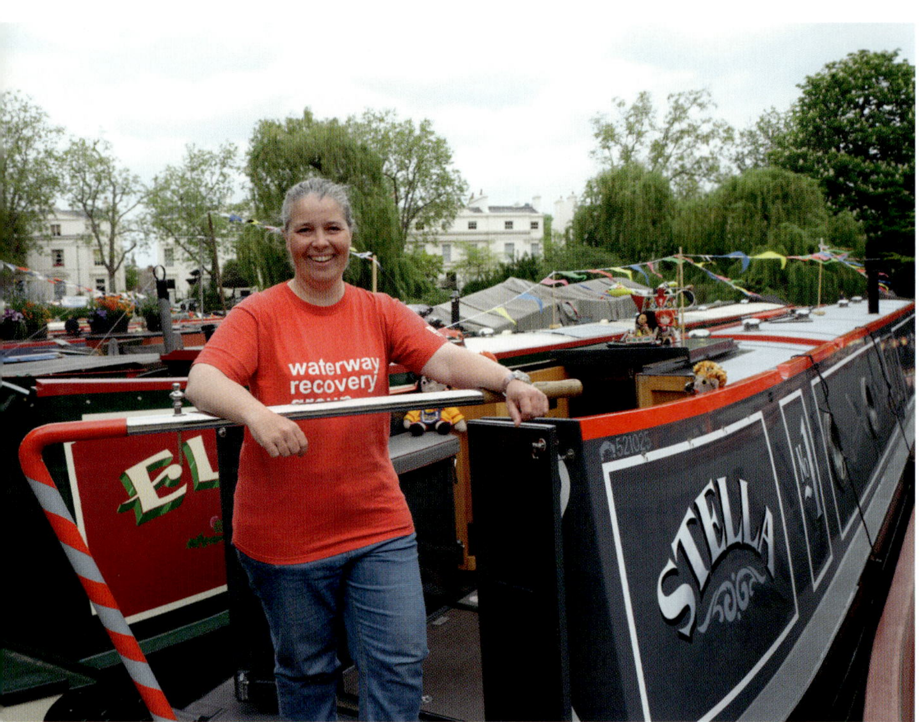

I live a busy life. I often say to people that I have a job within a job: I am a daughter, a mum, a nurse, an officer in the British Army and I am a leader in various volunteering organisations, and to continue with my lifelong learning associated with being a nurse, I am currently studying yet another university module. I have deployed onto many operations overseas and it was during these deployments to Afghanistan, Iraq, and Kuwait that I realised I needed to have a safe place to escape to.

Fifteen years ago, I decided to start planning to build my own 58-foot narrowboat. I had already chosen the name for her; she was to be called *Stella* after my grandmother, which means 'star'. Unfortunately, she died before the boat was completed. I visited Crick in Northamptonshire in 2011 and chose a builder who was going to realise my dream. The shell was built by Tyler Wilson in Sheffield and delivered to the boat fitter in November 2011 – Aqua Narrowboats in Derbyshire. She was placed in the water in early 2012. She was handed over to me at the end of May 2012 when the boat was on display at the Crick Boat Show.

The final details were managed by my parents, who I appointed as project managers – at the time, I was deployed with the Army to Kenya from March to June 2012. I received regular updates and found that the mobile signal in Kenya is far better than the UK! I spent a few weeks afloat and then deployed to support the Olympics in London until the end of September. Once this was completed, I had some well-earned leave and we had the coldest winter and the boat was frozen in for three months. Many people ask me 'Is it cold on the boat?' It is a home from home with all the mod cons: washing machine, full-size oven, hob, fridge, freezer, and wine cellars under the floor and not forgetting the central heating and a comfortable double bed.

I love my boat; it gives me time to relax, take stock and reset before having to focus on the next posting. I am grateful for my escape and realise that I am lucky. My boat provides a break away from technology and the stress of everyday life. Being close to water and nature provides many benefits and one that is so important is mental health. I think over the past few years this has become important to most people. The canals are unique to Britain and something that needs to be preserved for future generations.

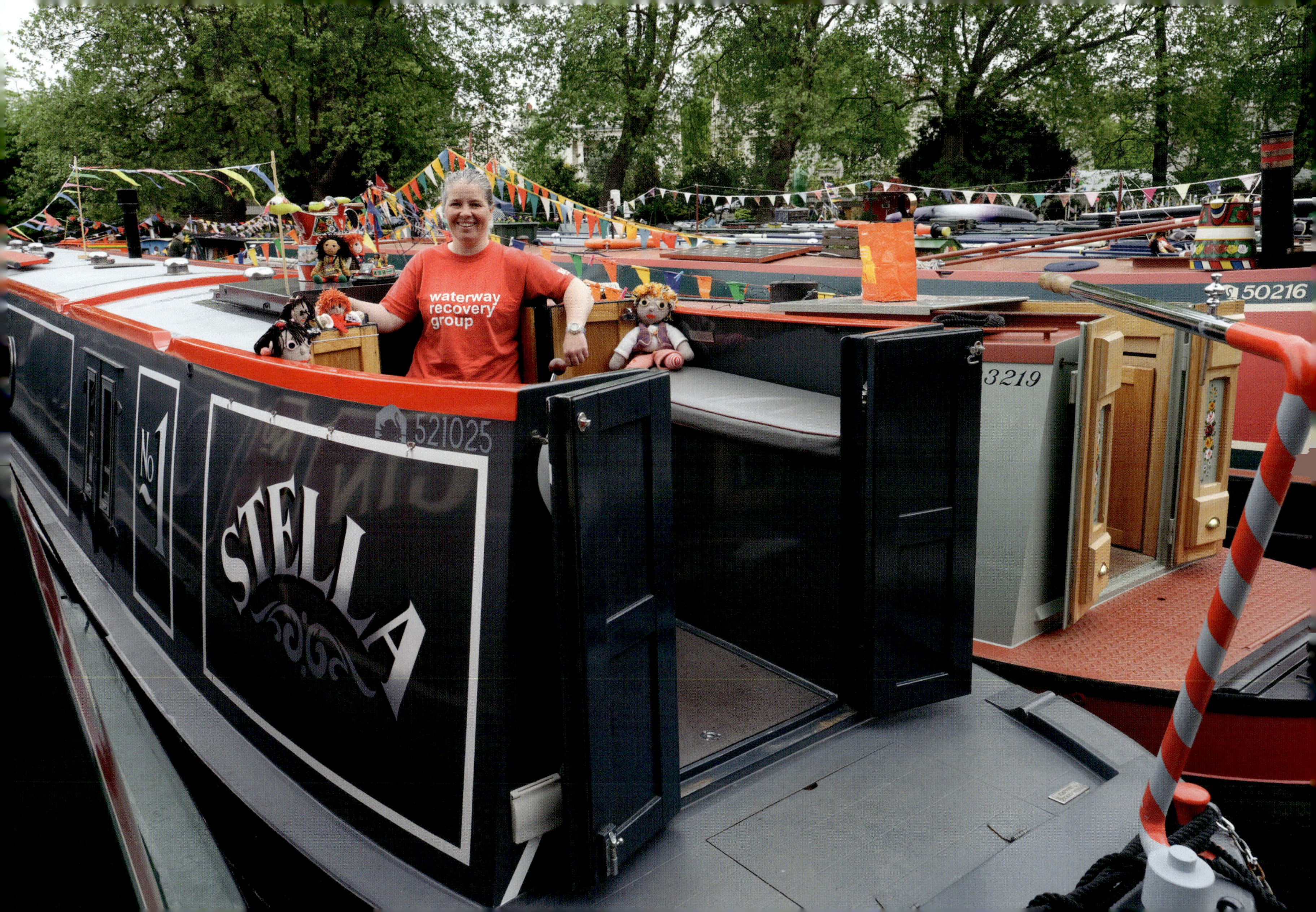
waterway
recovery
group
No 1
521025
STELLA
50216
3219

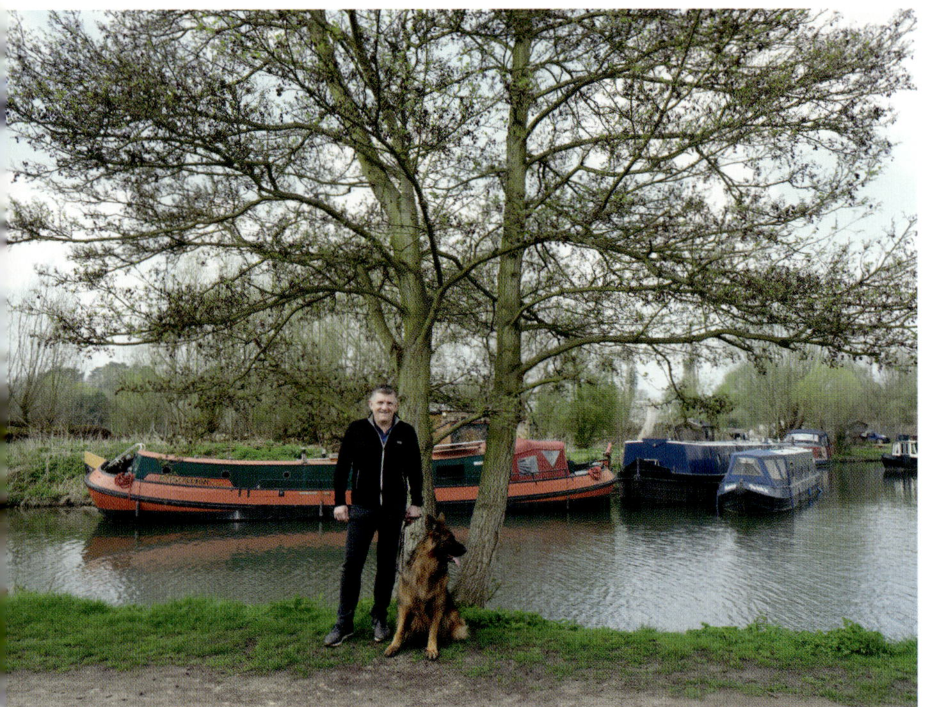

I believe the health of our canals and rivers, which provide such enormous support in helping so many species flourish, is such a worthy cause. The trees, plants, mammals and fish all deserve our help in maintaining their habitat. Hopefully we can all appreciate and enjoy these wonderful environments. Many enjoyable hours have been spent walking our dogs along the canals in Hertfordshire, enhancing our appreciation of nature, increasing our own well-being in the process.

Myself and my children, Georgia and Henry, have spent many enjoyable hours with our dog Scampi along the canals in Hertfordshire. And Scampi thoroughly enjoyed this euphoric walk, constantly scanning for any wildlife that may appear.

Every outing brings its own unique experience.

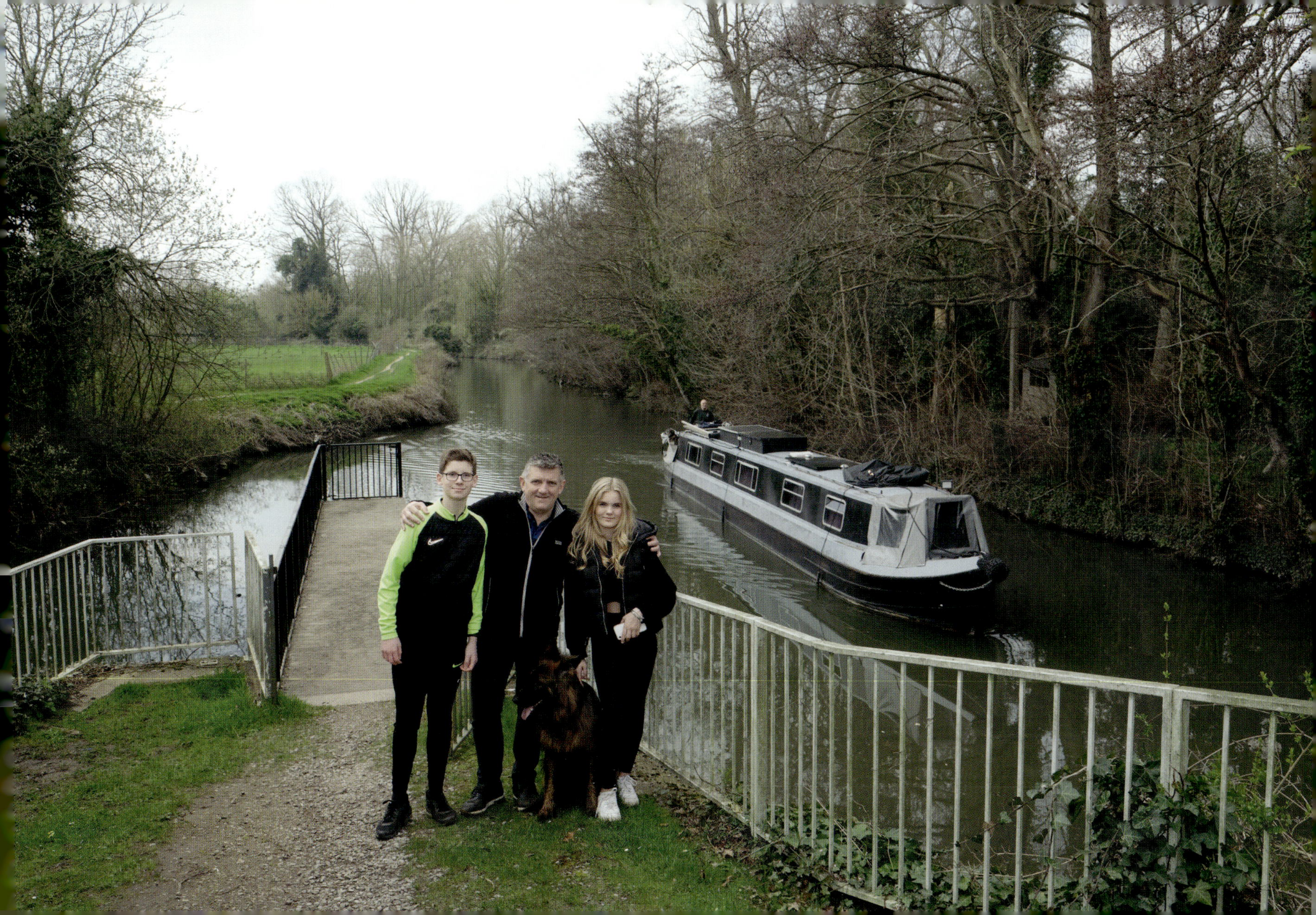

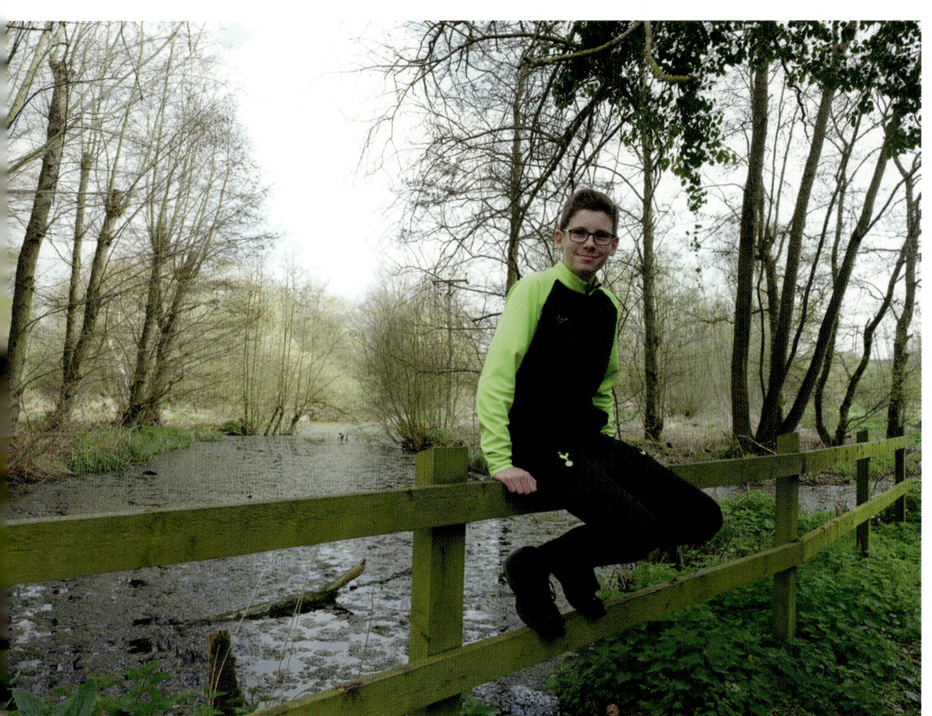

A few years ago, when Dad first suggested that we go down to the canal for a walk, all my sister Georgia and I wanted to do was to stay at home with our modern lifestyle of mobile phones and computer games, but reluctantly we went – kicking and screaming. How glad we were!

Whilst strolling along the canal we experienced some fascinating wildlife such as rabbits and squirrels running through the woods and swans swimming elegantly through the calm water, which provided a welcome experience to our walk. The birds chirping and the leaves crunching beneath our feet opened up the natural sense of being outside. Now many years on our walks by the canal are the perfect way to start the day with the sun blazing down on us and watching boats and canoes travel along, definitely clearing our heads, which in turn helps us to get back to studying.

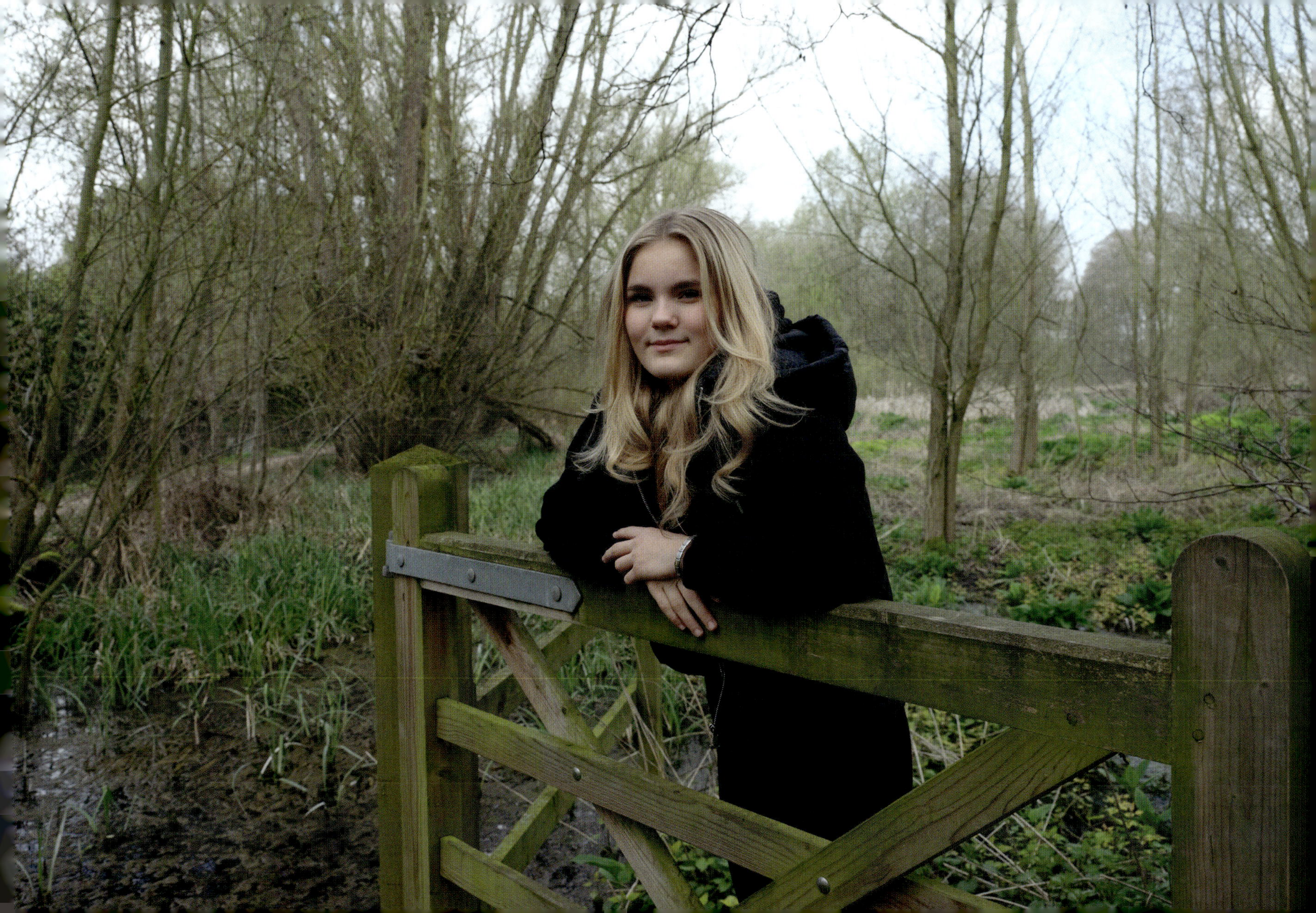

Kevin Still & Saffy

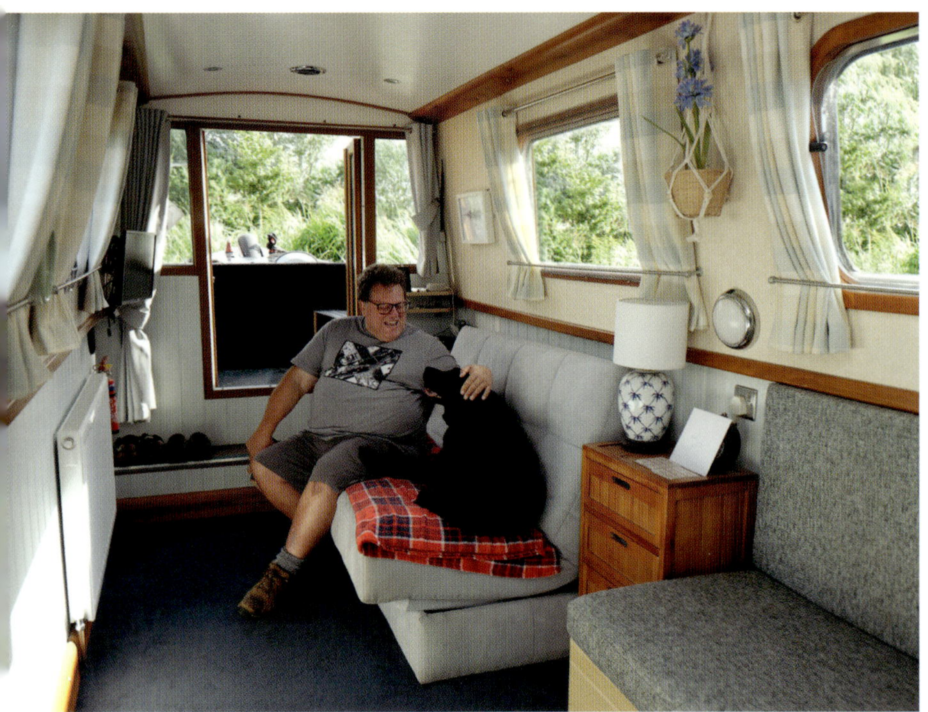

Everybody that chooses to live on a boat has a story as to how they got there … this is mine.

I was in the Royal Navy for nine years as a clearance diver (CD) and travelled extensively and certainly saw quite a few exotic locations! After the Navy I joined BT and lived with my wife and two stepdaughters in a three-bedroom house in Sandwich in Kent, until sadly my wife Beth had Covid complications and passed away in 2020 when the first lockdown occurred. What do I do now? I thought. I cannot just sit around this house, so I made a decision to rent my house out and sold all of my Morgan classic cars, which was my hobby – I loved tinkering and going to car shows…

In a flash of inspiration, I thought why not buy and live on a boat, but at the time canal boats were at a premium and everyone wanted one. They were sold within minutes of going on the market, so after a lengthy search I found a contact through a canal boat holiday company which sold their boats every so often, found this boat *Utterly Rudderly* and have not looked back since. My wonderful faithful dog Saffy and I love every minute of our carefree lifestyle. Long may it last – adventure before dementia.

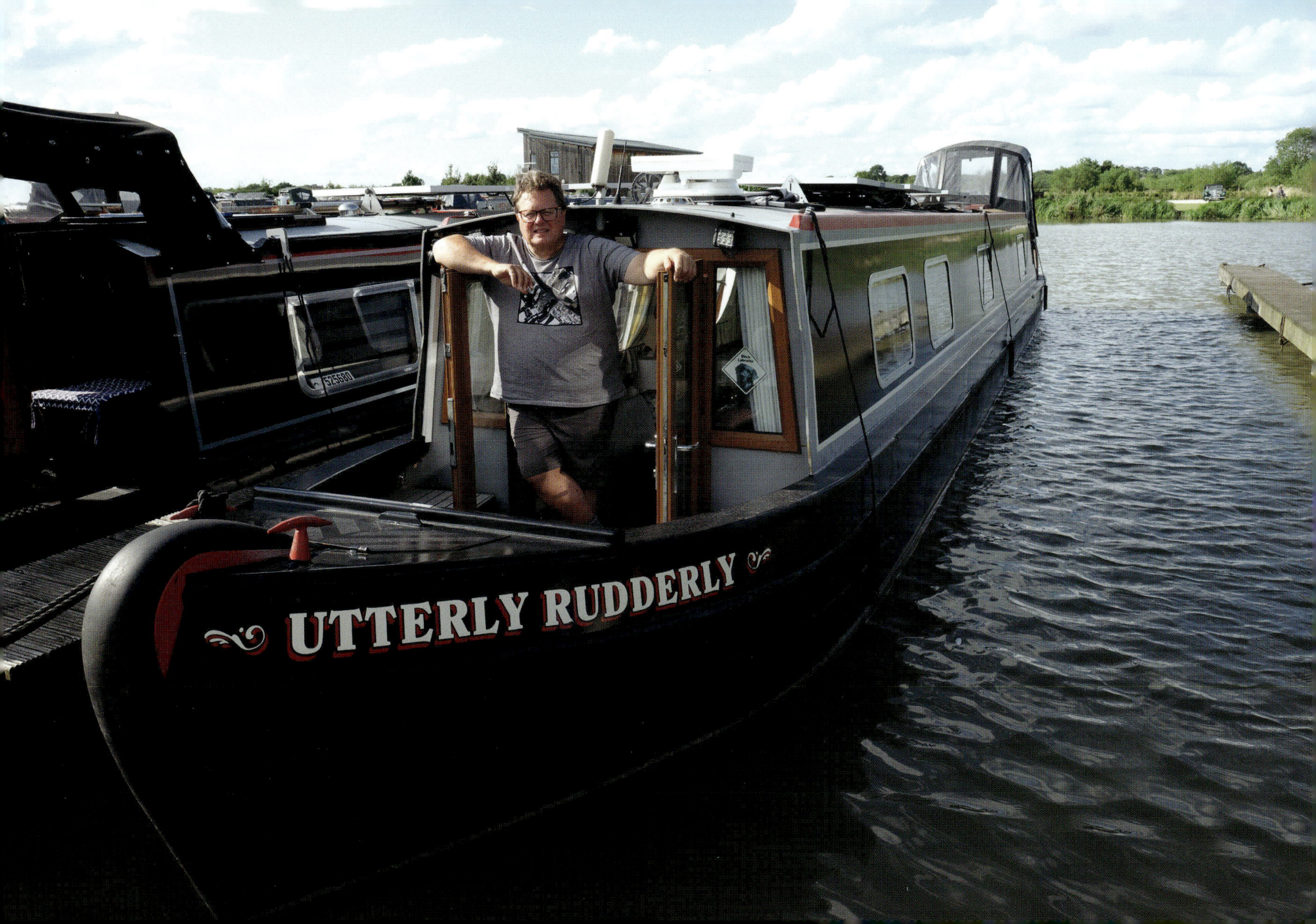

UTTERLY RUDDERLY

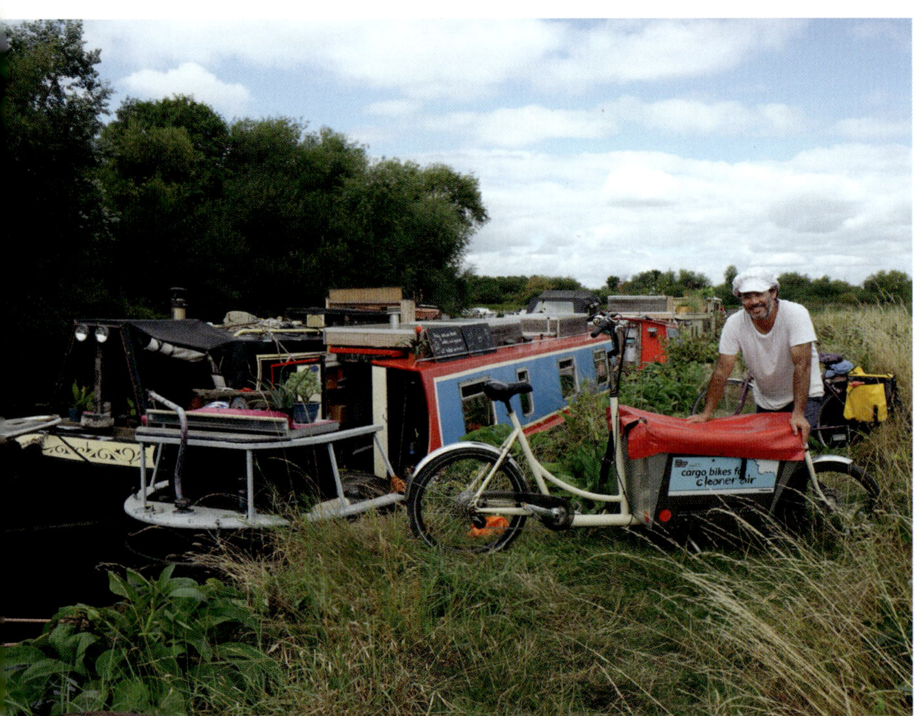

Originally, I came from Chile. That was thirteen years ago and I have had boats for eight years. I started baking on my boat five years ago.

I have a beautiful wife, Mercedes, who is a Spanish teacher and our daughter, Matilda, who is now eight years old. I love my life. It is a really peaceful life. I have a continuous cruiser licence, so we have to move every two weeks. The communities wherever we go are fantastic and the people always help each other out. Everyone tries to help if you have a problem.

I get my energy from the sun. I have solar panels that run the lights, fridge, water pump and charger for my phone. As for cooking, my gas cooker is run by calor gas.

Everything I bake is handmade – no machines involved at all. I used to work at Spence Bakery in London until my wife and I decided to have a child; then I wanted to spend more time with them.

My life is so very peaceful, so simple, that I feel completely fulfilled.

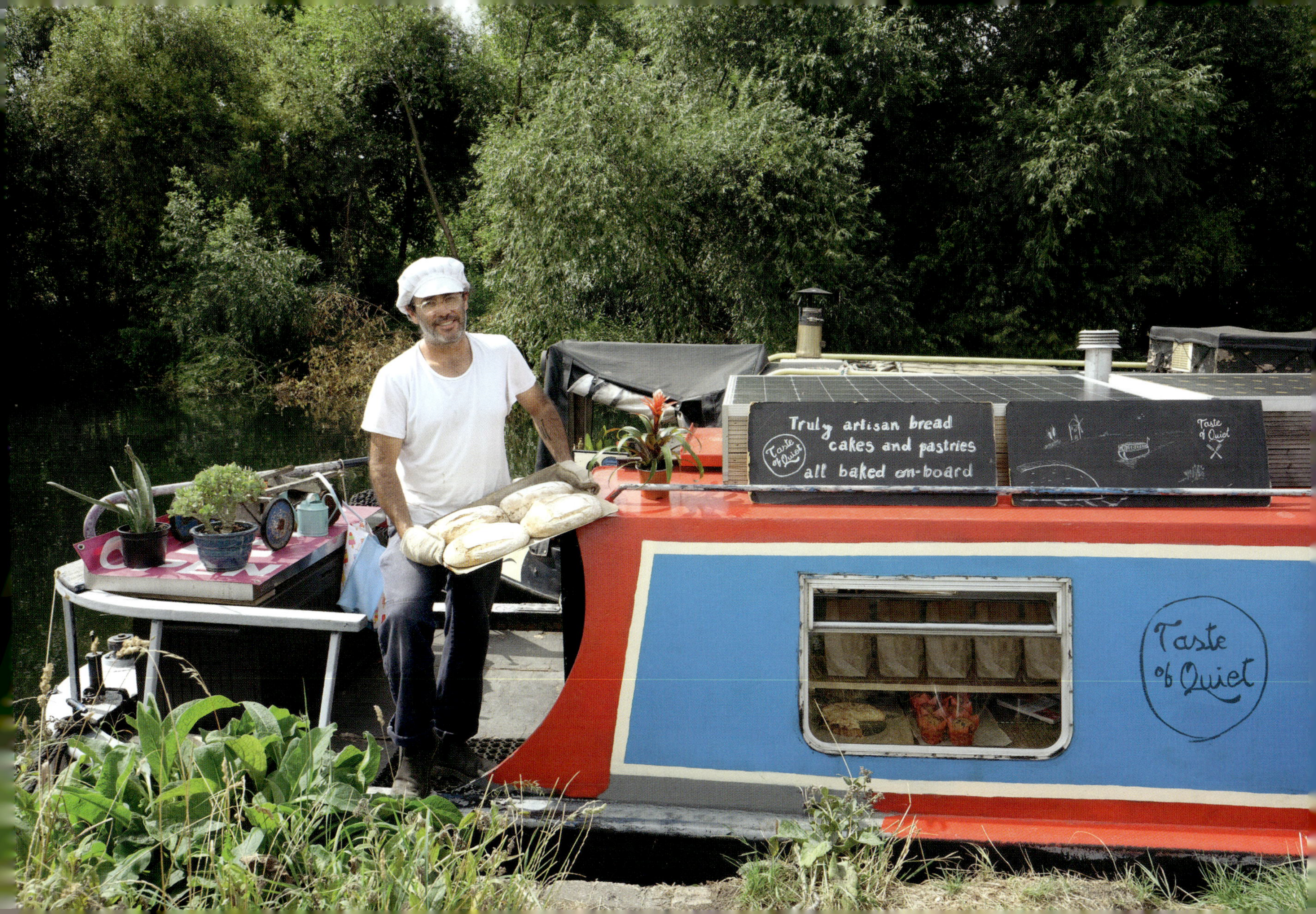

Truly artisan bread
cakes and pastries
all baked on-board
Taste of Quiet
Taste of Quiet

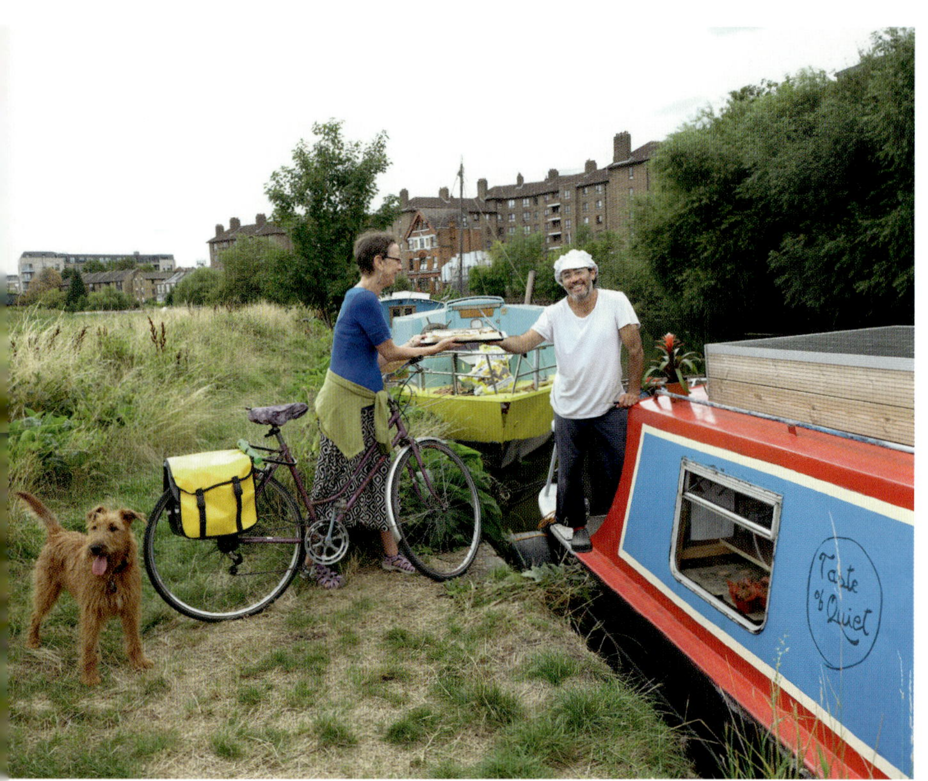

I've lived in a flat overlooking the River Lee in Clapton for nearly twelve years now and love looking out from my window at the river, the bird life, and of course the colourful houseboats. I've also got to know several 'boater' families. Some that come to the neighbourhood include yummy baked goods (thank you Pedro), bike repair, dog treats! It's a great community and their presence adds another interesting layer to living here.

Lilla Flicka Bakery – Baerbel Eckelmann

My story is very simple:

I was out running around Stonebridge Lock and the smell of baking grabbed my attention. I stopped and discovered the amazing floating bakery. I got chatting to the master baker and noticed an accent, so asked where he was from. When I heard he was Chilean I ran straight back to my partner, who was waiting by the lock.

My partner happens to be Chilean and was so excited to hear there was a Chilean baker along the canal. They met and a conversation developed as if they were long-lost siblings. We tasted the cakes and it immediately reminded us of traditional German kuchen – a traditional cake.

In the south of Chile, there is a huge German community and my partner knew that delicious taste and texture only too well. Since that first meeting, we have got to know the whole family and we support Pedro by eating far too much cake and bread wherever he may be along the canal.

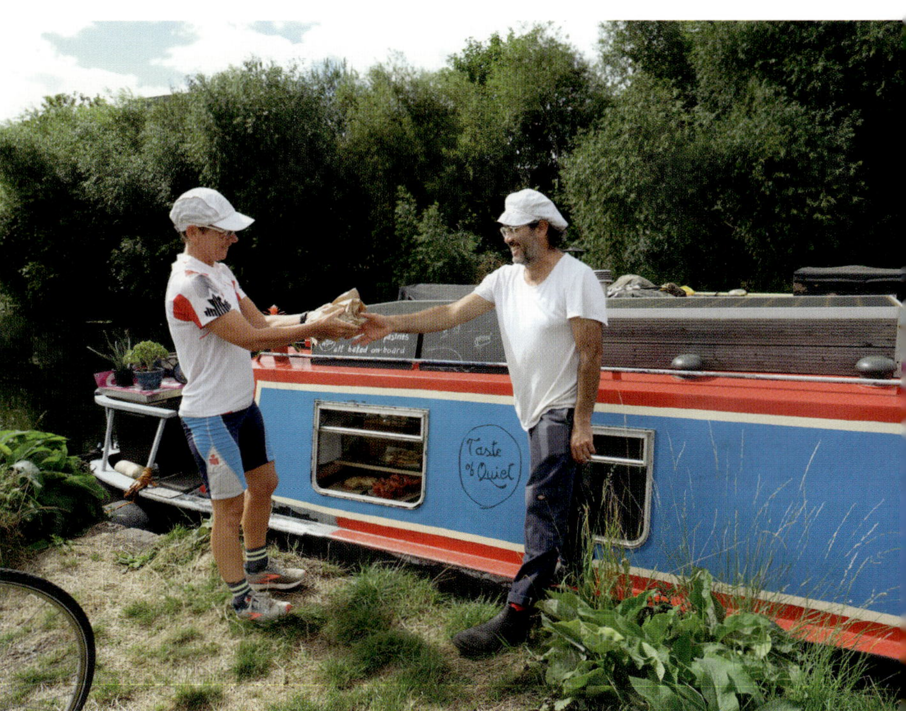

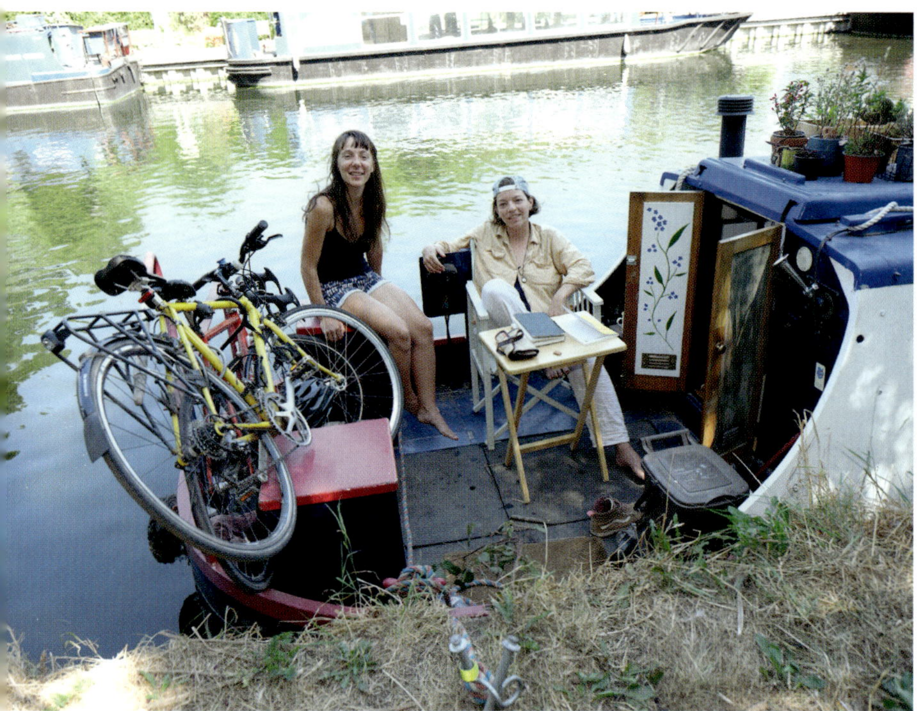

Boat sitting has been an incredible experience, a lesson in resourcefulness and a very special time.

We have had the opportunity to get closer to nature and to see a completely different side of London. Time stops the second you get on the boat. It is very magical to experience so much peace within the canals in the centre of London. Something to recommend for the soul!

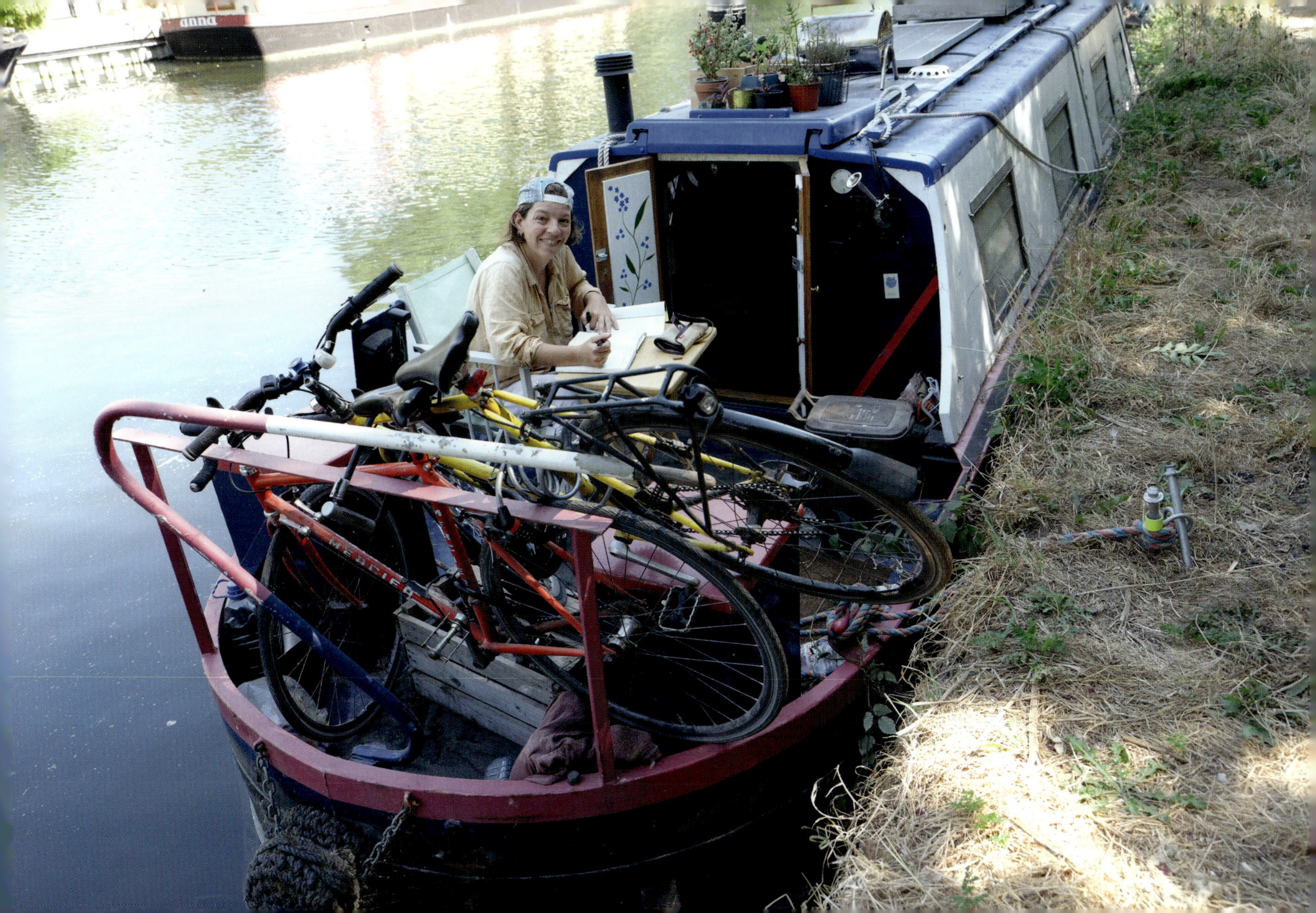

Martin Bourne

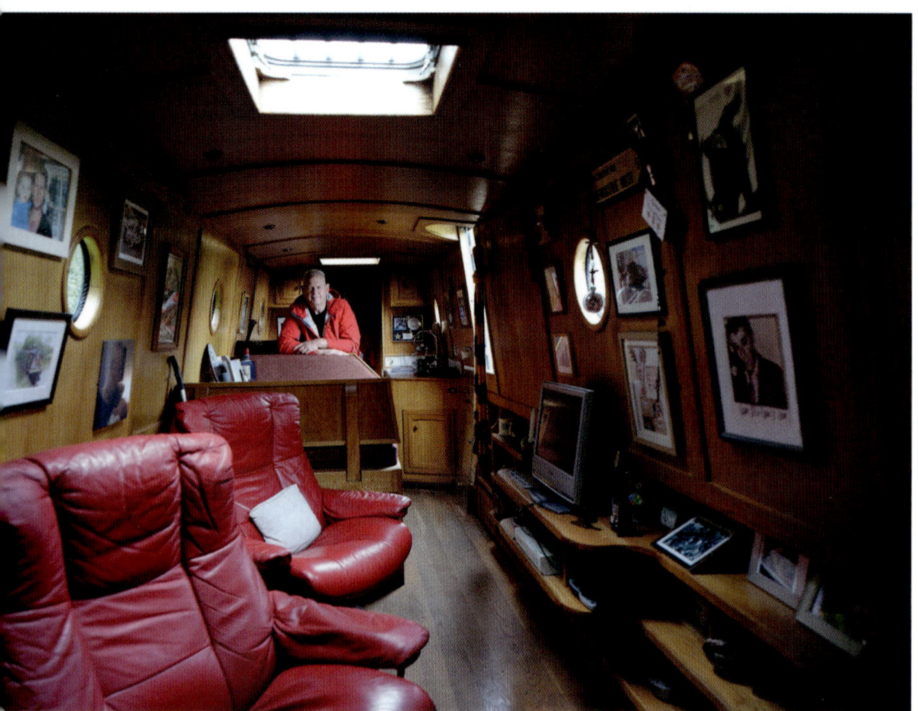

After my divorce I had a bit of cash, so I was determined to buy another house. I sorted the relevant details out but unfortunately just before it all went through I was made redundant. Determined not to rent a house for a quick fix, I thought 'buy a boat'. On the hunt I came across *Willowbrook*. It cost a whole lot more than I was expecting to pay but I had to have it.

After eight/nine years it was looking a bit shabby, so I put it to my partner Justine to do it up or get another. She decided to get another, so we sold *Willowbrook* to a friend and bought *Cowslip*. We lived together until we split about six years ago (amicably). We were together for almost twenty years and had moorings in Cropredy Aynho but for the last seventeen/eighteen years in Heyford. Justine died in May this year, sadly.

For me, being a bit of a nomad, life on the cut is perfect, especially as the wild times of youth are a distant memory. Peace and tranquillity is the way forward. There's always stuff to remember, the main thing being make sure you've got all your chattels with you when going out – walking back 500 yards in the rain to get car keys is a right pain.

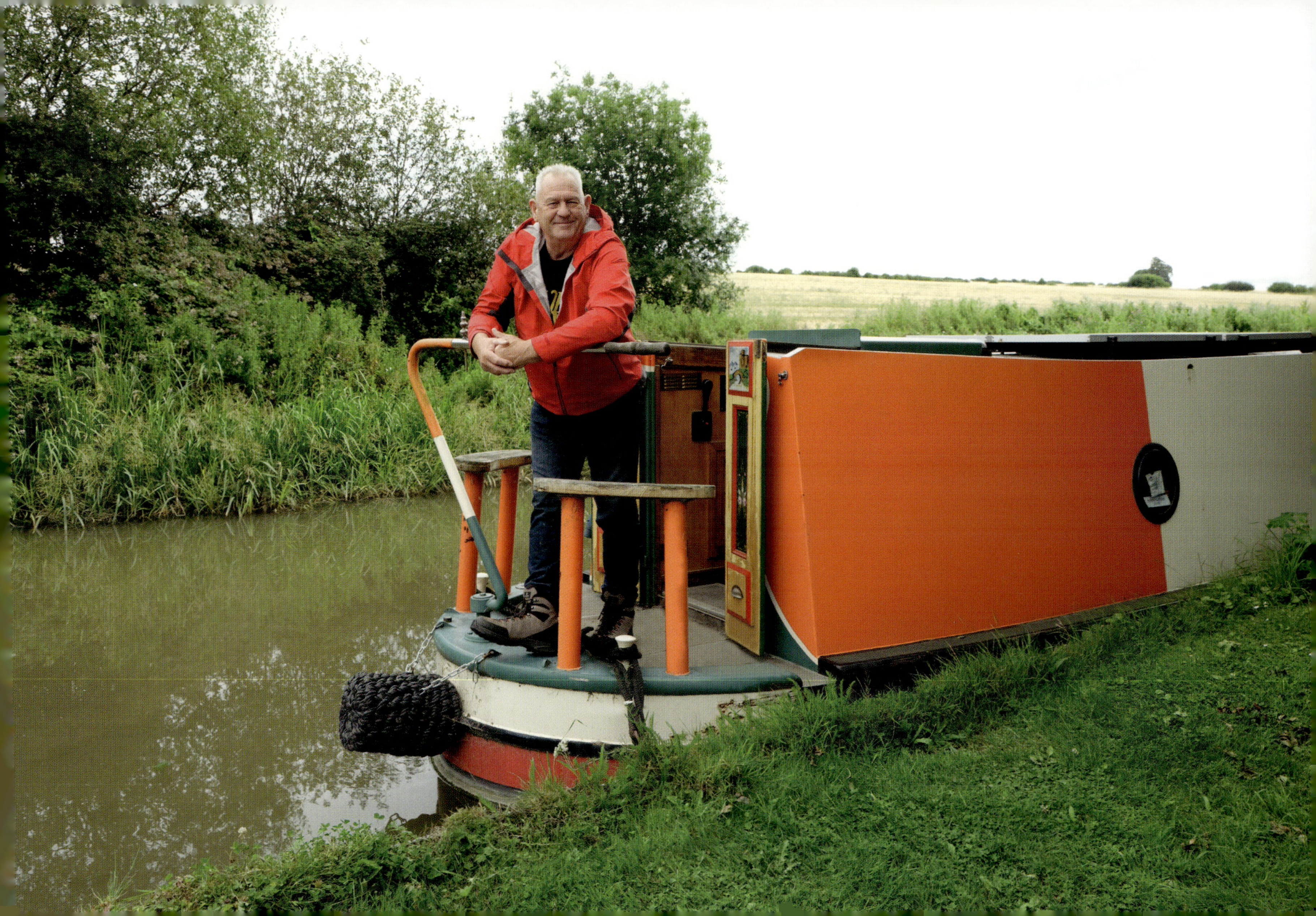

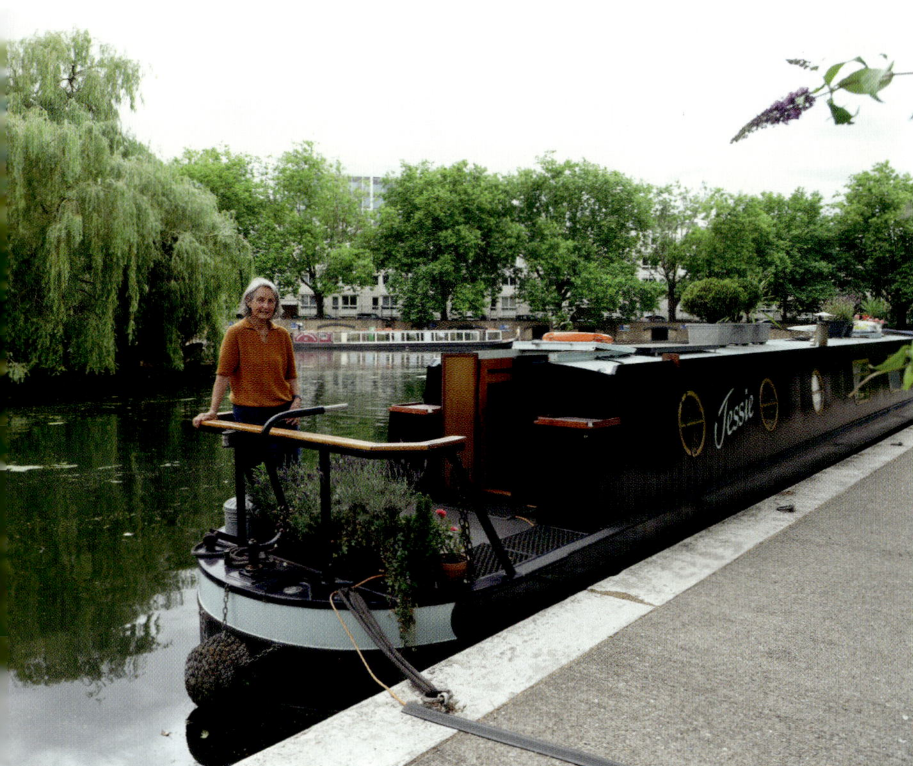

I can hardly believe it's been ten years now since I secured this amazing mooring site in Little Venice. People have been staying on a B&B basis ever since on *Jessie*.

It's really hard work keeping a boat in good order inside and out, but I do get much satisfaction from the surprise, pleasure and excitement of guests on arrival. It is compact, off-grid living and it takes a moment to adjust, but the juxtaposition of the city and the waterway environment is very special.

The local wildlife is always a hit.

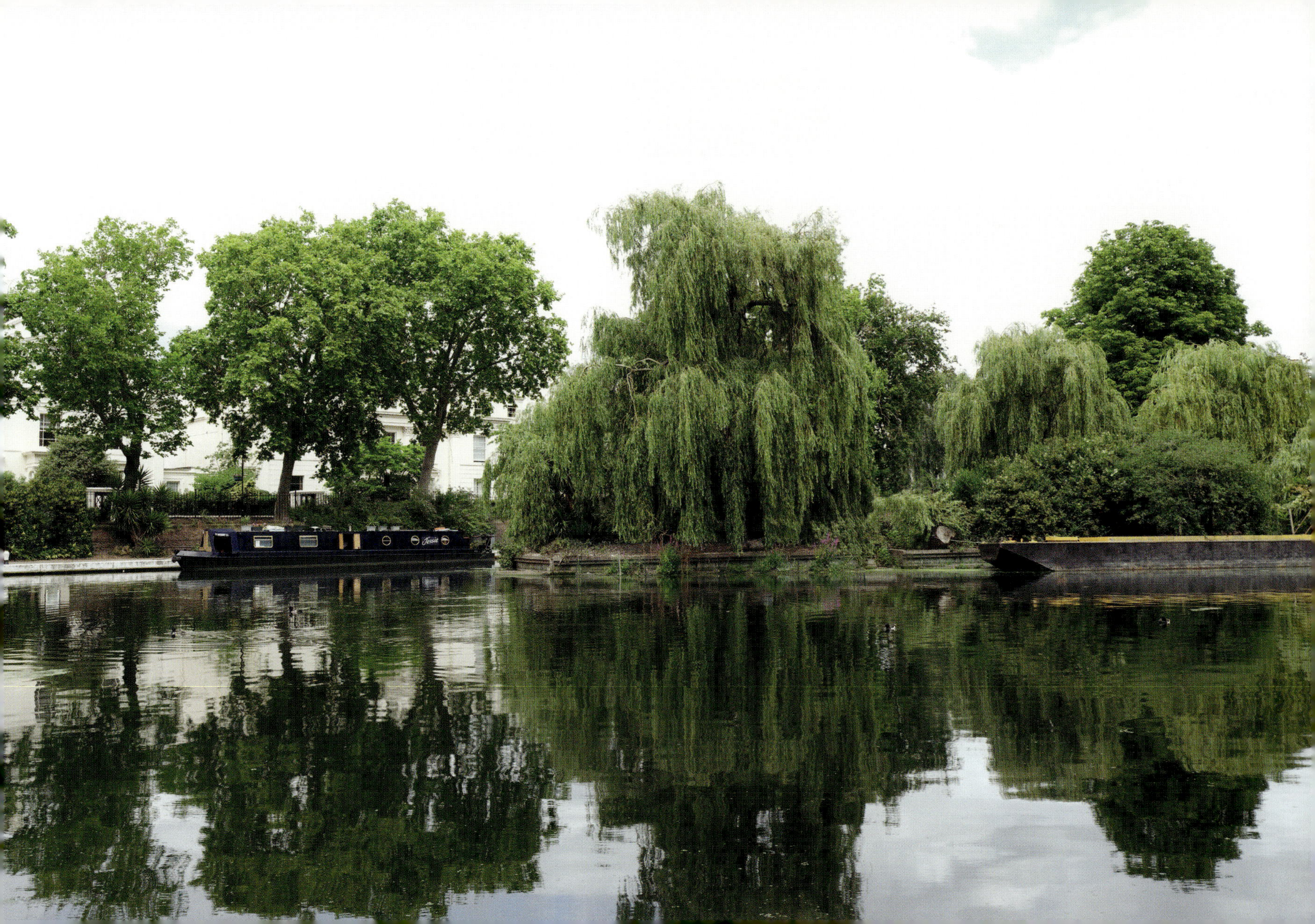

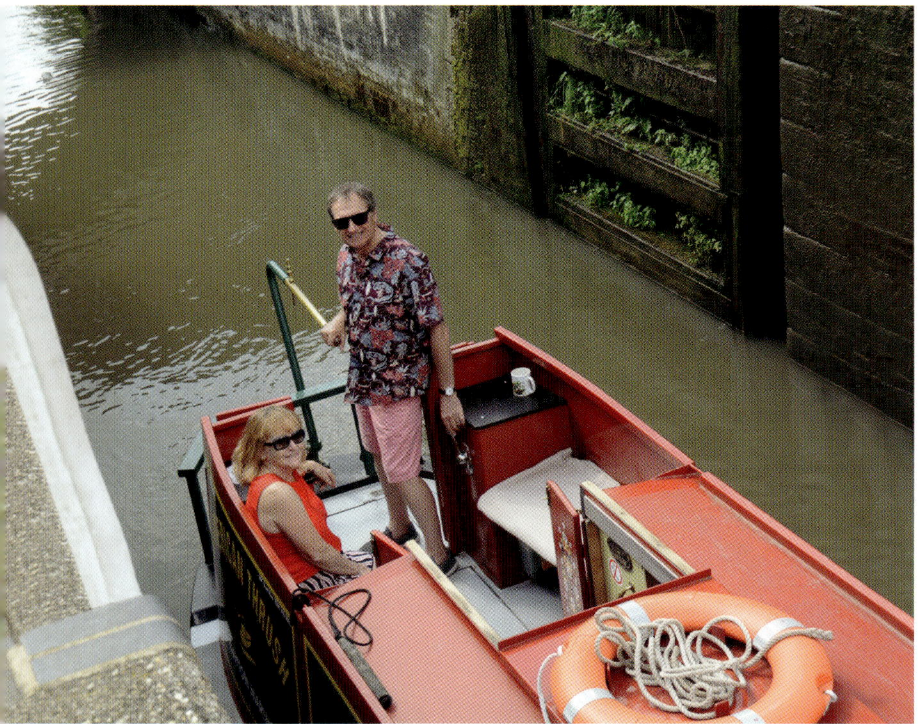

We have had three holidays on canal boats, on different UK canals, all of which we very much enjoyed.

Days spent on a narrowboat are relaxing and peaceful – a complete stress detox. We enjoy every aspect of a canal trip, meandering along, mooring up and navigating the locks.

Going through the locks is fun; some boaters don't like them, but we love them.

Hassles on the canal are few, but in particularly dry spells the Canal River Trust have been known to ban navigation through the locks until sufficient water is in the canal and the pounds or water storage areas, to enable movement again. So, if that happens, we moor up and wait.

It is easier if two boats work the lock together, if the locks are big enough to accommodate two boats. It is also a better way to manage the water – locks use roughly 153,000 gallons of water every time a boat uses one of them, so two boats saves a lot of water.

Our favourite canal, and the best one for dramatic scenery, wildlife and tranquillity, is Llangollen. Travelling across the longest aqueduct in Wales – the Pontcysyllte Aqueduct with eighteen cast-iron arches spanning the River Dee – was amazing. It was completed in 1805 by Thomas Telford and William Jessop and is now a World Heritage Site.

The canals really became important during the Industrial Revolution as major highways to transport goods and materials. Digging these canals was a huge engineering feat, and in order to move water to where it was needed, some extraordinary architecture was developed. The system of locks – used to move boats up and down steep inclines – needed 'pounds' to store water. Powerful water pumps were designed and housed in pumping stations to supply these pounds and many of those pumping stations are still in use today.

So, as well as being areas of natural beauty, our canals and the technology that developed over 200 years ago is still in use today. That is extraordinary!

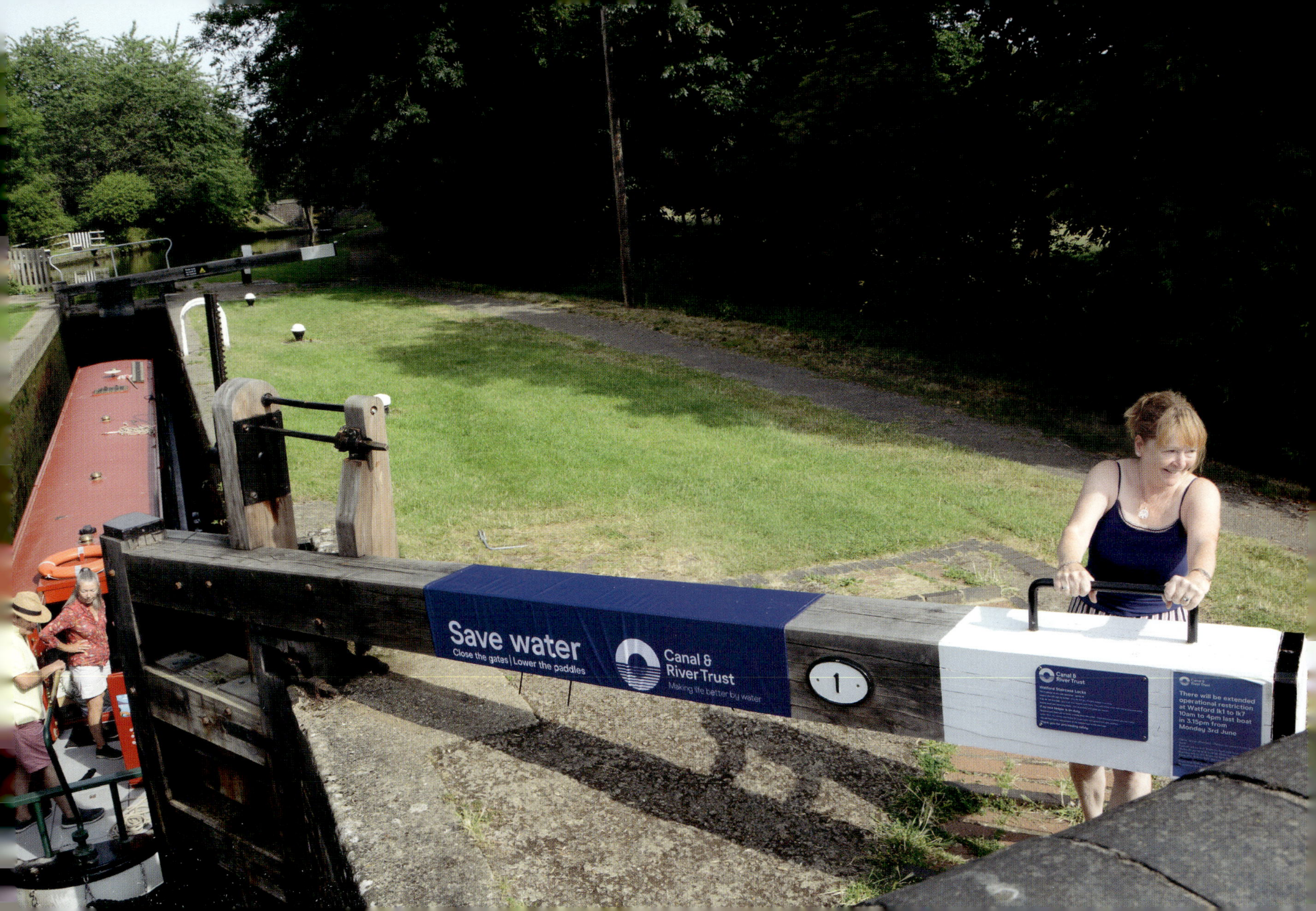

Save water
Close the gates | Lower the paddles
Canal & River Trust
Making life better by water
1
Canal & River Trust
Watford Staircase Locks
There will be extended operational restriction at Watford lk1 to lk7 10am to 4pm last boat in 3.15pm from Monday 3rd June

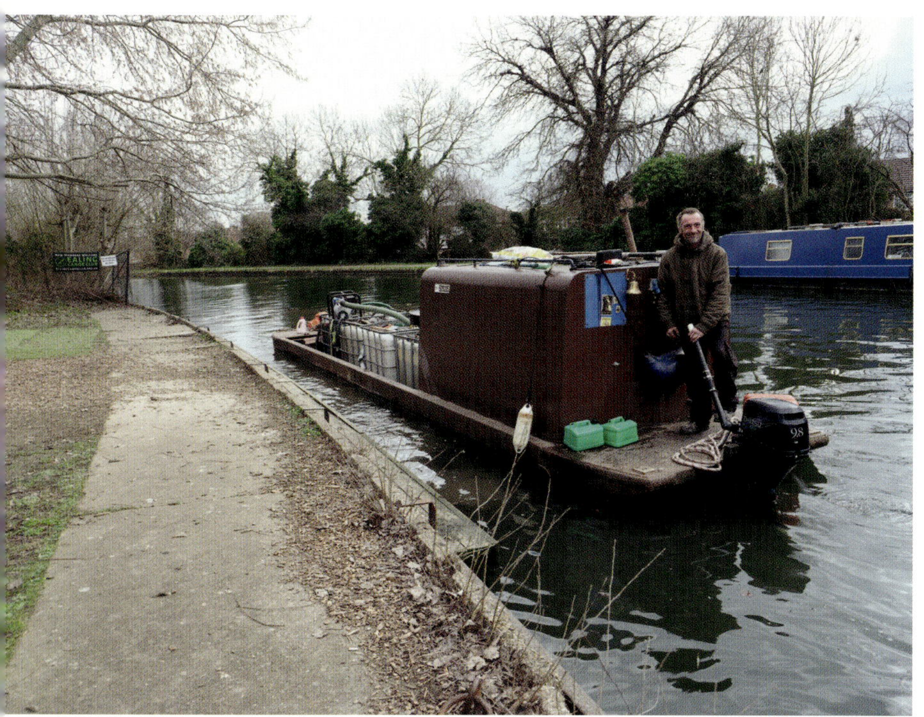

I'm thirty-five years old and originally from Bradford, West Yorkshire. I started off working as a chef but changed to house clearance and waste removals, which I was really interested in.

I bought this boat called *Effluence* about two years ago and my company name is Excremental Effluent Services. This is actually my first year of trading and I'm about eight months in.

I mainly do pump out of waste cassette, Elsan emptying and compost toilet disposal. I also sell chandlery, toilet products and kindling.

When travelling one day somebody informed me that I had a pipe trailing in the water. As I lifted the pipe from the water, I accidentally snapped off the manifold to the pump. This caused an enormous volume of poo to poor down my leg! Oh, the joy of working upon the water.

But I really do love my work! I really enjoy meeting new people every day and solving their problems.

There are more boats on the waterways now than there was 150 years ago but the facilities for these boats have not increased. They are few and far between. I am proud to provide boaters – both on moorings and constant cruisers – with a really essential service. This is especially important in the winter months, between November and March. During this time, the Canal River Trust close areas of navigation for maintenance. I obtain a list of the planned closures in advance and can warn my customers if my journey is going to be delayed.

Also, in bad weather when the canal is frozen, I can usually get to my customers and supply them with everything they need. I am always assured of a warm welcome!

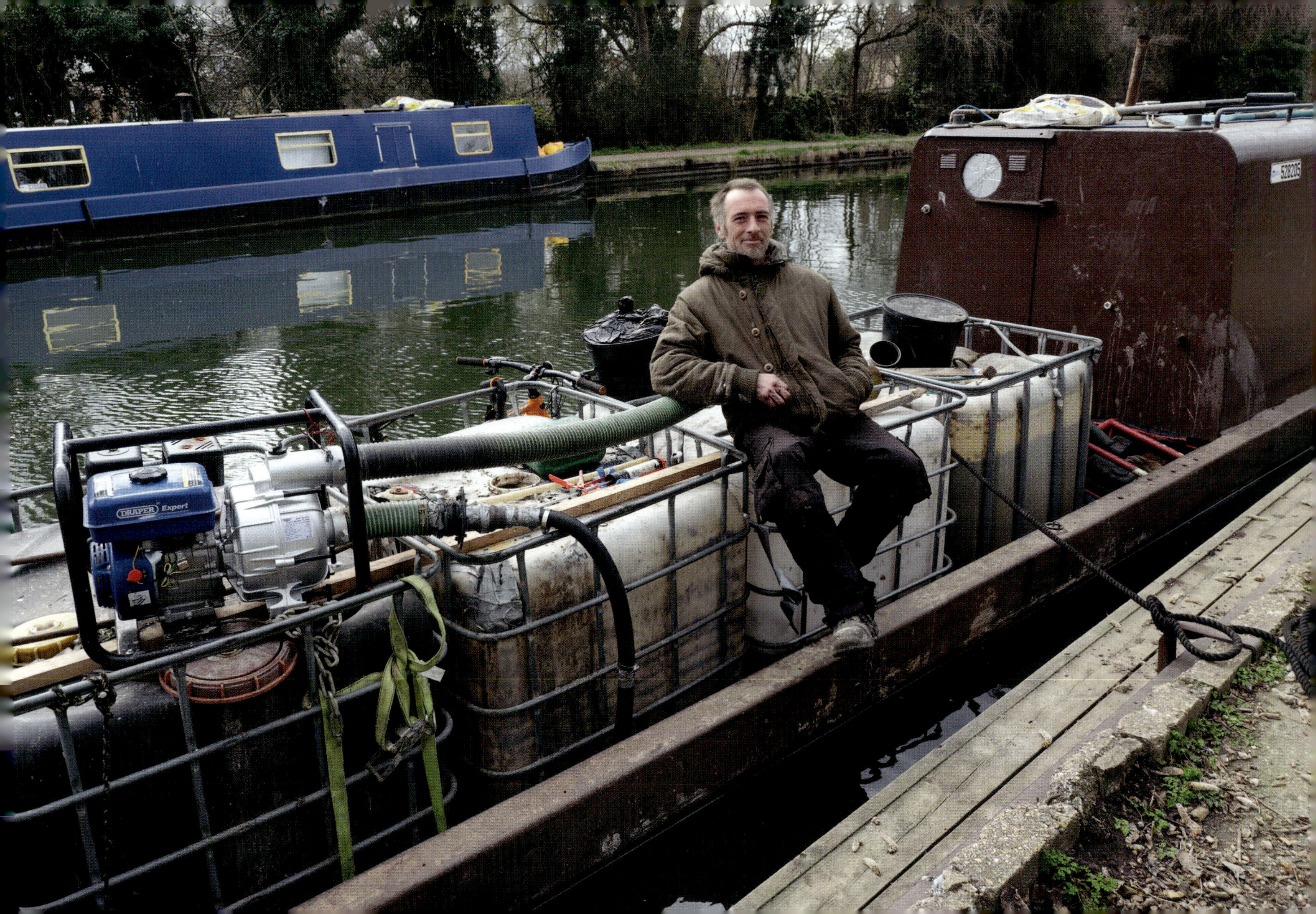

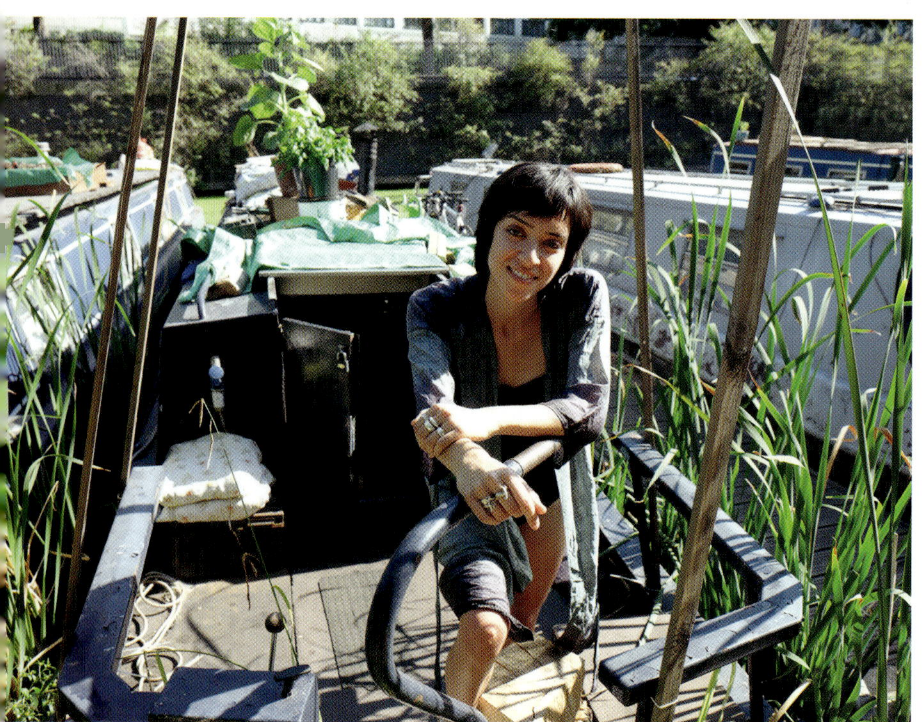

Behind the walls of London's most beautiful canal boat there's a writing desk. It was there that my debut novel unfolded. The gentle lapping of the water, the calls of coots, and the rhythmic rocking of the boat created an atmosphere of serenity, allowing me to delve into the depths of my imagination. Within this sanctuary, my words flowed freely, crafting worlds.

But sometimes, the desk transformed into a workbench, and I became a silversmith. Silver dust, delicate and ethereal, would escape through my windows, floating upon the canal's surface, leaving a silvery trace behind.

At the end of a day's writing, I'd discover remnants of silver dust on my wrists. A whimsical excuse could be made, claiming I spent the day crafting jewellery instead of weaving tales. But let us keep this secret between us.

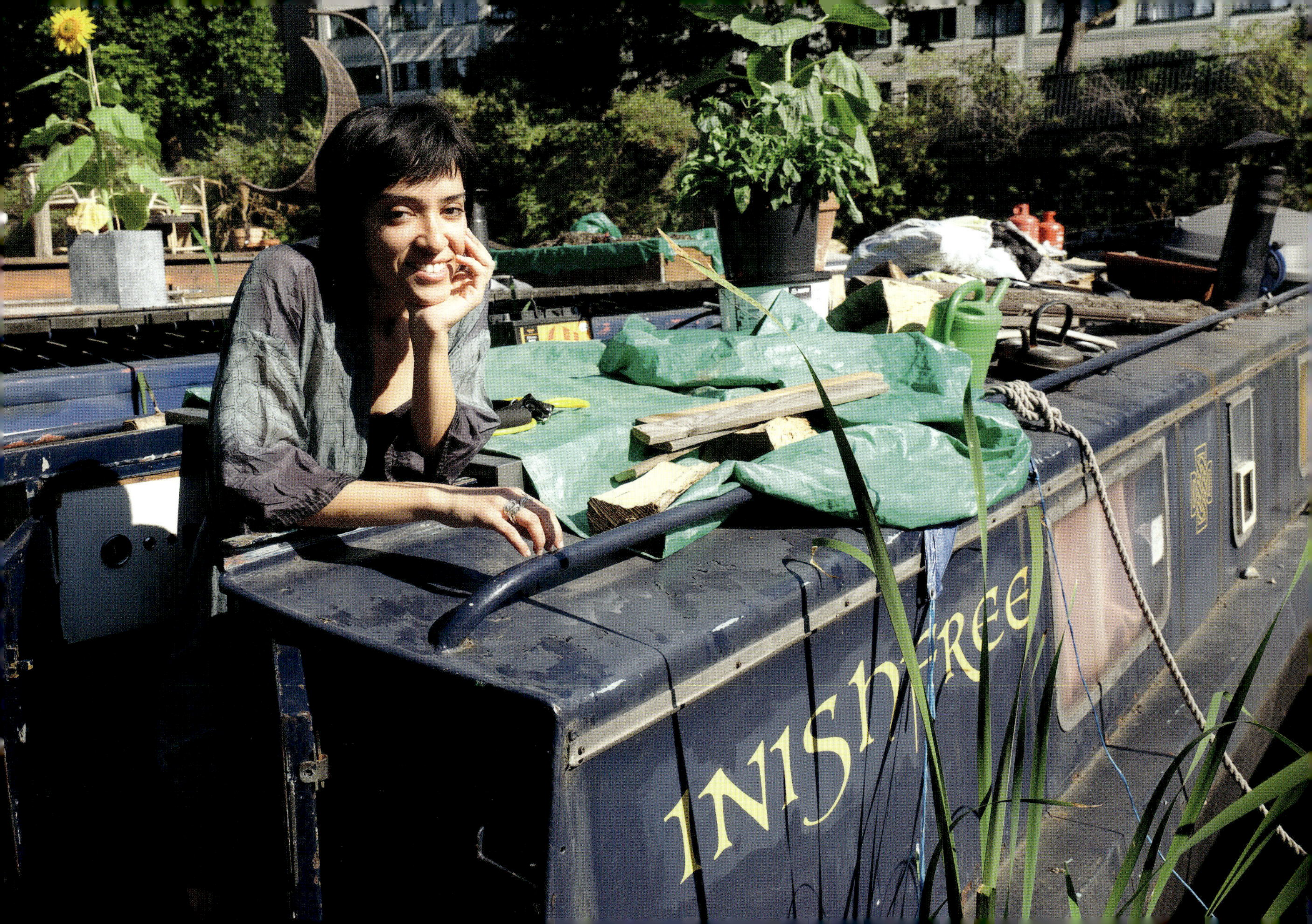

INISHFREE

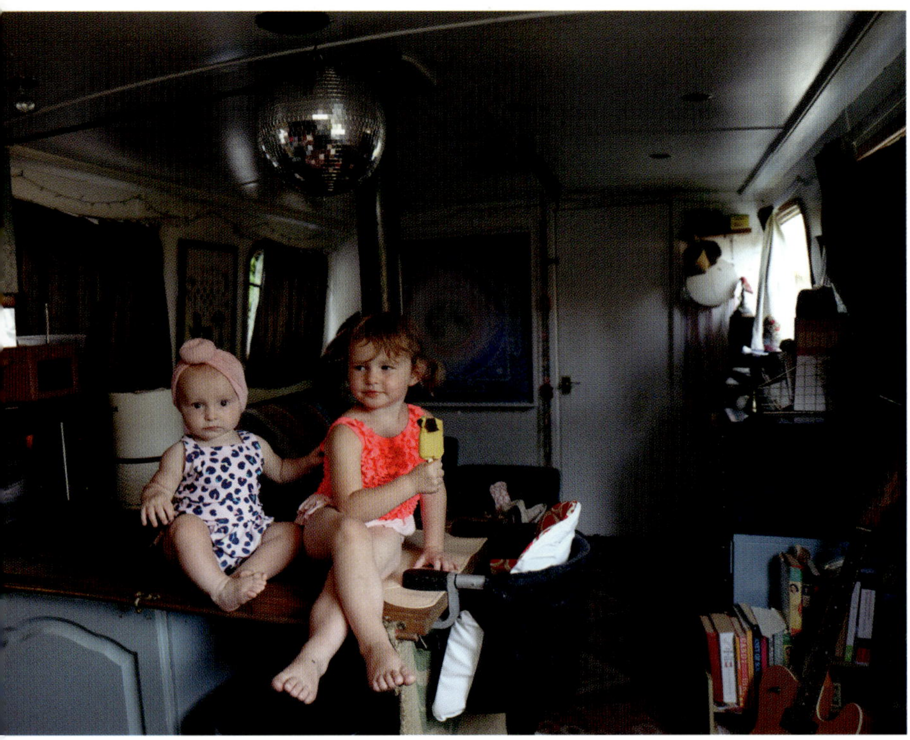

I think most people who have boats are looking for an alternative way of living. When we met, I was staying on a boat at this mooring for three months over summer. Chris fell in love with boat life at the same time as we fell in love with each other.

We were married under the willow tree by the east gate, and this boat is one we bought together while I was pregnant with our first daughter. We found our boat up north. She came from a charity called The Sobriety Project, and that is the boat's name – *Sobriety*.

We pinballed her to Wakefield and down the Humber and she got lifted onto a truck by crane to make the rest of the journey to London. Chris spent a year rebuilding her and making her our own. When my parents came to visit, my dad got involved with painting and building too.

In winter we make it warm and cosy with the wood burner, and in summer the mooring really comes into its own with music nights, outdoor dinners and paddling pools set up along the towpath. It's been an opportunity for Chris to try out projects like connecting solar panels and building safe play areas for our two girls. Almost everything he's built has been recycled or found.

We have become very conscious of our footprint – our water and energy usage. It's definitely more work when we're on the boat, but it's an incredible experience for our girls to have in their childhood.

We love having a community and an outdoor space that we can escape to. And all this is a stone's throw from Regent's Park and a half-hour walk into central London.

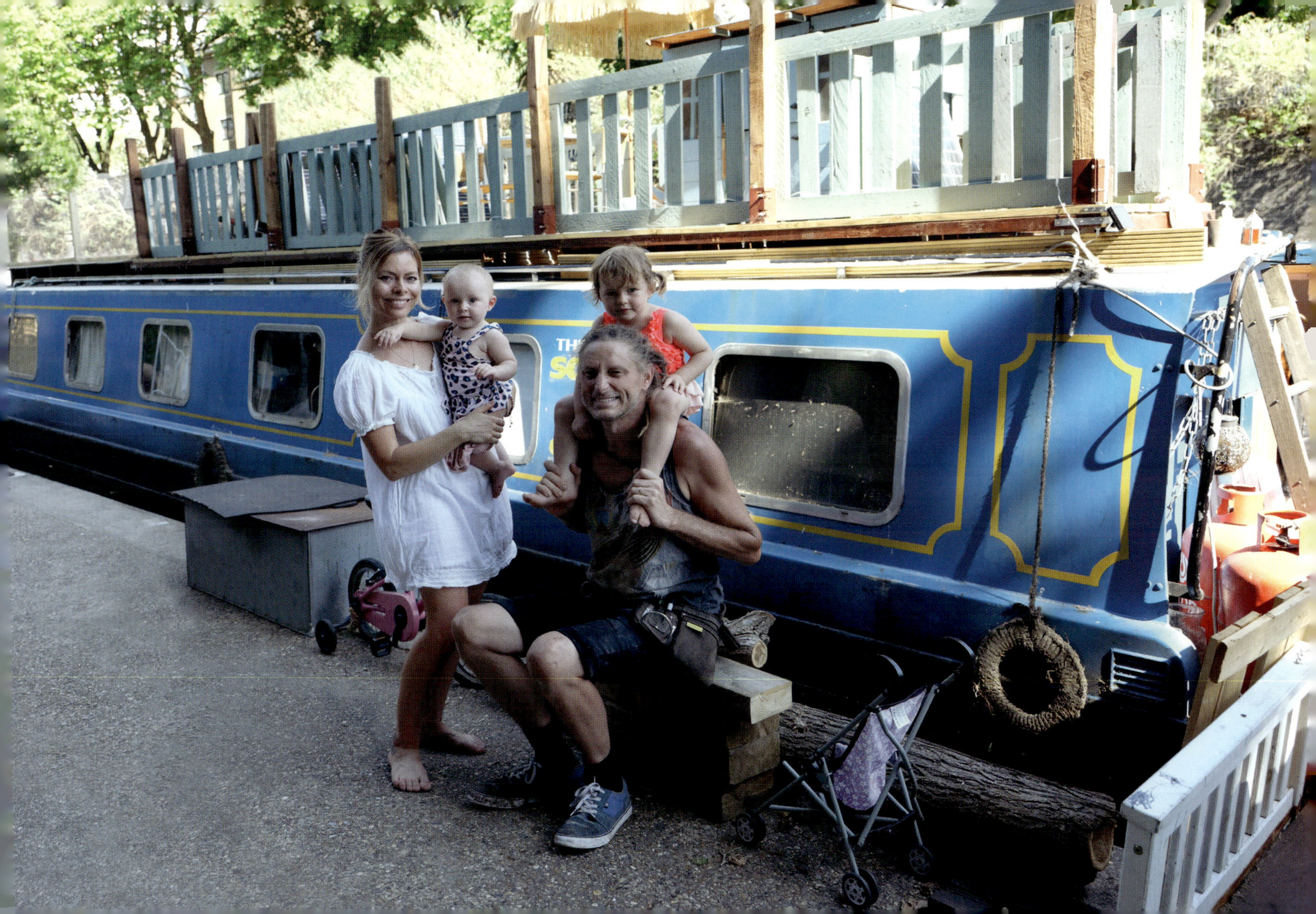

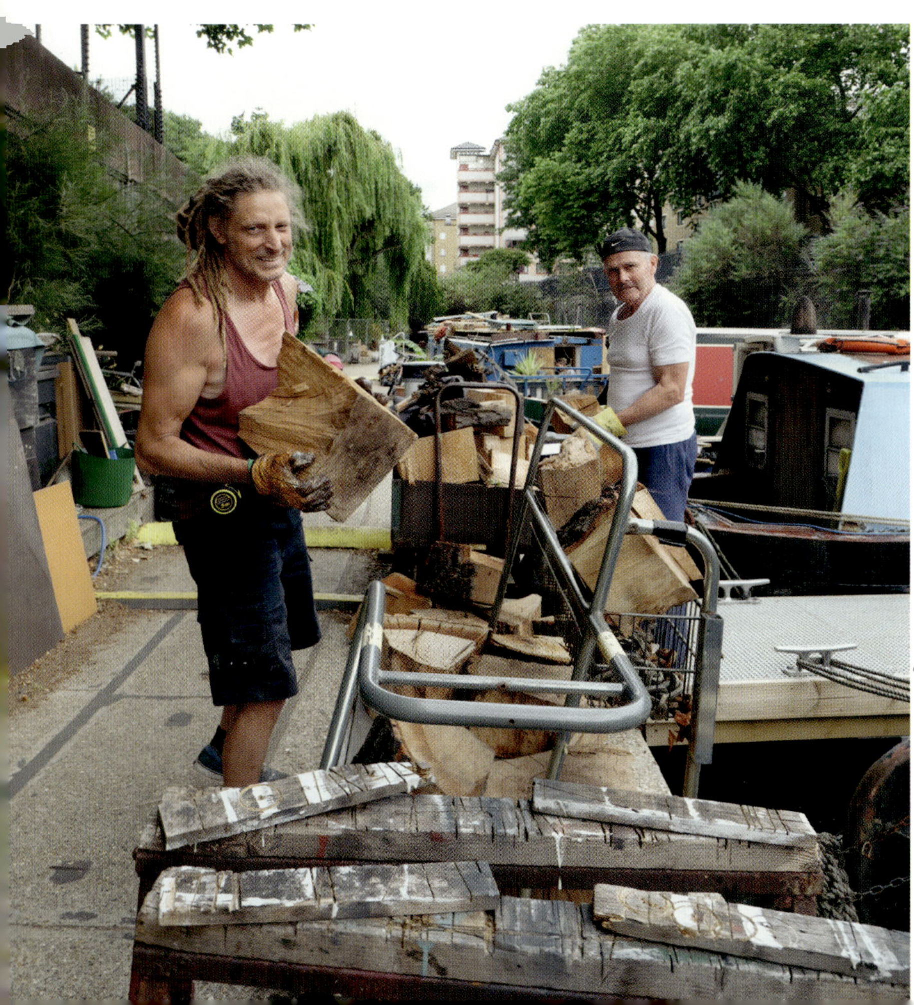

Chris and Steve hard at it, taking charge of the renovations on *Sobriety*. Everything takes longer than you think. The other problem is always the lack of space – a traditional narrowboat is 6 feet 8 inches wide – to get through the lock gates, which are 7 feet wide! Trying to work in a such a narrow space means that you have to contort yourself into back-breaking positions just to get a screw in the right place, so finishing the interior was a great reason to celebrate.

At the end of a long day, there is usually a beer and a barbeque to look forward to – and of course our lovely boating community join in.

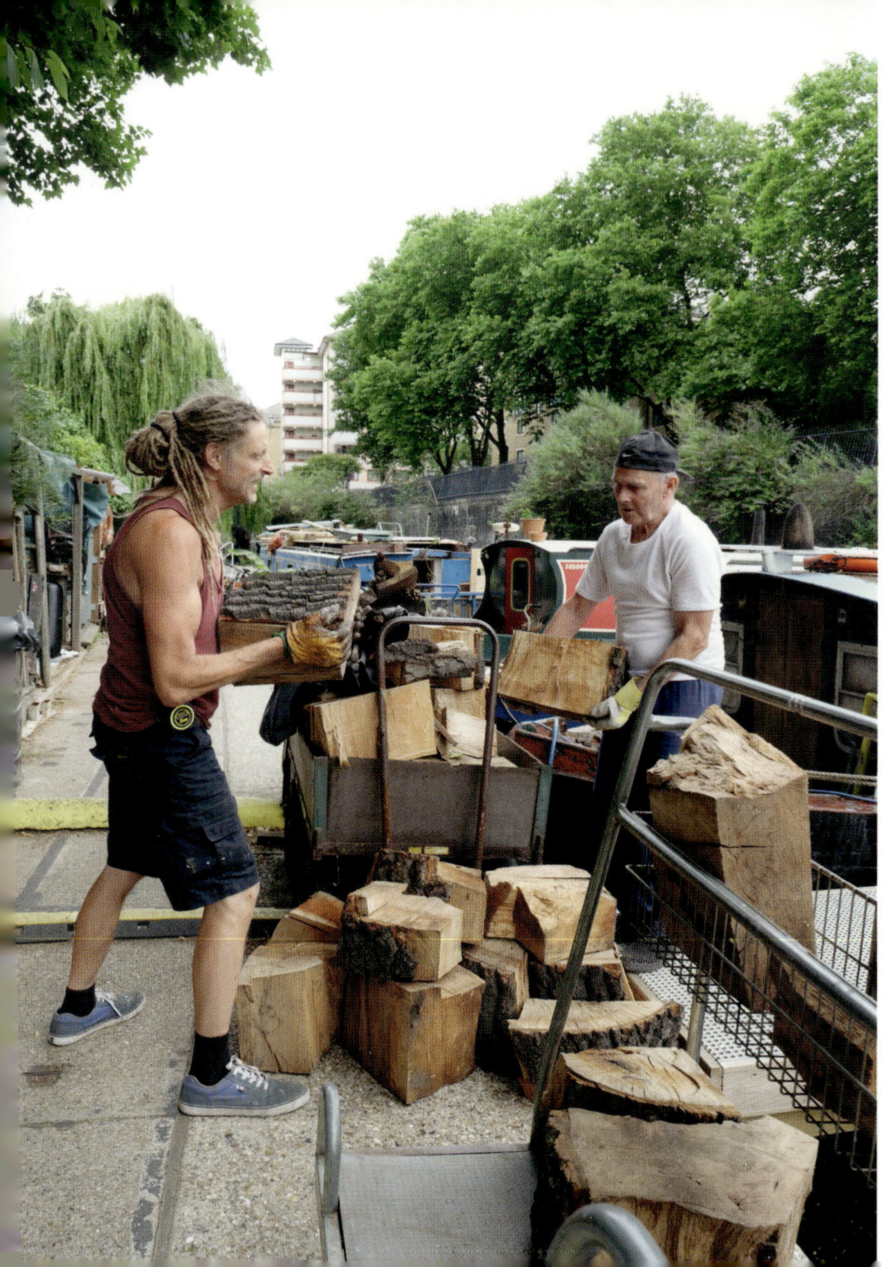

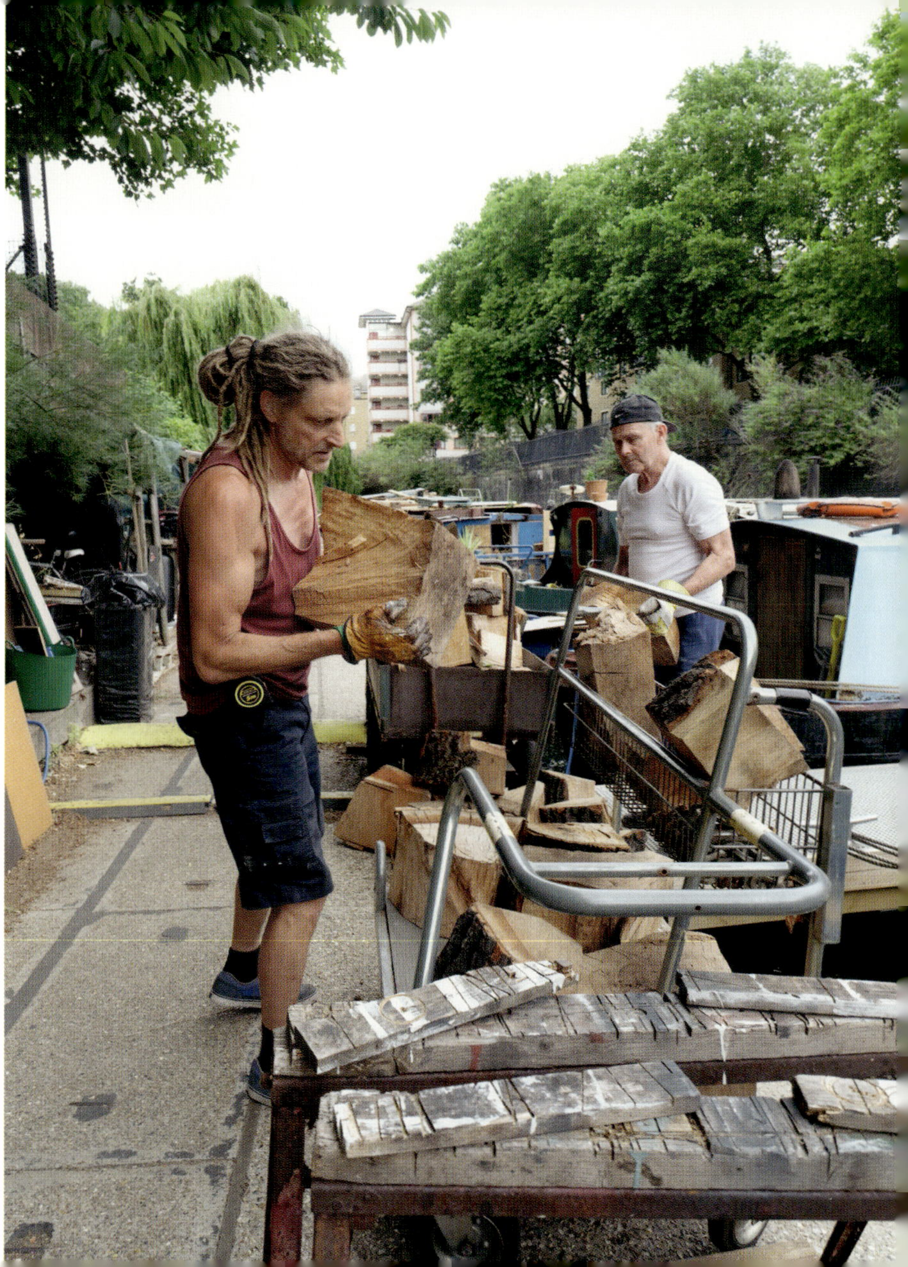

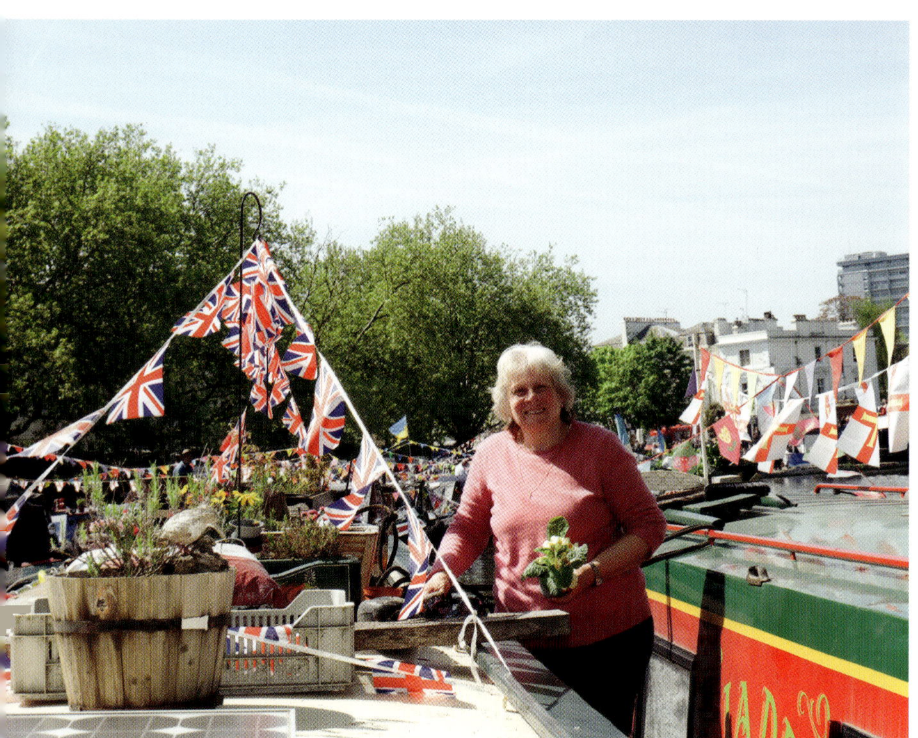

My husband Roger and I bought our boat, *Salar,* in 2012 and we moor her in Ivor in Buckinghamshire.

Since then, we have taken *Salar* to nearly all the Inland Waterways Canal Cavalcade in the Pool of Little Venice, West London. It is a vibrant canal festival in the heart of London's waterways and kicks off the season of water festivals and events across the country. It is an enjoyable, fun weekend for families, with a big display of colourful boats – sometimes one of the historic boats owned by enthusiasts makes an appearance. A frequent visitor is *The President*, a restored steamboat, and it is usually possible to visit the boat and talk to the team about how it works.

A multitude of unique stalls are set up on Rembrandt Gardens, selling chandlery for boats: ropes, macramé mats, or decorated buckets and jugs traditionally painted with castles and roses. There are real ale bars and delicious food, much of which is made by boaters for boaters.

There is also a safe area for the children with music and activities. And over the whole weekend there are performances on Puppet Barge for the big (grown-up) kids and little ones.

There are two boat processions over the weekend. The first is on the Saturday afternoon and that kicks off the Cavalcade weekend. The second is the torchlight procession when the boats are lit up and dressed for the occasion. That is held on the Sunday evening. After that, there is a jazz band to entertain us all.

This is an annual social occasion for us and it is great to be a part of a weekend celebration to meet up with old friends. It is held over the first of the spring bank holidays when people want to cast off their winter gloom and meet new people on new boats. The weather is nearly always glorious – so we really look forward to it. It feels like we are welcoming spring!

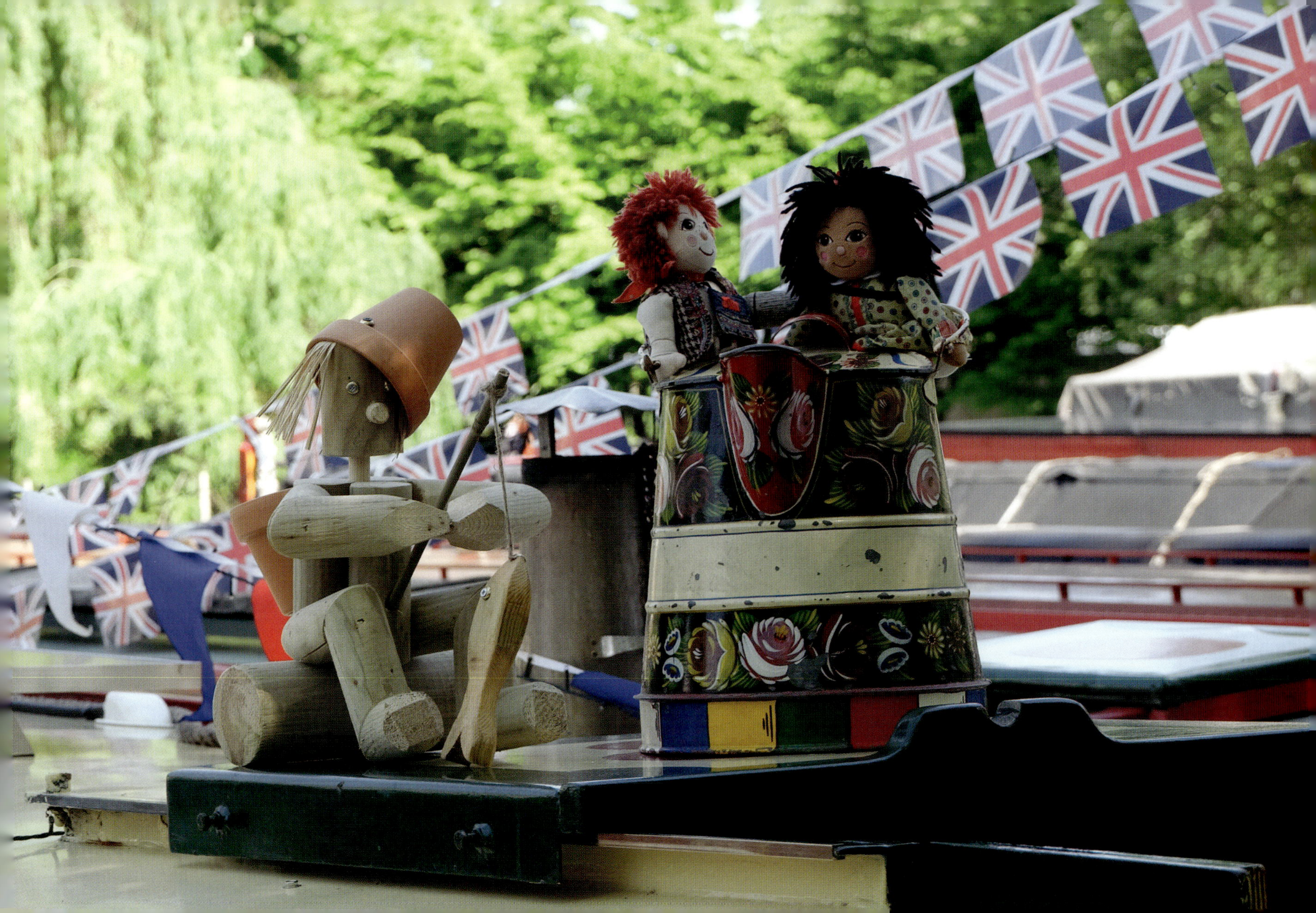

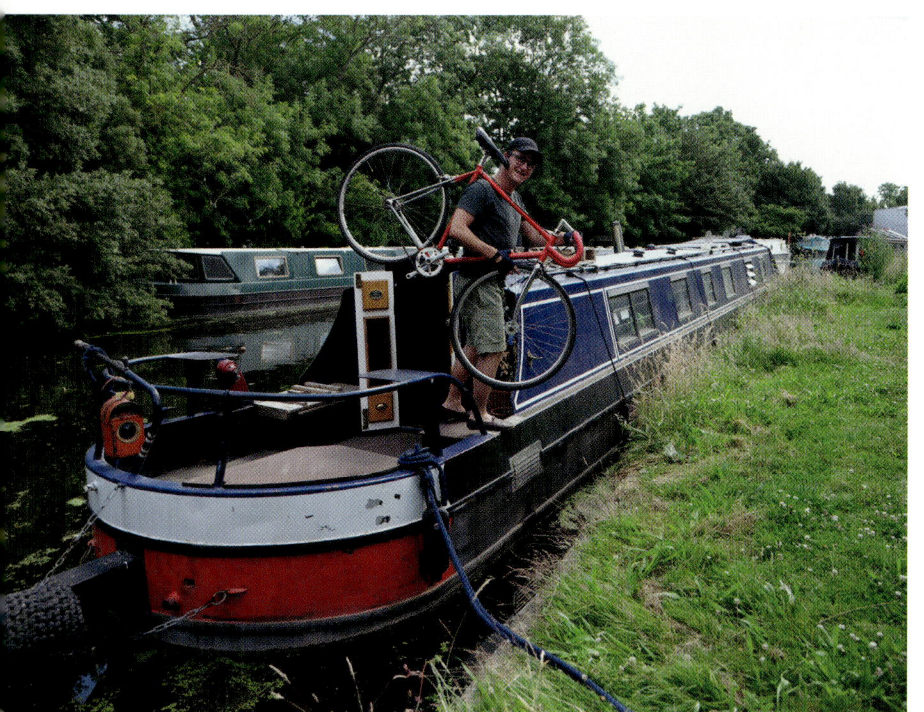

I've lived on a narrowboat for about two and a half years. I really enjoy the variety, living in different places throughout London and the South East.

I have to move every two weeks to comply with the terms of my 'continuous cruiser' licence and the canal never quite feels like central London, even in Kings Cross. I've taken the boat on holiday to the West Country, down the Thames and to the Midlands without ever having to pack a bag! I have mobile internet and plenty of solar panels, so working from home – home being wherever I happen to be – isn't a problem.

Moving the boat every couple of weeks means I end up living all over London. I cycle everywhere so I don't rely on public transport. So that means I'm not limited in my choice of location by having to moor near tube or train stops. I enjoy the freedom of knowing I don't have to rely on TFL to get me to work!

In my spare time, I make jewellery and the boat also doubles as my workshop. I have a workbench and everything I need for metalwork onboard, and a lot of the skills I am learning are useful in boat maintenance too.

I started learning to work with iron and steel last summer, but I don't think I can fit a forge on-board, sadly.

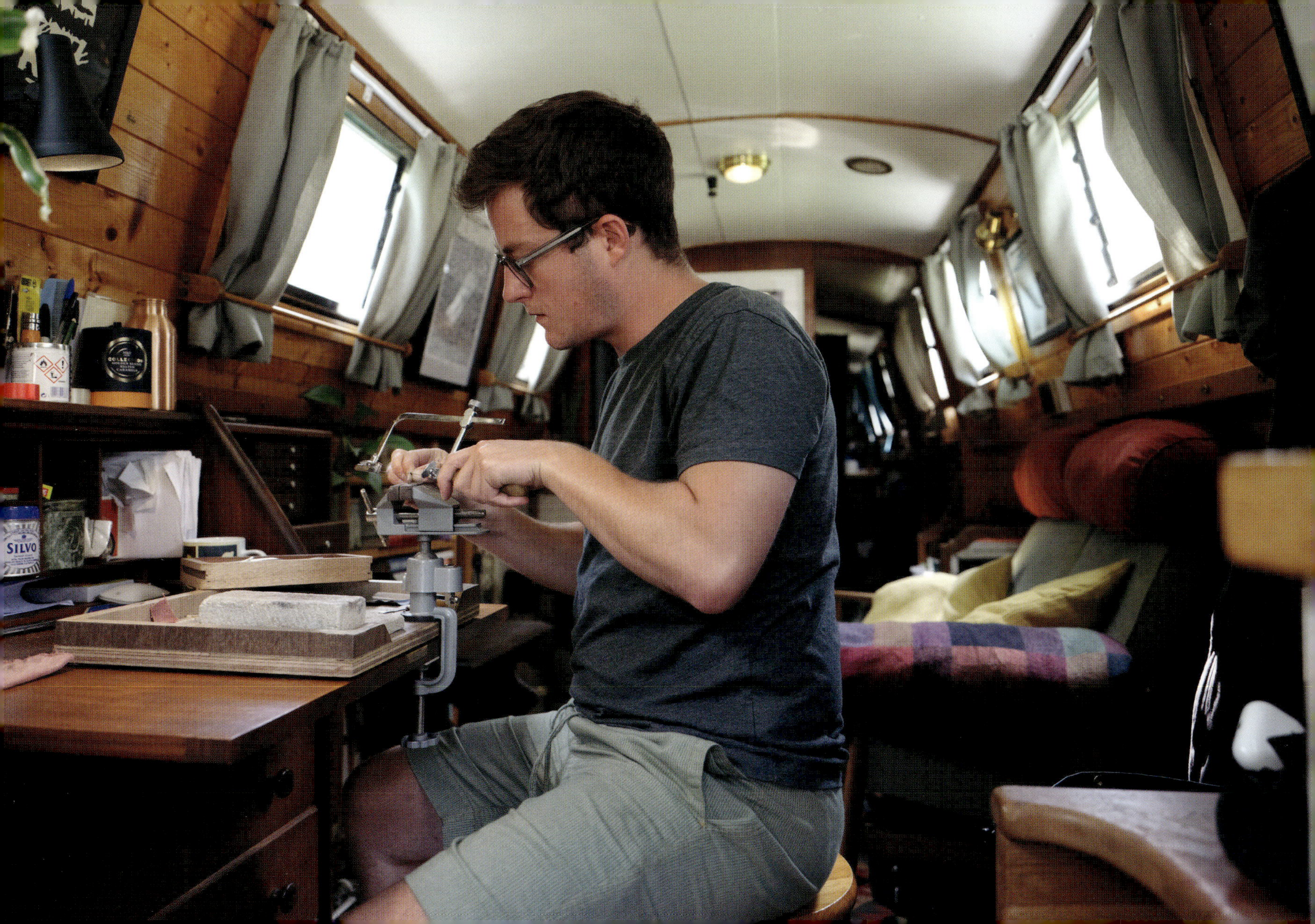

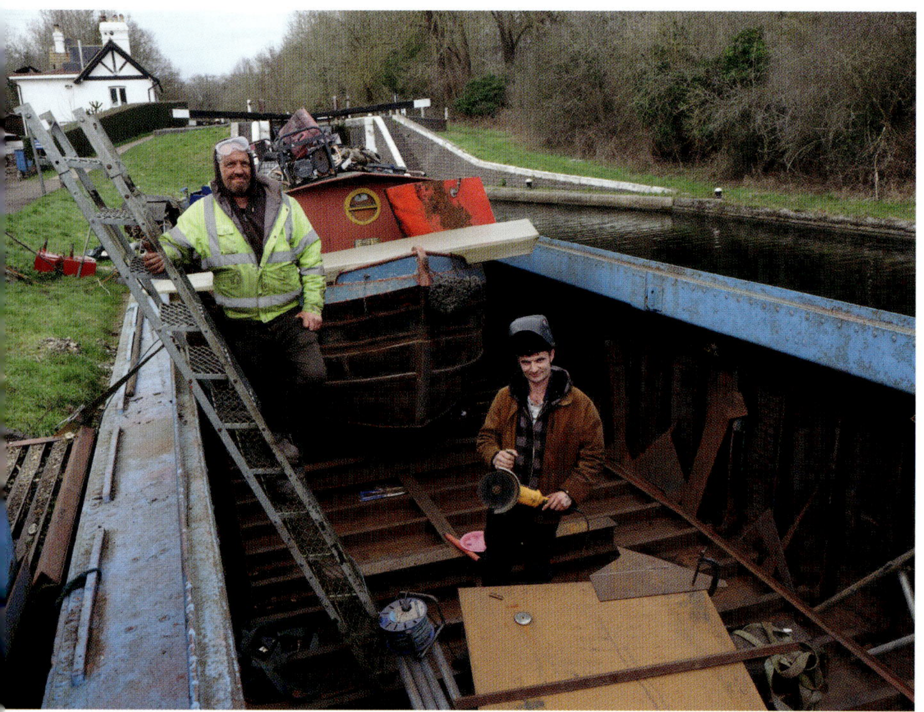

We are the fifth generation of Wakehams and have been around boats all our lives. We live in a cottage at Denham Deep and have a dry dock – and as you can see, we are welding the bottom of this boat and painting it for a customer.

We also have fuel boats that travel along the canals of London selling wood, kindling, coal, calor gas and diesel to canal boat owners. Some constant cruisers wave us down, but we also have a round of regular customers on marinas and leisure moorings.

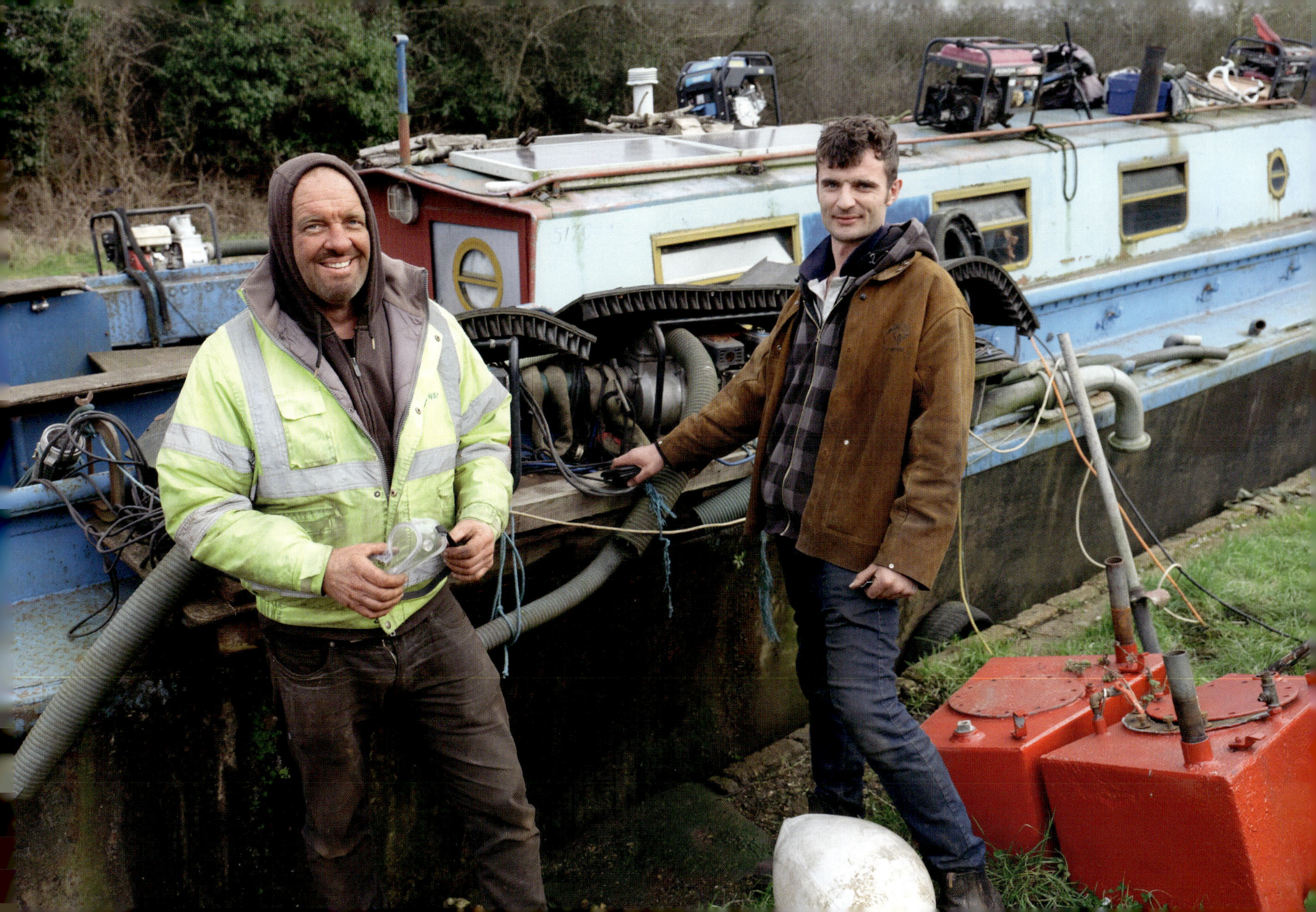

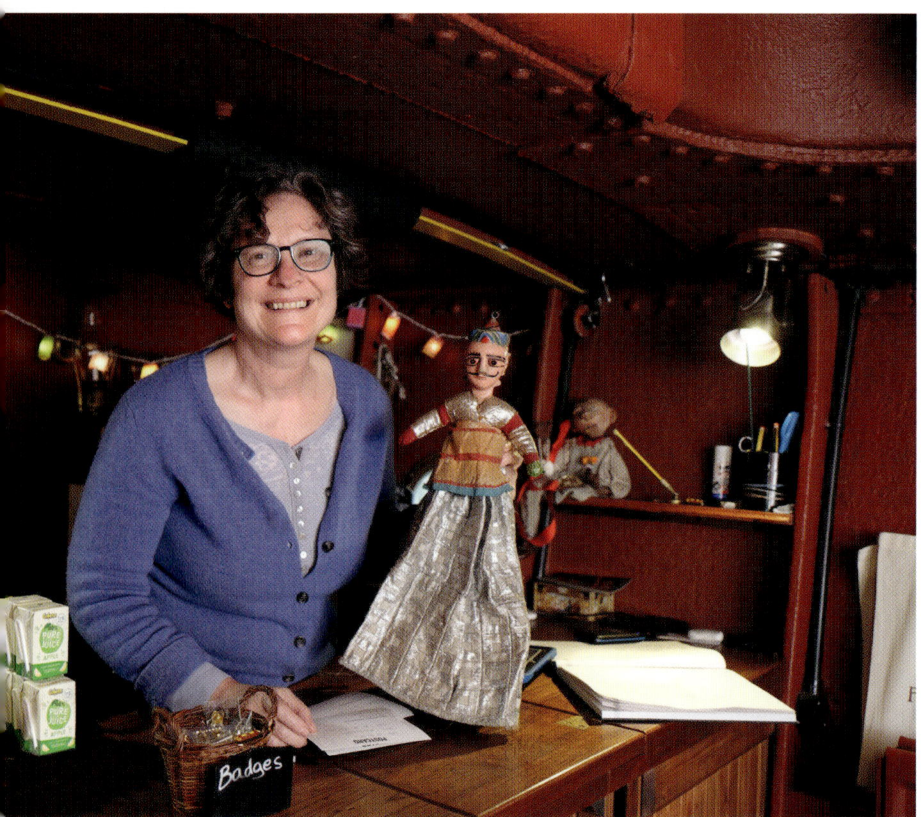

A family business! Kate and Stan Middleton, the second and third generations, stand on the deck of the Puppet Barge.

We are moored in Little Venice on the Regent's Canal for most of the year but head onto the Thames in July and spend the summer in Richmond. We have shows throughout the year and you can book online at www.puppetbarge.com.

Running a theatre on a barge isn't always easy. We once dropped the box office phone and all the tickets over board and on another occasion it was so cold that the toilet froze solid!

Mostly the theatre runs smoothly but we always remember the old boater saying 'don't buy a boat if you can't take a joke'.

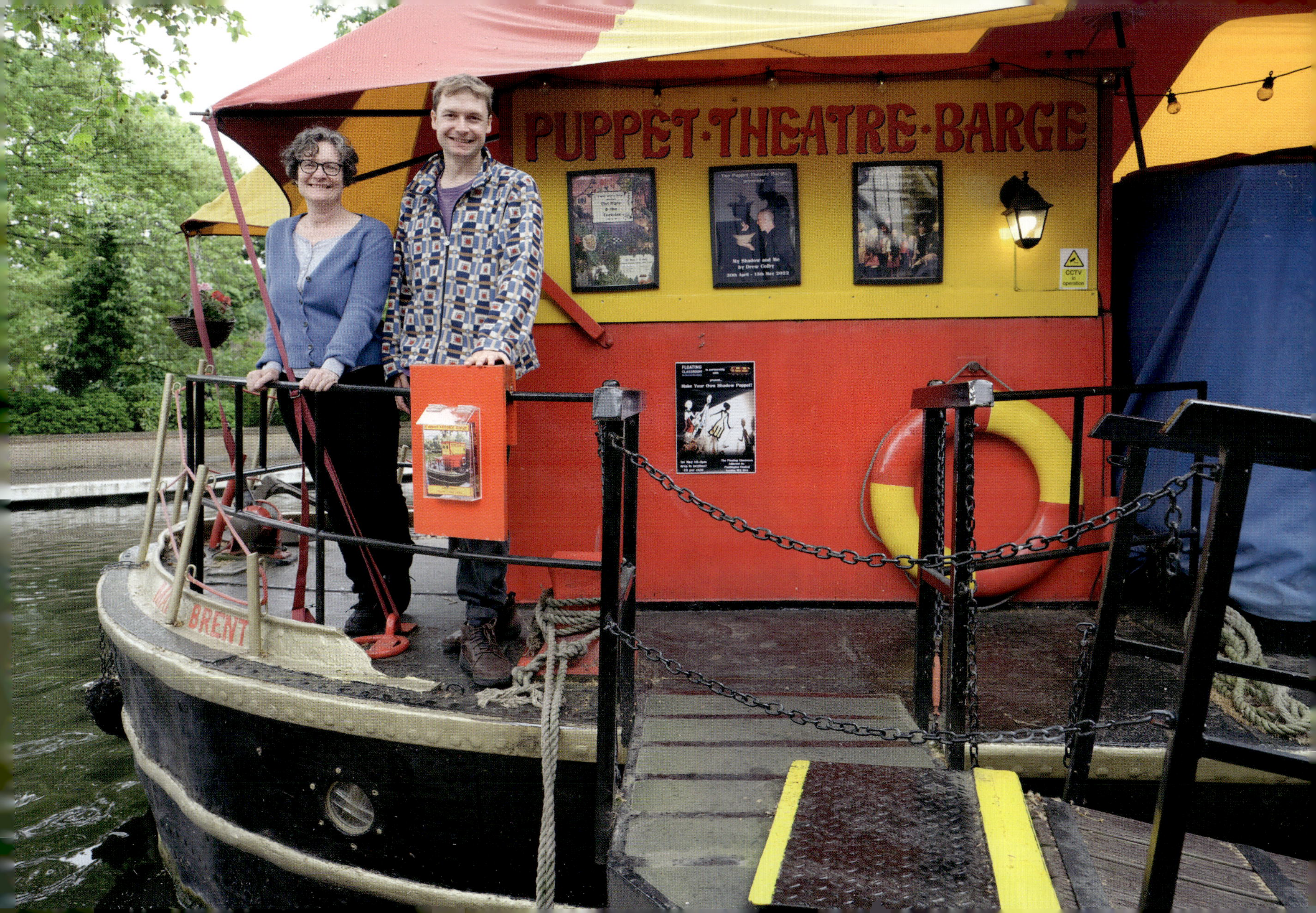

PUPPET · THEATRE · BARGE
CCTV
in
operation
BRENT

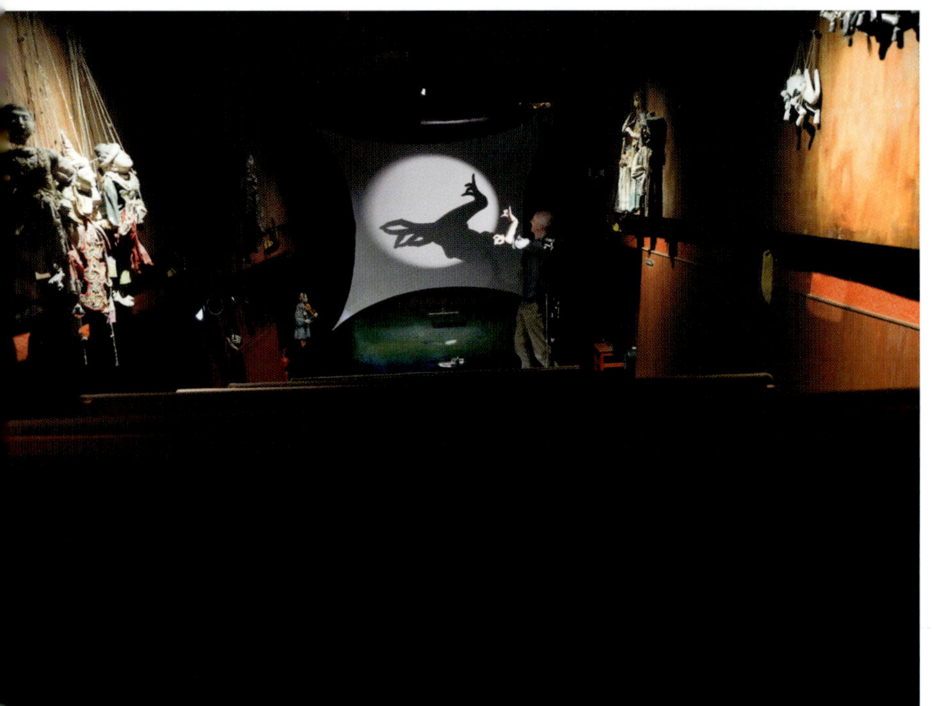

Being in tune with the movement and flow of the canals helps me to develop a sense of flow with my shadows.

It's a great pleasure and a challenge to perform on the Puppet Theatre Barge – although it is bigger than the narrowboat I lived on, it is a small space, and yet, with such close proximity to the audience, there is a magical sense of the shadows immediately communicating to the audience. Sometimes the barge moves slightly, or you hear the lapping water as boats go by, which all adds to the unique experience of performing on the boat.

There is something about being part of a natural environment on the boat. I am able to observe wild, farm and even domestic animals that help me to make shadow animals such as the rabbit.

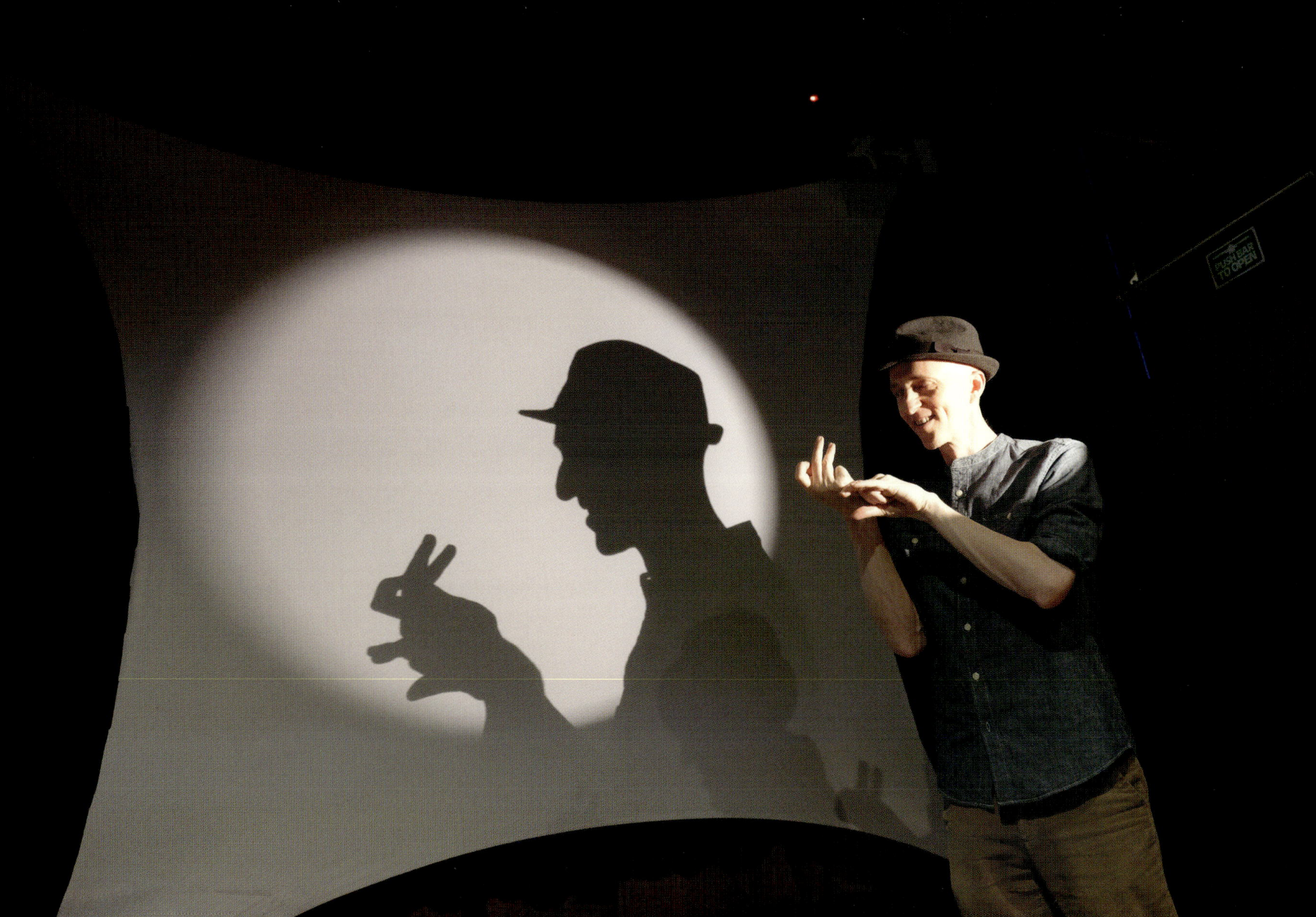

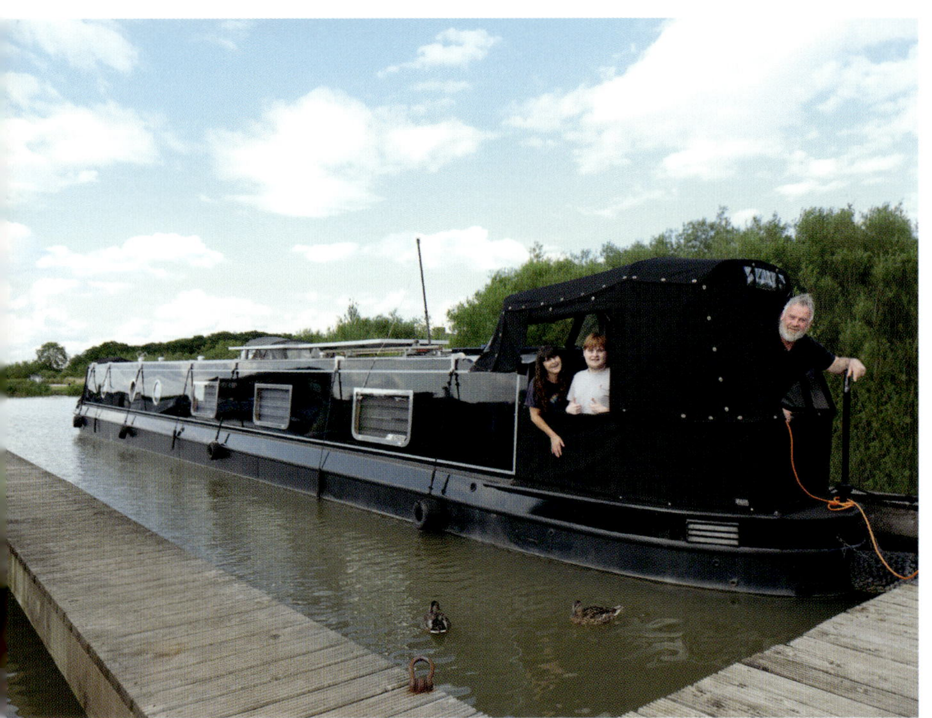

We are Steve, Rachel, Johnny and Will. We sold our three-bed semi five years ago and had our boat built. We escaped the hustle and bustle of residential chaos and now live a more relaxing and calming life on the water. Since then, we have never looked back! Over time our eldest flew the nest and now there are just the three of us – although he never misses an opportunity to come out cruising with us!

Steve and I are still working and Will is autistic, so we need a base to moor and meet all our needs. We have swapped and explored marinas over the last five years and have also enjoyed six months living canal side. Having no plug-in electric, water on tap and place to empty your toilet makes you appreciate all the things you would take for granted in a house.

Steve delivers healthcare and I support children with special educational needs in school, so every holiday or weekend we can, we escape into the countryside.

It wasn't easy at first for Will with his autism as he struggles with change and anything new, but being strong and persistent has given him a life which has brought the best out of him, and after two weeks you would think he'd lived on a boat all of his life. We cannot get through life without change and we feel we have given him so many changes that he will cope with challenges a lot better in the future. He loves the wildlife and nature, observing all the hidden gems off the beaten track that we would not normally see. Through the boating community he has really come out of his shell and we have all made new friends for life!

Life is about experiences and they don't just fall in your lap; you have to go and get them. We always say 'life is too short and do today what you might regret not doing tomorrow'. If we can do it, anyone can.

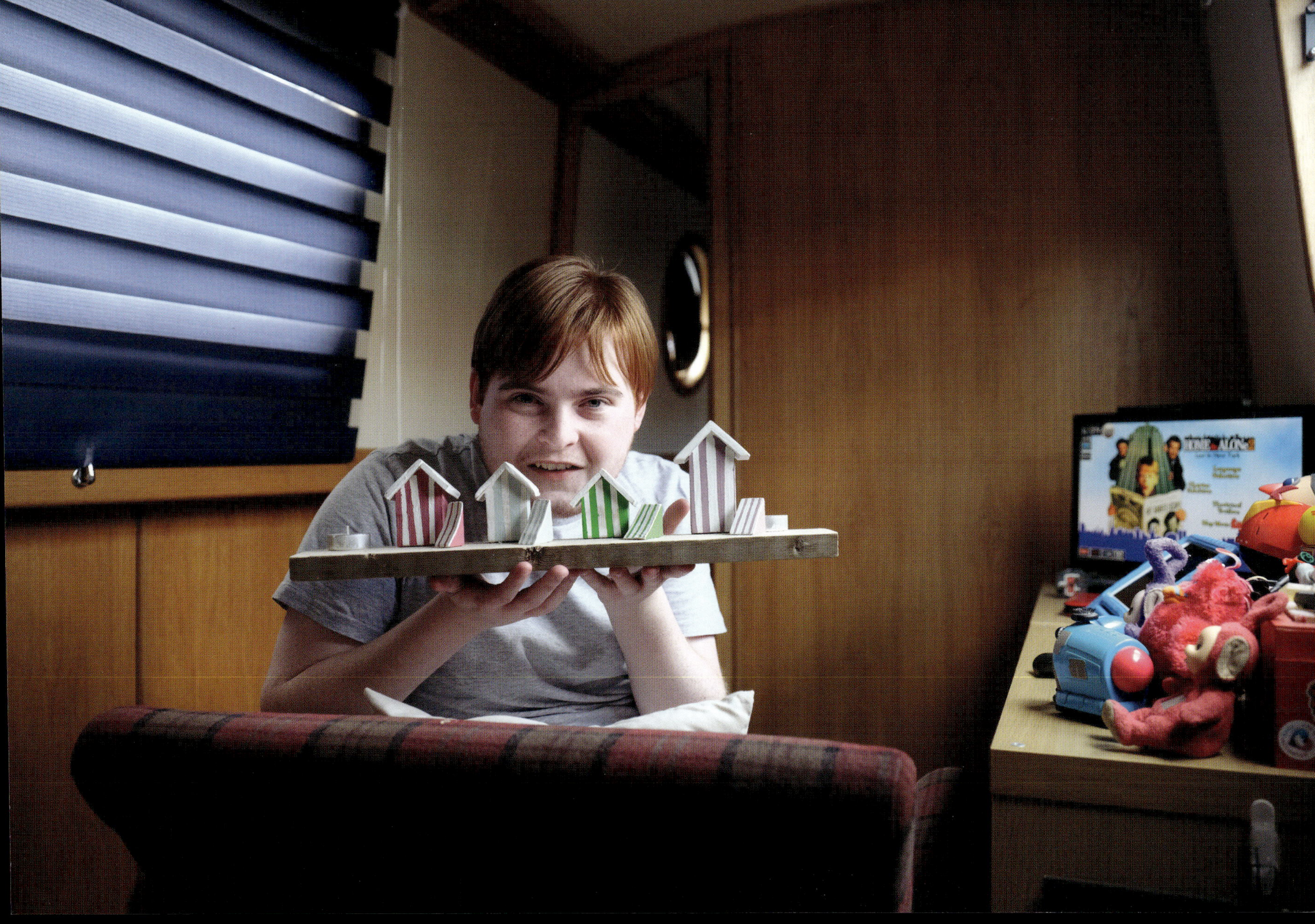

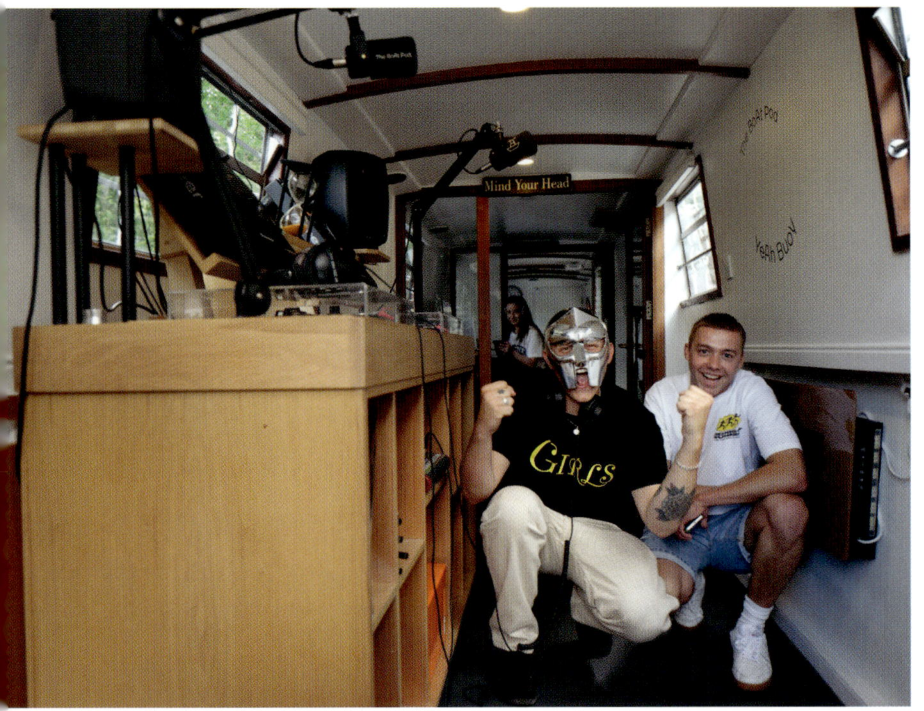

We are Ralph Bazaar and Bobby Pratt – collectively known as Midnight Runner. We are a DJ duo hailing from North London, with a passion for collecting and sharing underground music. But we are not just two traditional disc jockeys plugging hit records. Midnight Runner is also a radio brand that strives to support like-minded DJs and artists through on-air shows, guest mixes and curated club nights across our city.

Although we are at the beginning of a journey, Midnight Runner is dedicated to building and nurturing a global music community, a creative platform to share music, knowledge and talent.

We discovered *The Boat Pod* through the social media and were immediately intrigued by its uniqueness. As our background was radio, we were very keen to find out more about the space and whoever was behind it.

So we arranged to meet Sophie Callis on her boat, moored in Little Venice. Sophie is the captain of the ship and brains behind this project. We talked at length about music, arts and our experiences within the music scene/industry. Sophie gave us an opportunity to pitch and perform a pilot show on *The Boat Pod*, which was thankfully a success.

From there on, we were fortunate to be given a monthly breakfast show, which first aired at the beginning of July. Our show is called 'Sore Head Club' and features a wide range of soul, funk, disco, jazz and house music, designed to ease you into your Saturday morning and get you set up for the rest of your day.

It has been a real joy to host our shows on *The Boat Pod* as it is like nowhere we have worked before. Sophie has created a welcoming, unique and inclusive space with a beautiful energy and ethos surrounding it. We look forward to working and supporting *The Boat Pod* and its community indefinitely.

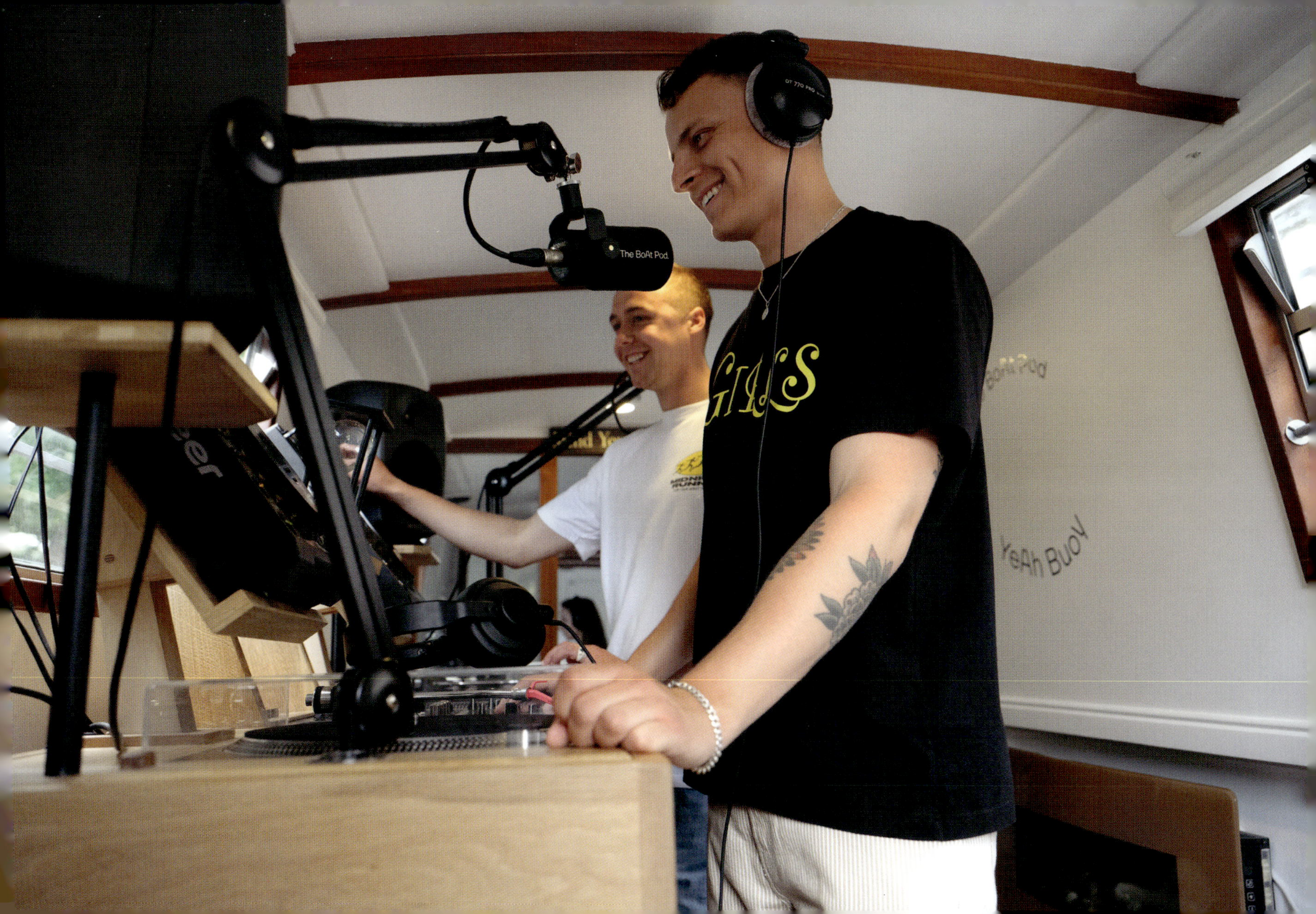
The BoAt Pod.
YeAh BuoY

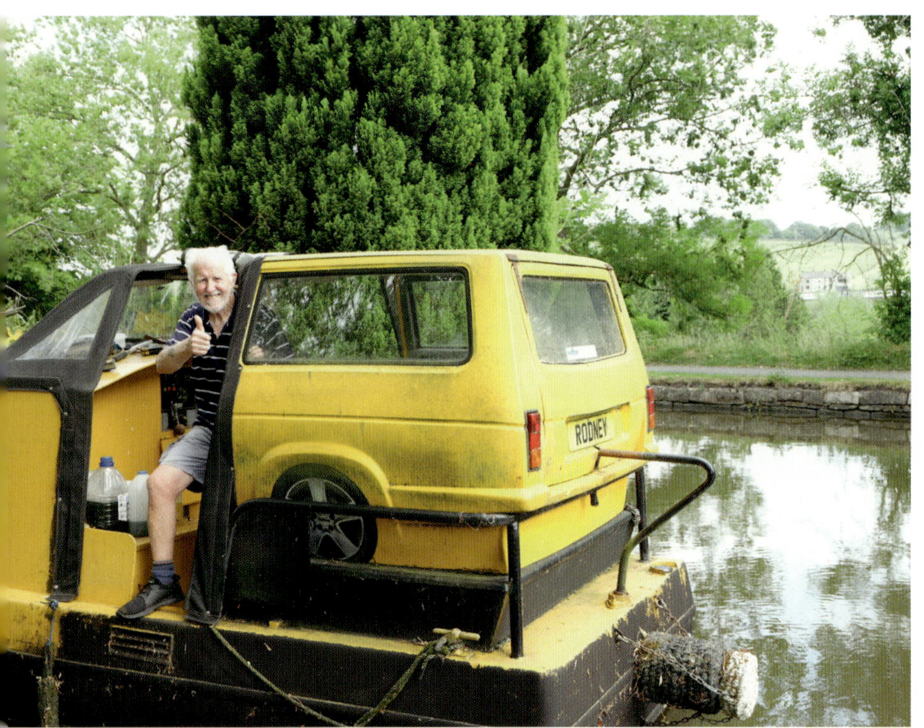

This boat came up for sale and it was berthed at New Mills. I had always wanted to own a boat but until I sold my house, I couldn't afford one. The canal has always been really important to me and when I saw it come up for sale, I thought 'right I will buy it!' I bought it off a guy called Tony Vaughan from Stockport, who had already converted it to *Trotters Independent, Del Boy & Rodney* – I take no credit for that.

When Tony sold it to me it was a real mess inside, so I decided to completely gut it. I have spent years planning what I would do to it. I always wanted a dinette for when my grandkids come so they would be able to sit around the table and play games or have snacks. I just started getting into renovating the boat when lockdown came, so I wasn't allowed on it; then just when I could get back on, the second lockdown came. At this point I had lost a bit of interest, so when I did get back to it I thought 'where was I up to', where are all my tools. The wood was all over the place and it felt a bit of an anticlimax, but then I got back into it and I'm pleased to say these last few weeks have been good – it has been nice and warm and I'm back into it now.

I live nearby in Whaley Bridge so it is easy to spend a lot of time here and work on this project.

My son Matthew and his wife Claire have two daughters, Katie and Sophie, and my daughter Nicola and her husband Colin have two children, Hannah and Connor (we call him Conboy). It will be great to be able to take them out on the canals in the holidays and have some fun when the renovations are complete.

This project will take me about six months to complete. I will of course keep the Trotters Independent name and it would be great if David Jason and Nicholas Lyndhurst could pop up and have a look when it is finished … so 'watch this space'.

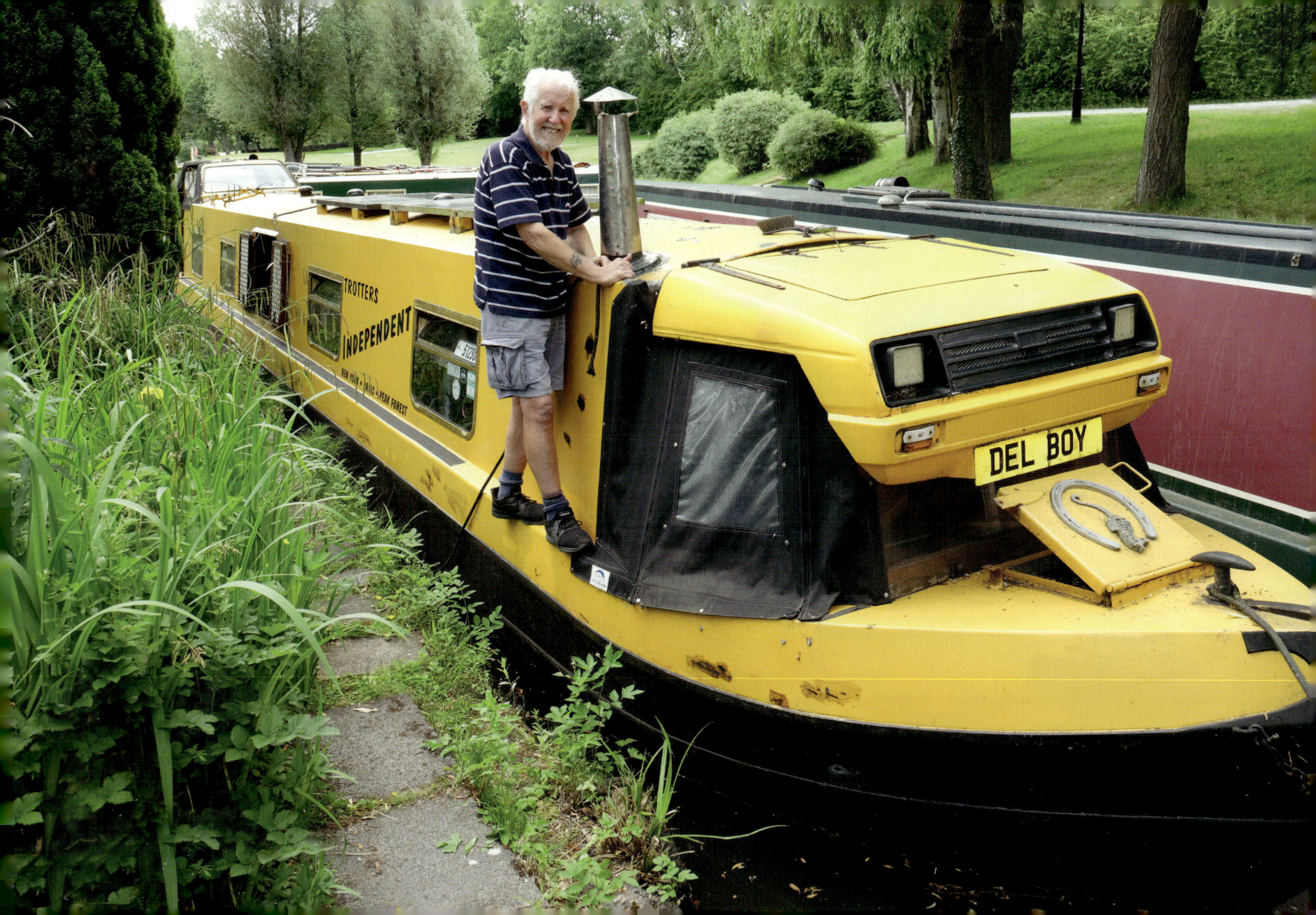

TROTTERS
INDEPENDENT
NEW YORK · PARIS · PEAK FOREST
DEL BOY

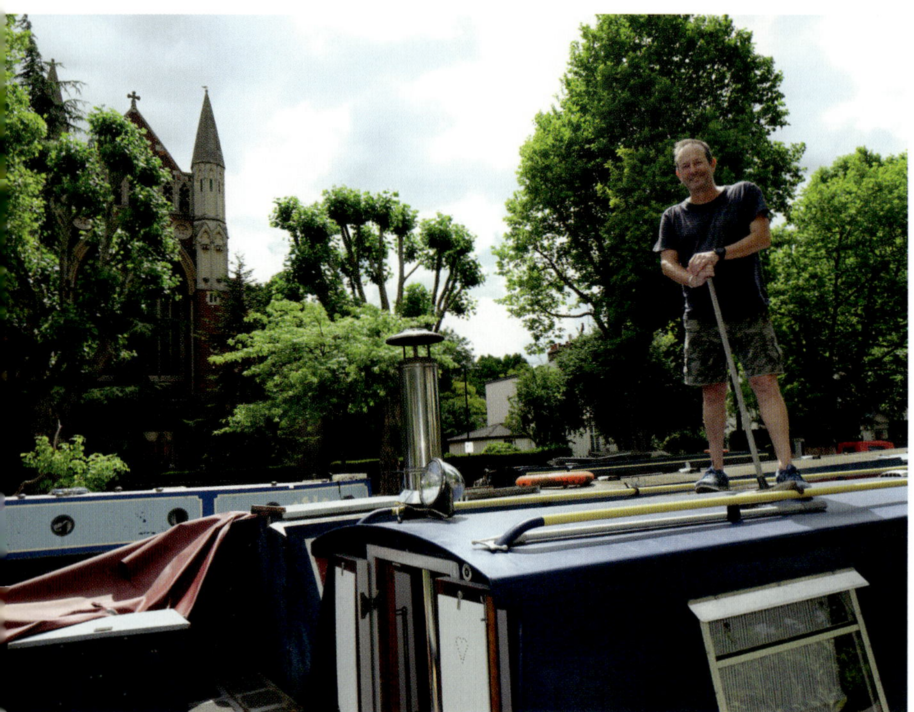

I'm often asked why I chose to live on a narrowboat (not a longboat – I'm not a Viking) and what it's like?

Well, I say 'It's like camping out in central London. You are very aware of the changing seasons and the weather. The rain on the roof, ice cracking in winter, the boat rocking in the wind and the swans pecking on the hull demanding breakfast in the mornings.'

The canal – or the cut as it is known to the bargees – is like a small floating village with a real sense of community that is hard to find elsewhere in London.

I also like living in a small space as it forces you to make hard decisions about belongings and whether they are really necessary. Having lived out of a rucksack for most of my adult life, I find the more belongings you have the more of a millstone you have around your neck. Nature abhors a vacuum – the bigger the space the more the accumulated stuff.

I cannot imagine myself living anywhere else.

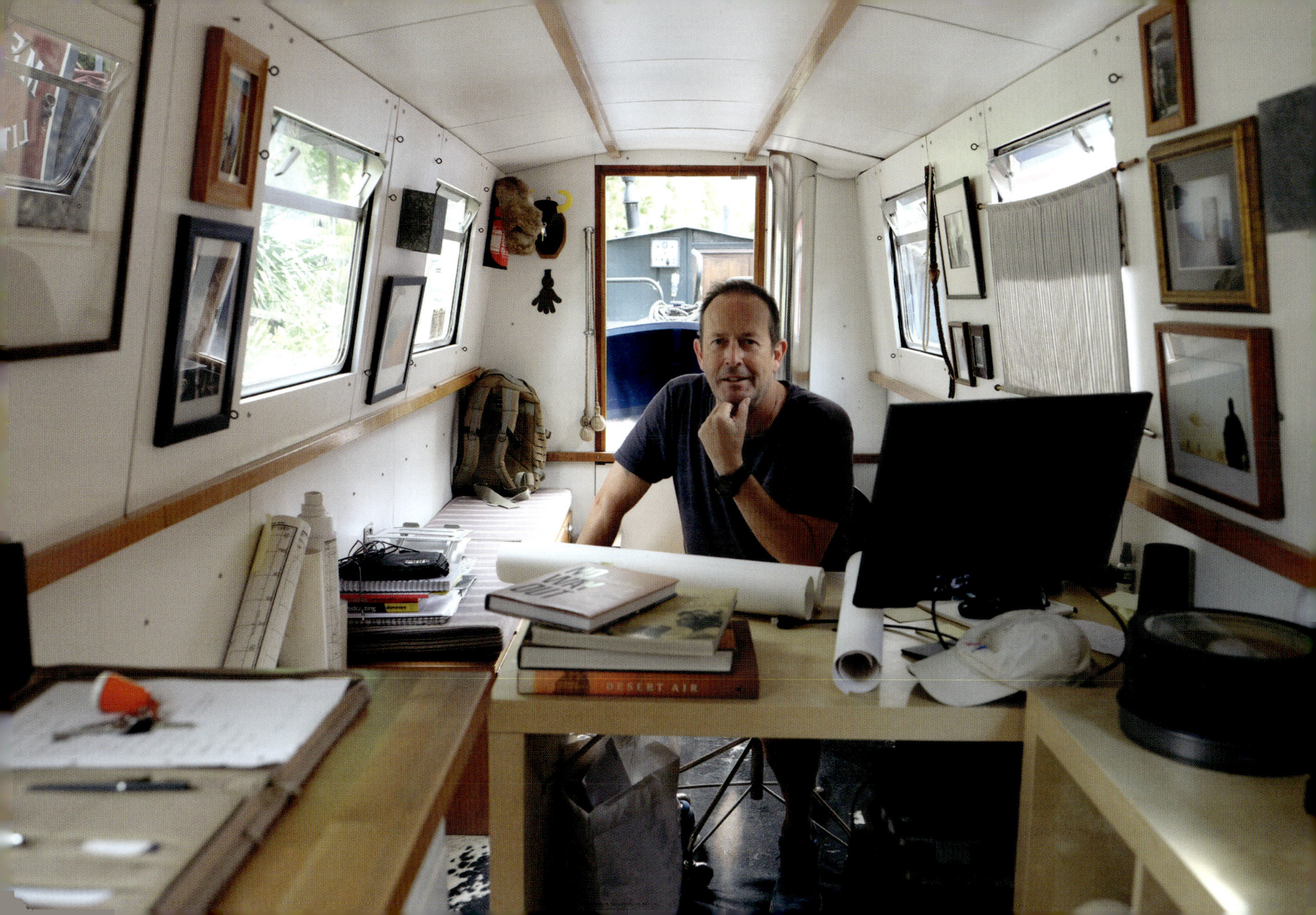

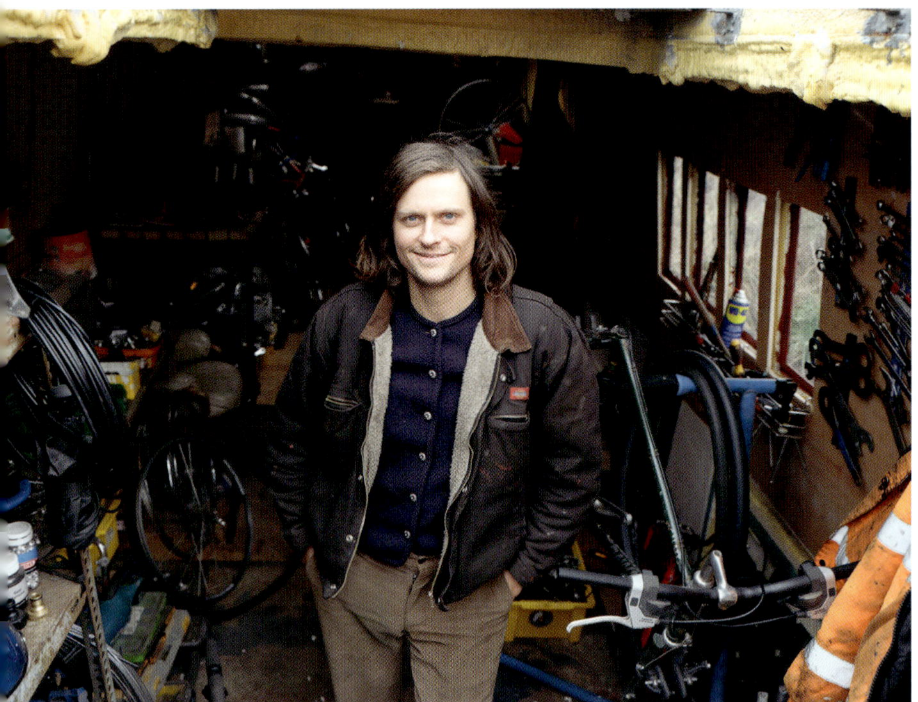

All aboard *Floating Bike Repairs*, the most whimsical bike shop in the world.

Mechanic and sailor Sam Skinner is bringing beauty and life back to London's canals, one vintage bicycle at a time. Light rain falls from the London sky, tinkling onto the corrugated fiberglass roof like mini chocolate chips.

Sam Skinner sits on a stool beside the vintage Dawes bike propped up in his stand. Wheels and frames, parts and tools, hang around the ceiling of this tiny canal boat, surrounding his head like birds after a cartoon character gets a good knock to their loaf. And this suits Skinner, a good-natured bike mechanic living and working full-time on his three-boat flotilla called *Floating Bike Repairs*.

Since he's floating and a constant cruiser, Skinner changes location every couple of weeks around the canal system in the UK. On sunnier days, he sets up his work stand out on the deck or on the boardwalk beside his moored boats. Many of his customers stumble upon him while he is working, by happenstance. The rest of them simply ask – his regulars know to send him a text, give him a call, or check his Instagram for his most recent location.

When Sam was about ten, he went to a sailing club and saw some really impressive boats that made him want to own one one day. So he just started working in the yachting world but then realised he really missed bikes and thought why not set up a business on a canal boat with no stress and very little overheads?

This is now the fifth year of trading and Sam's lifestyle is just to do what he wants and enough people will come by and find him! It is increasingly easy to find business and bike repairs are quite cheap. Some new customers come across him on Instagram and they just follow the pictures that he posts most of the time. Some find him by phone calls and he tells them where he is – which is usually anywhere along the River Lea. As he cruises around, moving every two weeks, they might have to try a little harder to find him but they do in the end.

Sometimes Sam just finds bikes that have been dumped in the canal, fishes them out and repairs them.

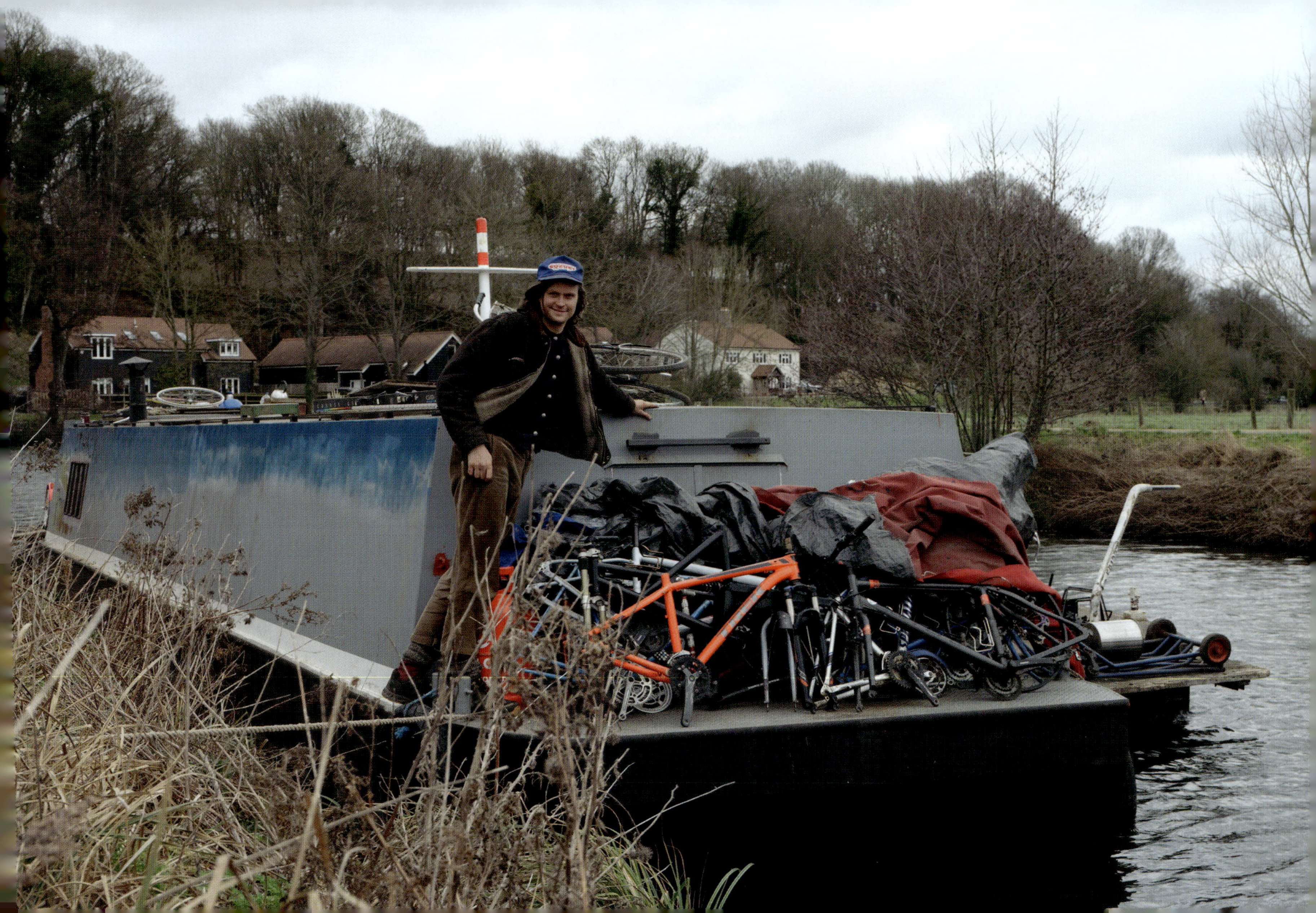

Sam Worrall

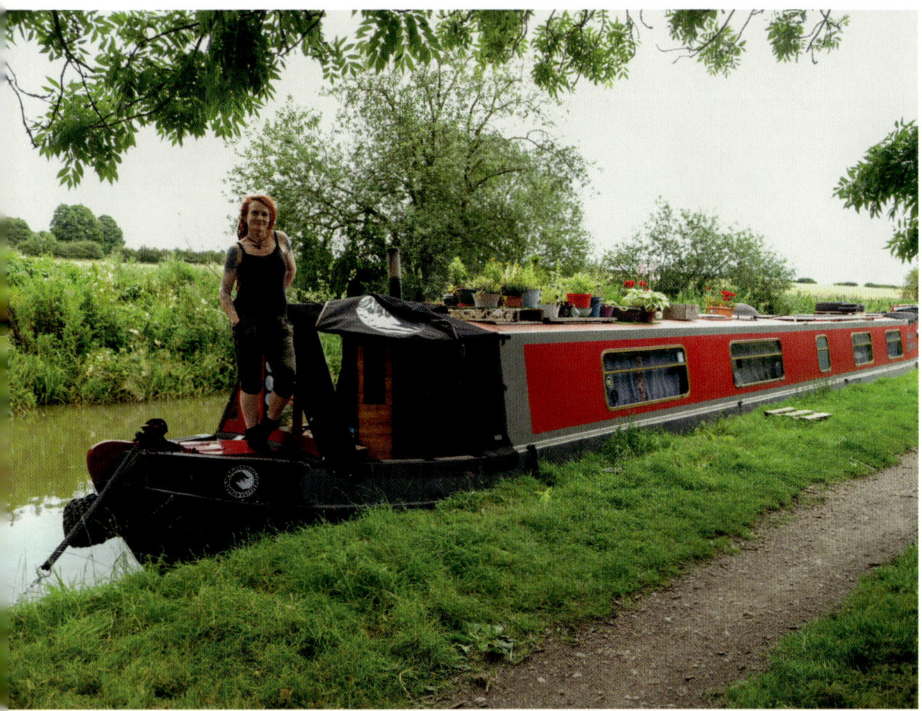

I've been a new traveller since the late 1990s. Ten years ago, I stayed on a friend's boat on the Kennet & Avon Canal and immediately I wanted to be a part of that community. So I bought my first boat.

I was a professional archaeologist, travelling to and from sites across the country and working very long hours. But as a constant cruiser, required to move every two weeks, my job and lifestyle were incompatible. I then started working for the Gypsy and Traveller advocacy charities, doing support and outreach work.

I left the Kennet & Avon in 2018, moved into my camper van and went to work and live on Orkney, working for Historic Environment Scotland as a tour guide during summer months, then back down to England in the winter to work for another advocacy charity, Friends, Families and Travellers (FFT).

After two years of this cycle, I realised I really missed living on the cut and being a boater, so I bought this boat. A week after I moved on the Covid-19 pandemic struck and we were in lockdown! I just made it to south Oxford in time, having cruised out of London, where I bought my boat from. I came to this canal as it is really beautiful and I knew it from previous visits. After lockdown I got a job in a local boatyard and a remote working job with another Gypsy and Traveller support charity. Three years on from that I am now managing the working side of the boatyard, running a team of engineers and painters, as well as working for FFT again.

I love the canals for so many reasons. The industrial archaeology that is still a working part of our landscape, the pace of life, the community, the nomadic nature of moving to another favourite spot every couple of weeks. The wildlife; here we have so many kingfishers, owls and otters. Beautiful Cotswold villages but also just a short distance from the centre of Oxford or Banbury. In summer I love my roof garden, towpath fires with friends, cruising up and down the canal. Winters can be hard but I have a winter mooring at the boatyard and that has helped make them easier. The boat I live on now is 57 feet and I renamed her *Shield Maiden* when I had her out of the water for blacking in 2020. I had her repainted at my yard that year too, so she's looking great outside as well as inside and I love her. To me my boat is like my snail shell. I can't see myself leaving the canal again until I really have to!

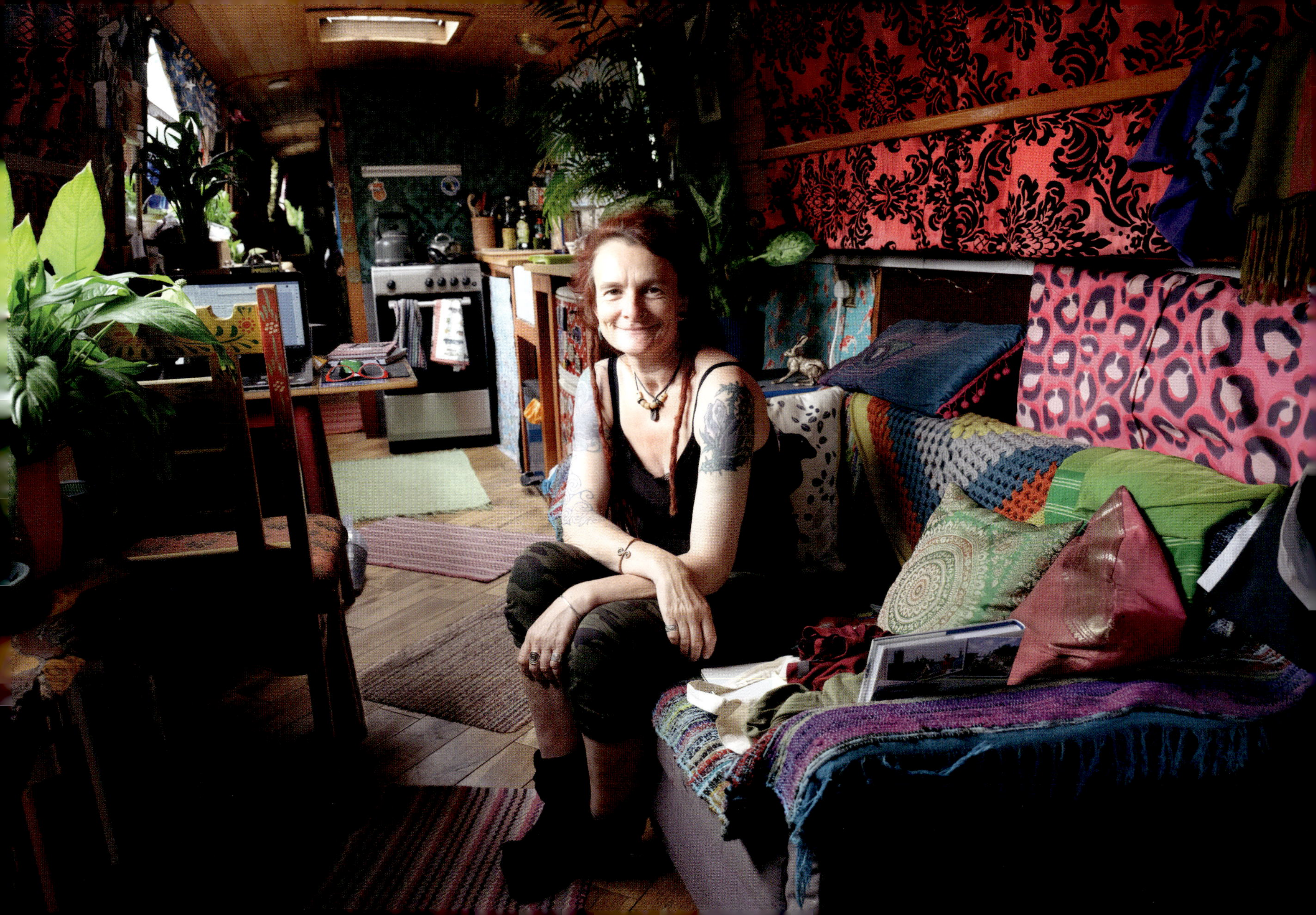

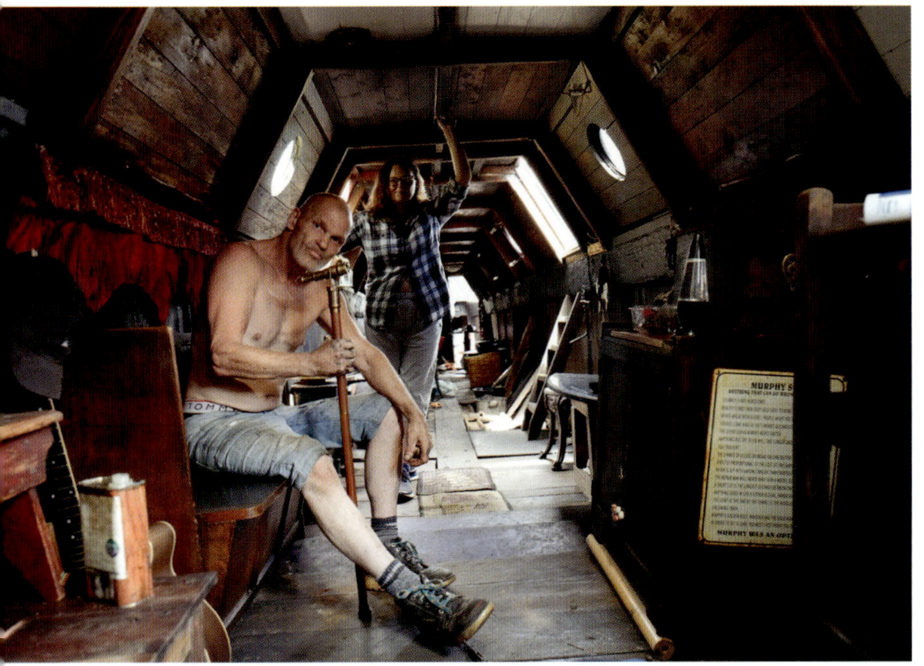

Our story revolves around our narrowboat, *Starcross*, which was constructed in 1936 by Walkers Brothers of Rickmansworth and was made entirely of oak. She is a deep-drafted, five-plank Ricky butty. Only sixty-two of these boats were commissioned by the GUCCC (the Grand Union Canal Carrying Company) – so she is a boat of great historical interest and a rare sight on 'the cut'. At the time, we didn't really understand how much of a historic treasure she really was, or how much work she would turn out to be!

We exhibited *Starcross* at the London Canal Museum in November 2022 and a veteran boater told us that these boats carried massively heavy cargoes of up to 50 tons, with a ten-man crew to handle her. Originally, she was a butty boat, towed by a Ricky butty tug or horses. In the 1980s, she had a cab fitted and 75 per cent of the original oak hull had to be replaced with elm, with a new keel. She was also fitted transom (a strengthening cross-bar) and her own engine. However, navigating this 71-foot, 39-ton vessel is like matrix – highly engaging!

Buying the boat three years ago was originally Tania's idea. She aspired towards a calm, drama-free life, with lots of outdoors, close to nature. Scott's qualifications, experience and drive meant that we were chosen out of a list of prospective buyers to be her new guardians.

So here is where the drama-free becomes free drama! After three years of caulking, servicing and repairing, witnessing every previous owner's panic-stricken botch to fix a leak and the nightmare behind the labyrinth of twee furniture, cute gimmicks and 'little house on the prairie' style, she sank! Scott thought she had been stolen. The only thing visible, sticking out of the murk, was the chimney.

As guardians of this historic boat, the onus was on us to rescue her. Lots of expert hands and wooden boat experience, coupled with big lumps of cash, were needed. And *Starcross* was raised and brought back to her former glory, if not better. The result is that she is now totally open plan, looking more like a stretch function room with Harry Potter overtones.

Chats with the locals and a bit of research established the cause of the problem. The Tottenham Hale pound has an issue with water levels. *Starcross* is deep drafted and so she listed very quickly as the water levels dropped. That enabled water to enter the boat through drainage holes.

Today, she is fully renovated and totally upgraded, including new pumps, electric wiring, solar panels and an engine upgrade. She is a very beautiful and peaceful boat now.

We are excited about our future, excited about showing off *Starcross* and confident that we have the knowledge to maintain and protect her for the future generations. We are guardians of a national treasure and a slice of canal history.

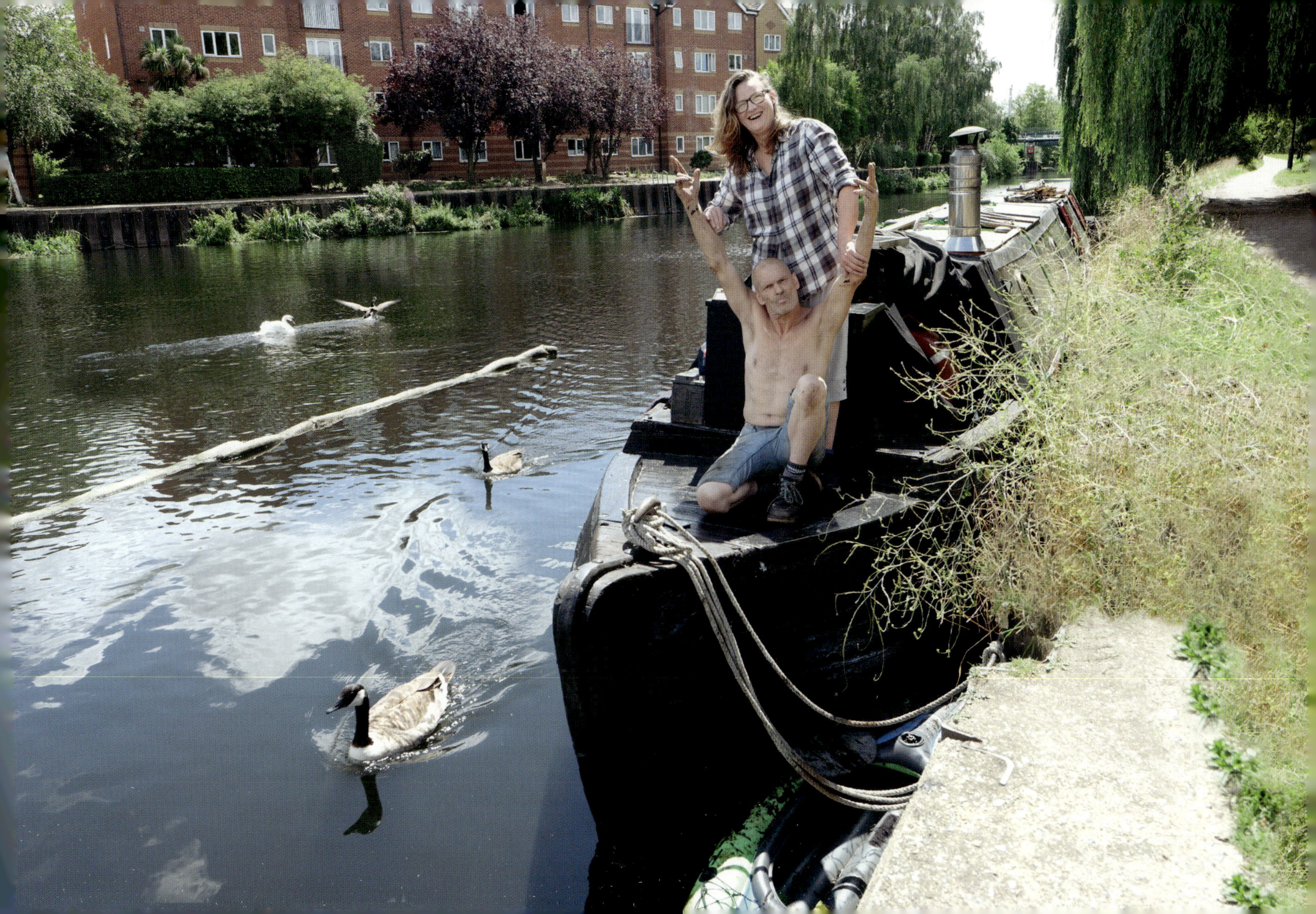

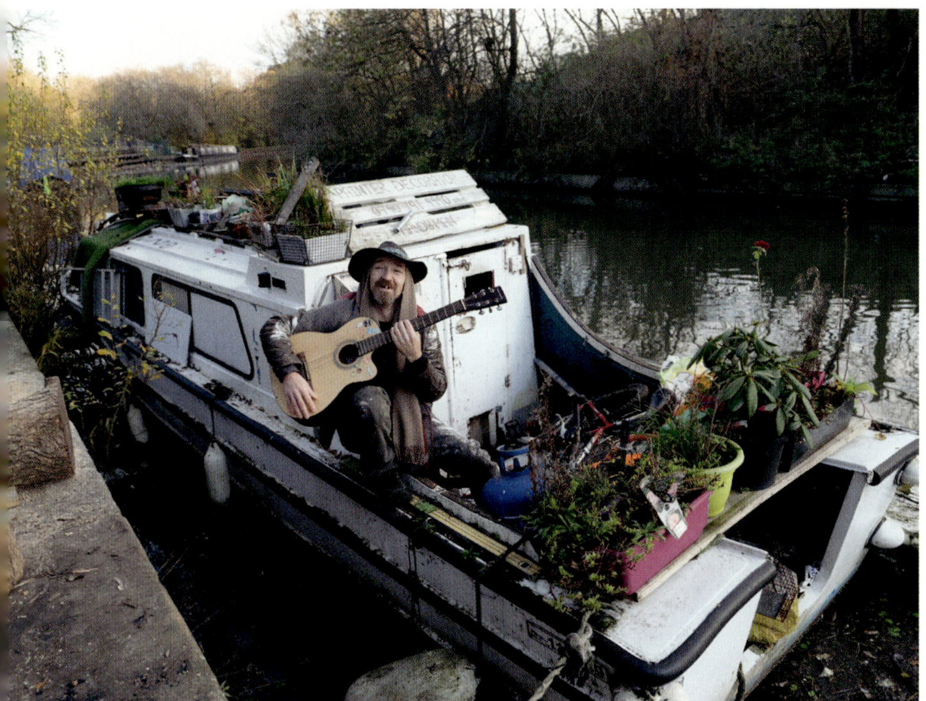

For what seems like an eternity, we dance and play, bringing time
and motion night and day.
The animals know of our loves embrace, they hoot and they howl
when I show my face.
Your seas are bound to me like arms open wide,
whilst we roll around in our playfulness and bring forth the tides
Where the night falls and no sun will arise,
I'll always lighten your darkness and brighten your sky
People take us for granted,
they do not see,
we two are working as one in love and forever shall be.

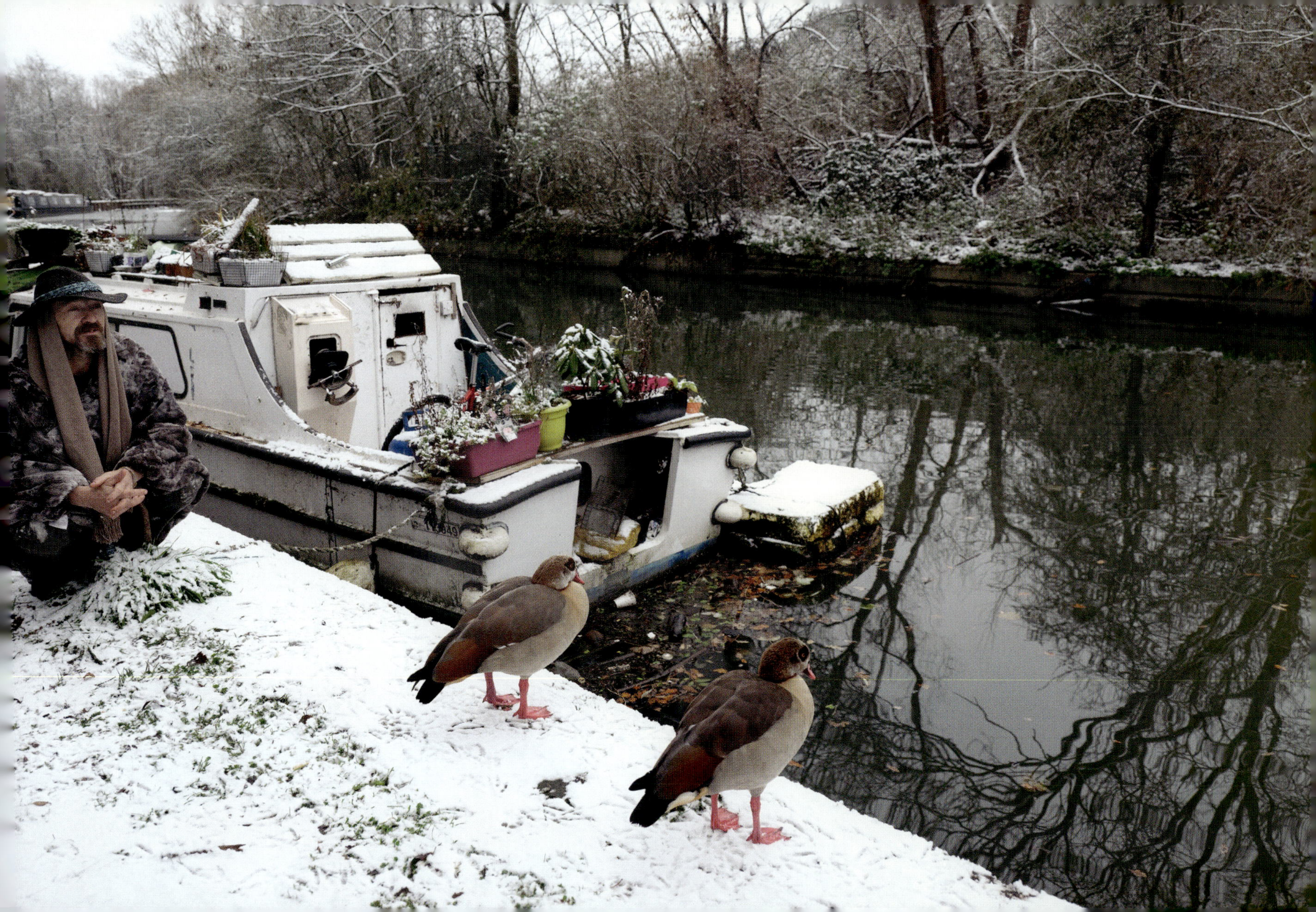

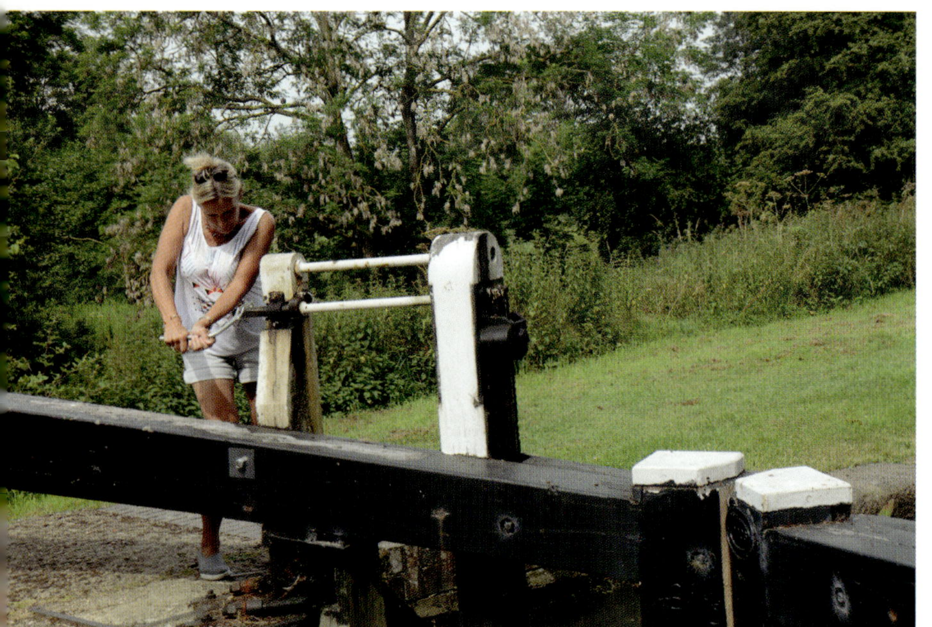

Life on water: I love the peace and quiet. On a narrowboat, the slow pace of life imposes itself on my own way of life. The enforced pattern of behaviour that we impose on ourselves in order to maintain a house, a job and a family vanishes the minute we begin cruising. I am so relaxed.

I don't need to read a book. I am just so happy just watching the world go by. We pass fields filled with cattle and sheep, see an occasional kingfisher, watch the herons fishing and the dabchicks diving for what seemed like an eternity. It is an amazing experience to simply sit and watch.

One of the things I love is laying in bed feeling the soothing rocking motion of the boat. I sleep so much better than I ever do on land. Really, when you are on the boat you cannot think of anything else. I enter another world.

A narrowboat today – a leisure boat rather than a working boat – is a mobile home on water. It is cleverly designed to fit everything in. Boats that are used for cruising need to have lockers and places to make your possessions safe when we are moving. Houseboats or boats that do not need to move can be more flexible in the interior layout. But the cruising boat owes its design excellence to the need for functionality.

Keeping life simple on board our boat is our key to happy cruising.

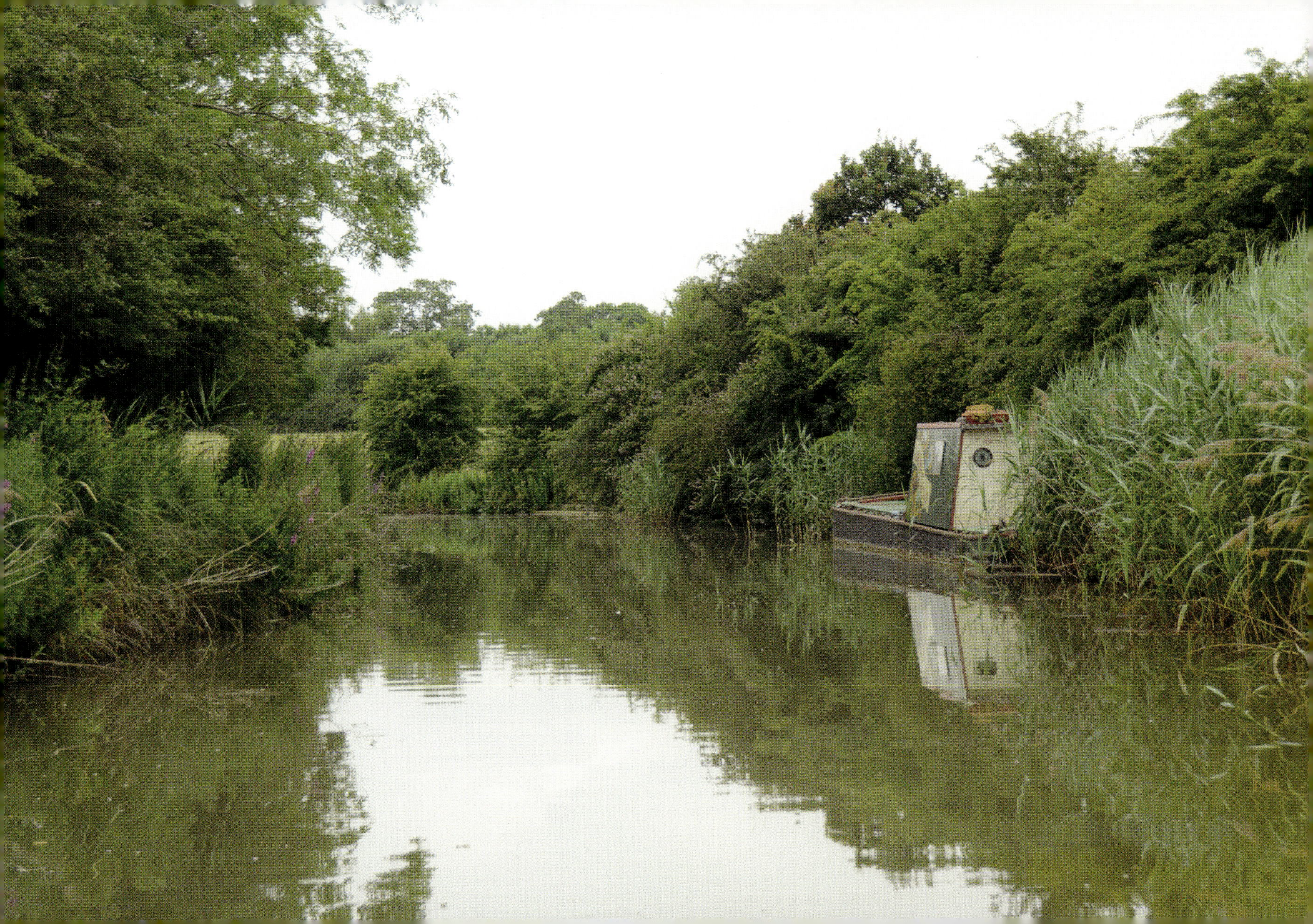

Susan Bookbinder

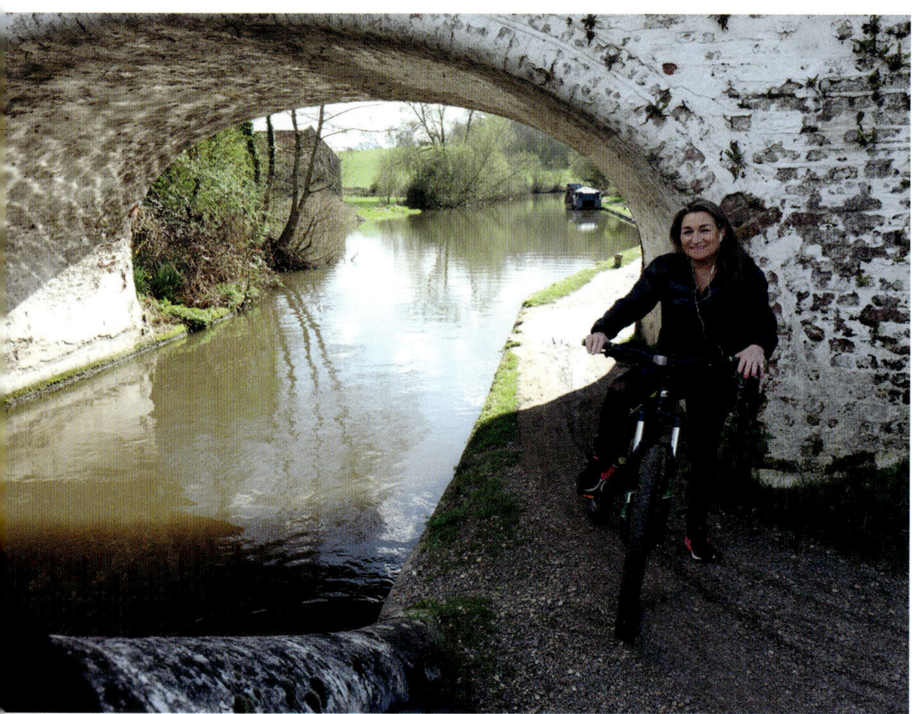

Since Covid, I have become a self-confessed workaholic and I find it difficult to stop. Riding my bike along the canal with music in my headphones is my precious switch-off time.

The name of each boat tells a story. *Just Because We Can*, *Skint Again*, *One Life – Live It!*. It is wonderful to see the spring flowers, the tiny ducklings and cygnets. By the time it comes to autumn, I have watched those babies grow up and I feel like they're my kids!

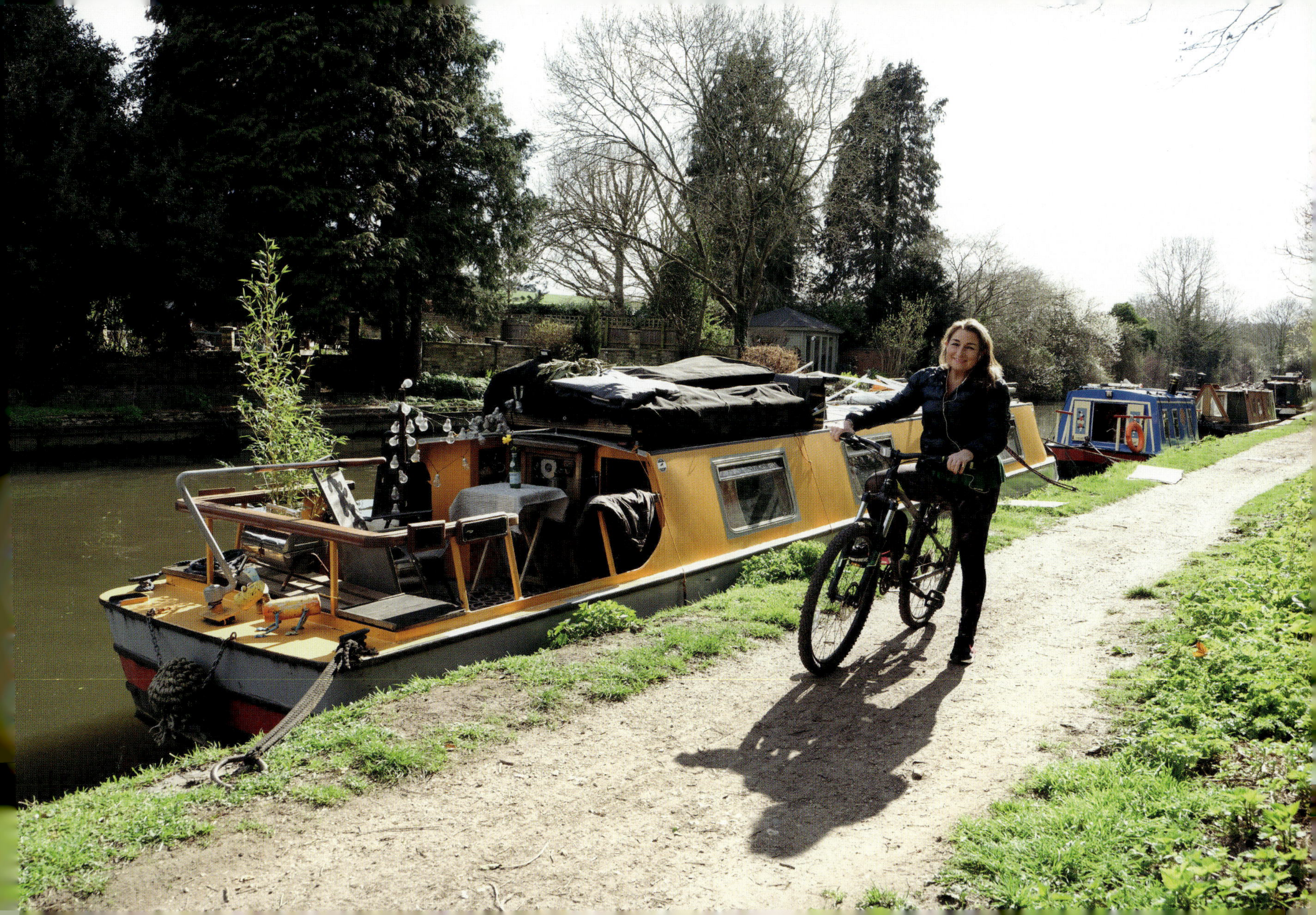

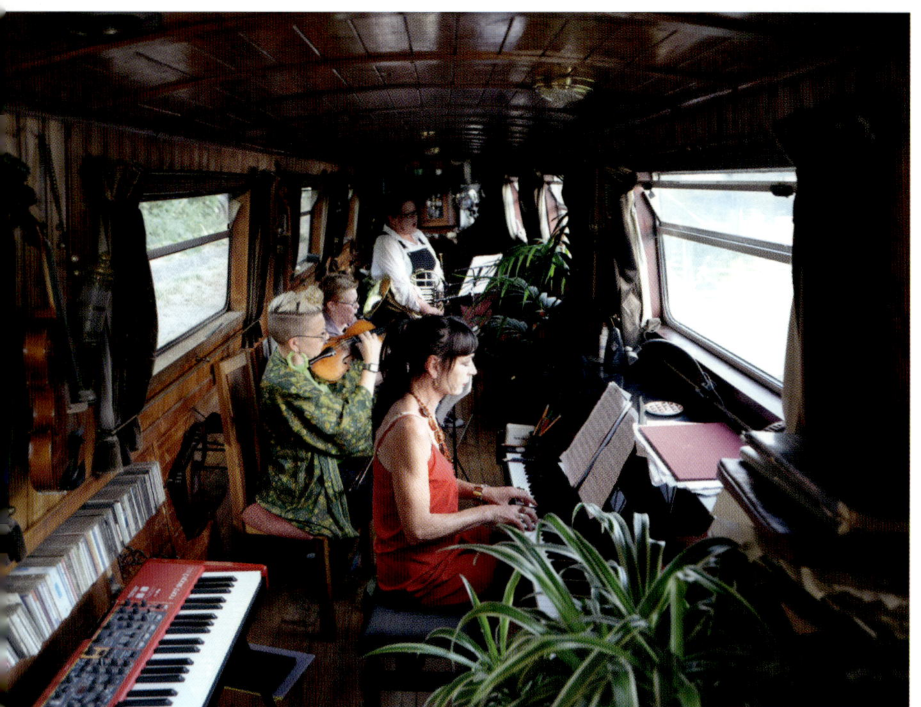

Risen from the ashes of The Cesarians, The Deviation could never be conventional if they tried. Featuring original compositions by their very own Justine Armatage and Alison Beckett, The Deviation rehearse regularly aboard a narrowboat in the heart of Hackney.

Initially, pieces were commissioned to accompany a book opening and exhibition for Sarah Finke. However, they soon realised that the joy in creating music together was something they just couldn't be without, and the repertoire continues to grow.

The Deviation are formed of Justine Armatage on the piano and cello, Alison Beckett on the clarinet and oboe, Chris Lehmann on violin, and Bev Crome on vocal, French horn and trumpet.

An uncountable number of gigging, touring and recording hours have already been clocked up by each member of the quartet in a number of different musical outfits and genres. However, the excitement of a group that creates its own niche somewhere in between avant-garde chamber music and acoustic rock 'n roll is propelling The Deviation forward into a new sort of unknown.

If the idea that the confines of producing music on a narrowboat – at best a mere 6 feet, 8 inches wide – seems like an impossible task, note that Justine has managed to fit two pianos into her boat.

In his youth, Richard Branson fitted an entire recording studio into a narrowboat and was so successful that the Virgin brand was born.

Bearing in mind how water has inspired some of the greatest and most memorable musical compositions, surely the future for The Deviation looks very rosy.

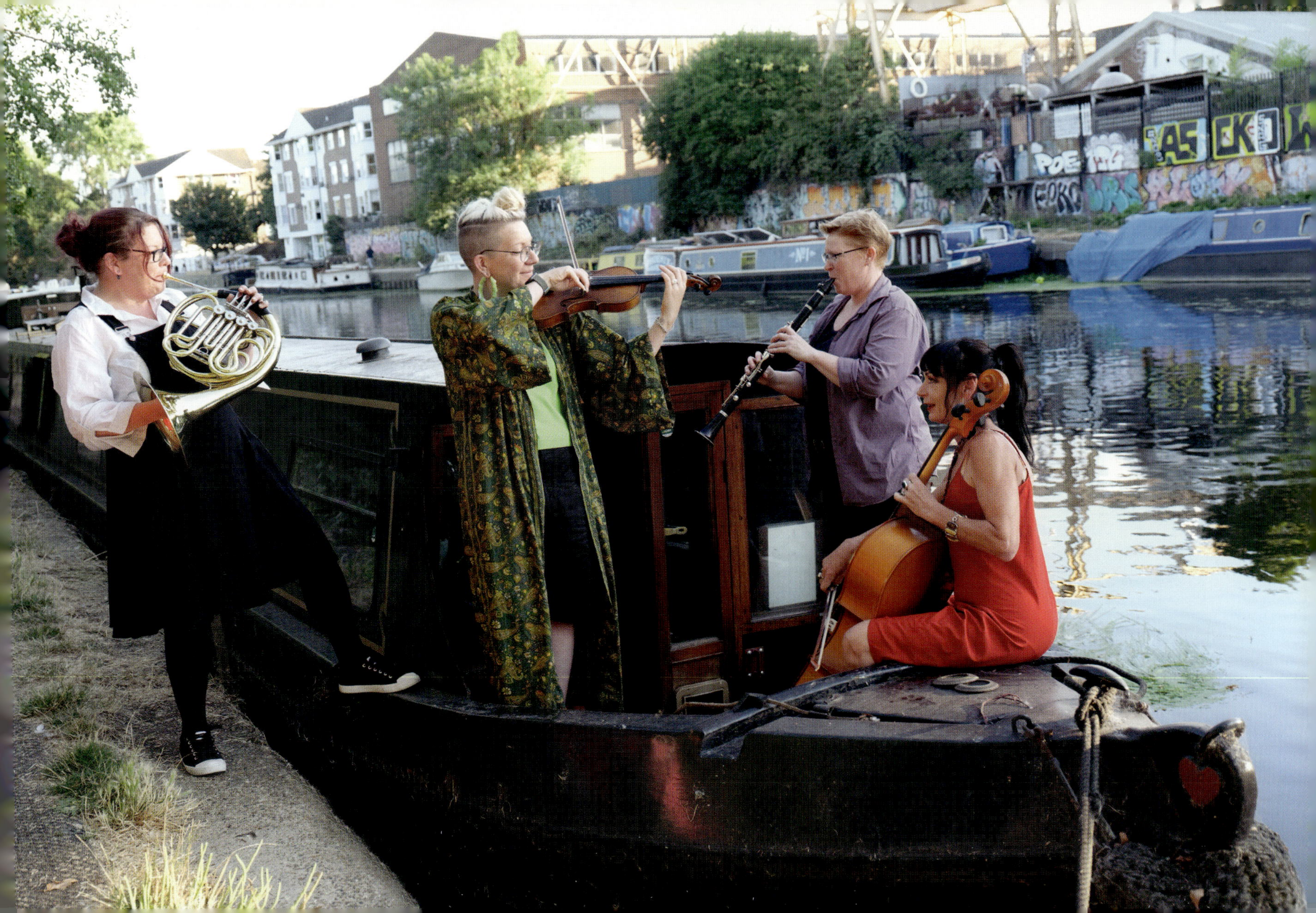

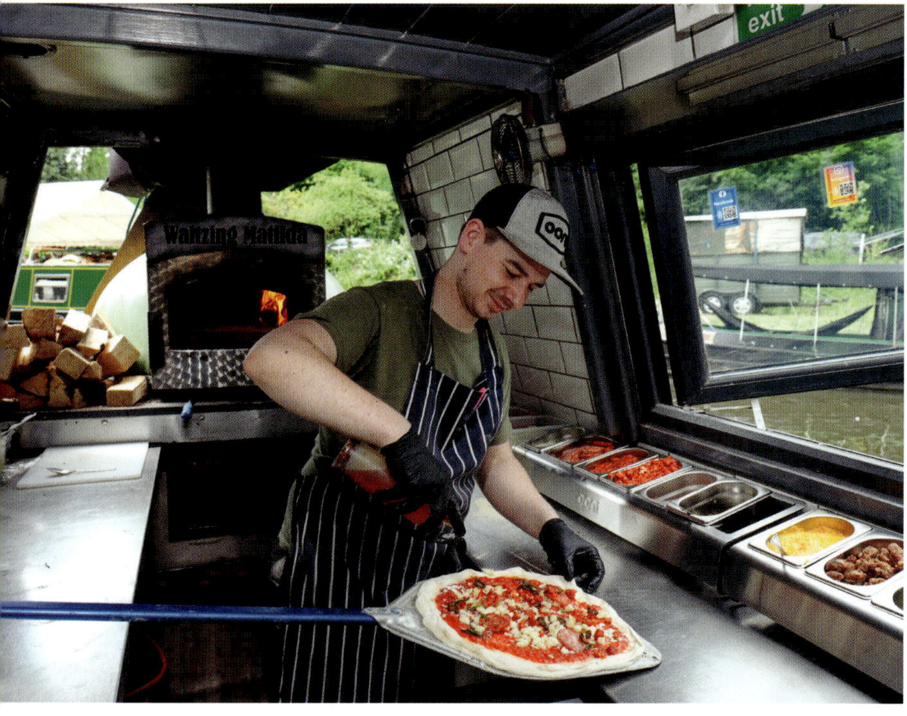

In the midst of the Covid-19 pandemic, my dad, my sister and I formed *The Waltzing Matilda* boat. It was a challenging time for everyone; both my dad and I were furloughed from our day jobs. Being unable to work and feeling confined was tough because we are both proactive people. I vividly remember sitting inside my dad's houseboat with my family, enclosed in our social bubble, grappling with a sense of loss and frustration. The conversation turned to what we could do given the current situation, and we noticed the canals becoming a sanctuary for many during the pandemic. That's when the idea of creating a community hub around our stunning canal system was born.

We set to work, planning what we wanted our community to see and what would bring people a sense of joy and escapism from the challenging situation. The idea of a café on the water began to form – a brew with a view, immersed in nature. Being a chef, I expanded this idea by integrating food. That's when the quirky idea of installing a wood-fired pizza oven on the boat emerged. We chose pizza for its simplicity – we wanted a food that mirrored life on the canals, stripped back from complication yet adored by all.

We were committed to using local produce. Small businesses were at the forefront of our minds, and we found an abundance of quality ingredients right on our doorstep. Even our coffee is roasted just a few miles away from the boat.

The boat's name, *The Waltzing Matilda*, came from an amalgamation of inspirations. My niece, Matilda, was only recently born when we were conceptualizing the idea. We wanted to name the boat after her and added 'Waltzing' as we waltz up and down the canal system. The name also resonates with the song 'The Waltzing Matilda', which we used to play for Matilda when she was upset, which always managed to soothe her.

Working with family can be challenging. We are often busy, work long hours, and survive on little sleep and sustenance. However, I can safely say there's no one I'd rather work with than my family. My dad's work ethic inspires me every day and will continue to do so for the rest of my life.

So far, the journey has been wild. We never anticipated the overwhelming success of our humble business. From selling out every week to featuring on TV, in books and in press articles, the community hub we dreamed of has never been more alive. We cherish being part of the canal's rebirth, and witnessing the community making memories at our boat is heartwarming. Knowing that the boat will forever hold a place in people's childhood memories fills us with pride. To us, *The Waltzing Matilda* is more than a business – it's a symbol of community, resilience, and family.

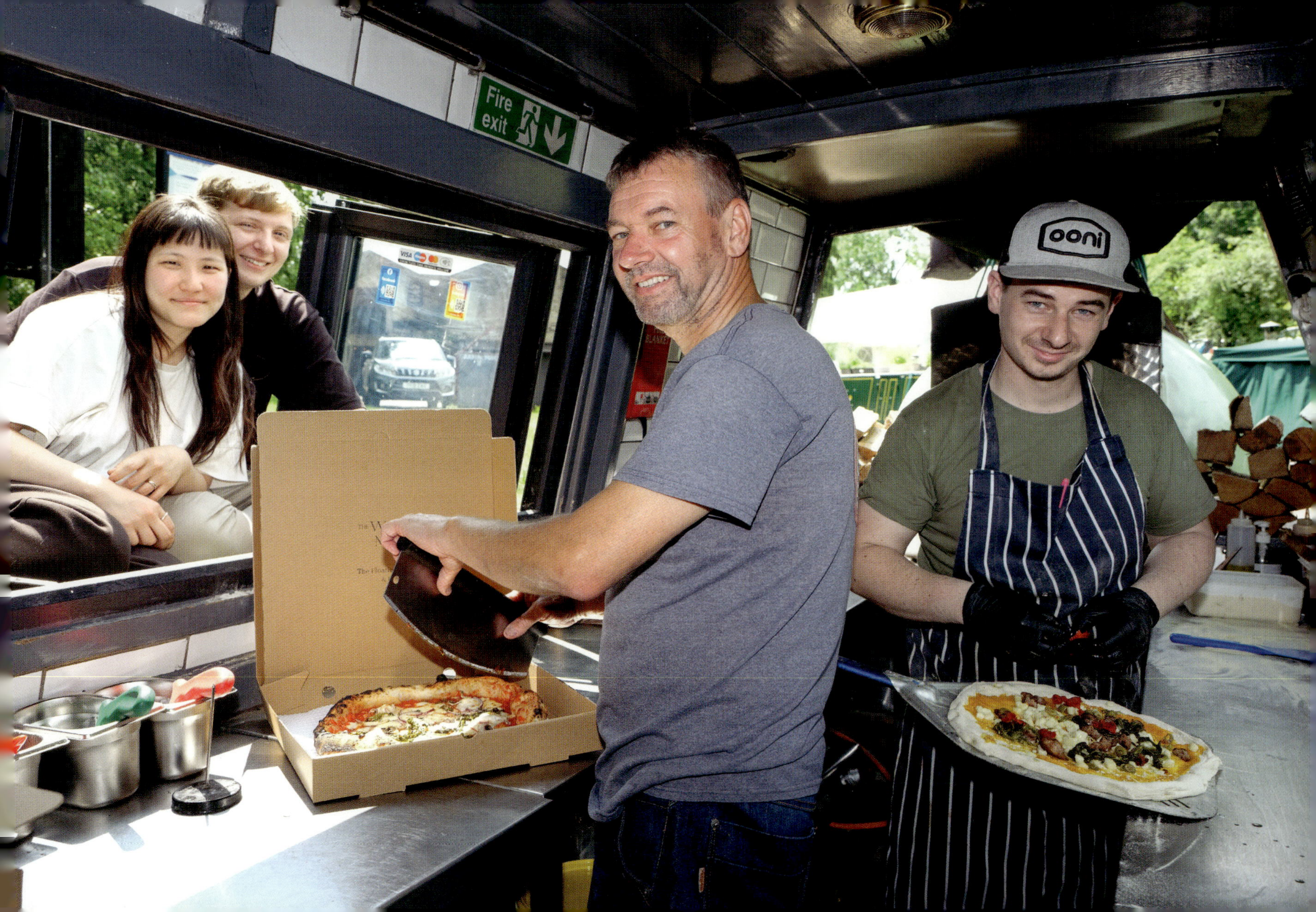

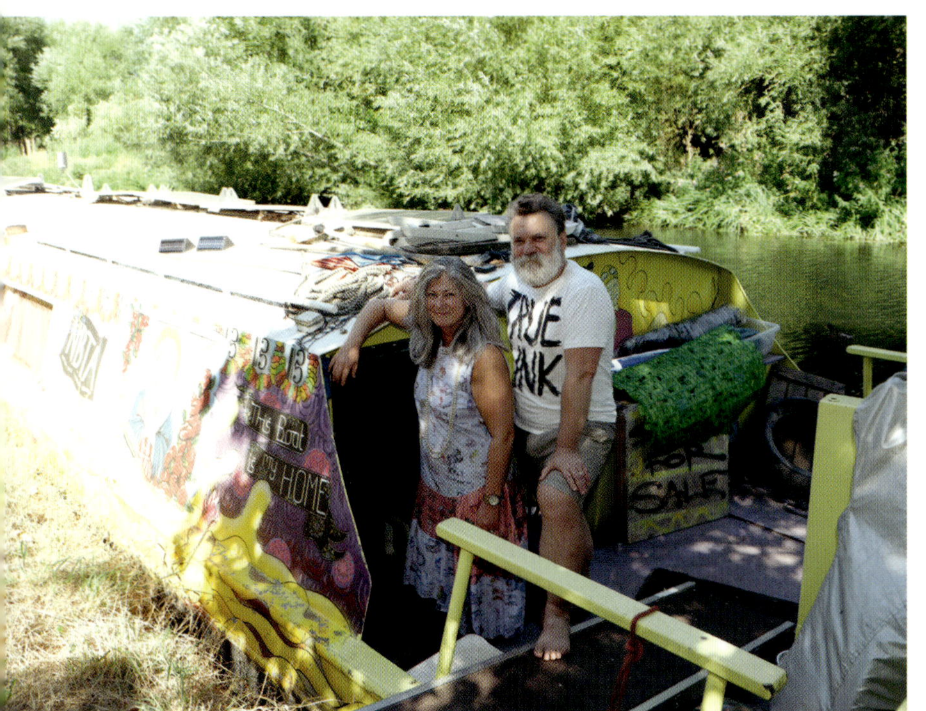

As itinerant boaters, our home is always situated near the public park, wherever there are towpath moorings. At the moment, we are on the Lee Valley Navigation.

We're members of the National Bargee Travellers Association, who campaign continuously and vigorously to save our nomadic way of life. We are marginalised by society – often refused registration with GPs because we don't have a home address.

We are banned from leaving our rubbish in public or towpath bins. We are continuously asked invasive questions by passers-by: 'Do you have a toilet?', 'What do you do with your poo?', 'How can you work when you live on a boat?'.

When land alongside the towpath is sold off for redevelopment, the moorings are frequently concreted over, or changed into private or commercial moorings. We have fewer places to moor up and no permanent home mooring. We feel as if our government is attempting to erase us from the inland waterways.

Boat life is very hard when it's super hot, or in winter when we contend with the rain, ice and strong winds. It has become especially hard since we began to experience the eradication of the public moorings. In the UK, unlike France for example, we have traditionally been able to moor anywhere for a short period. But prohibitive measures are making our travelling lifestyle harder to sustain.

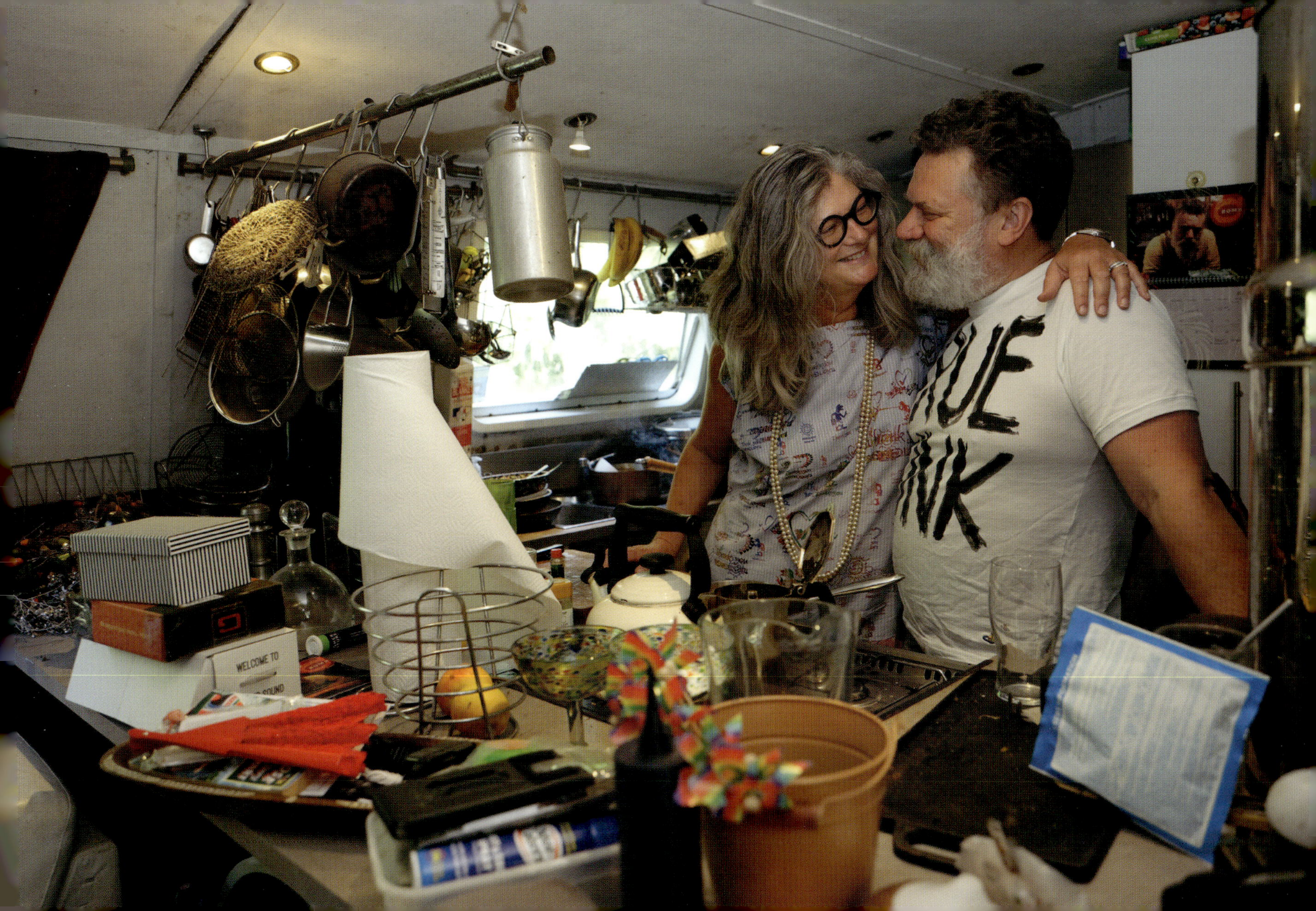

Tim & Sam Biglowe

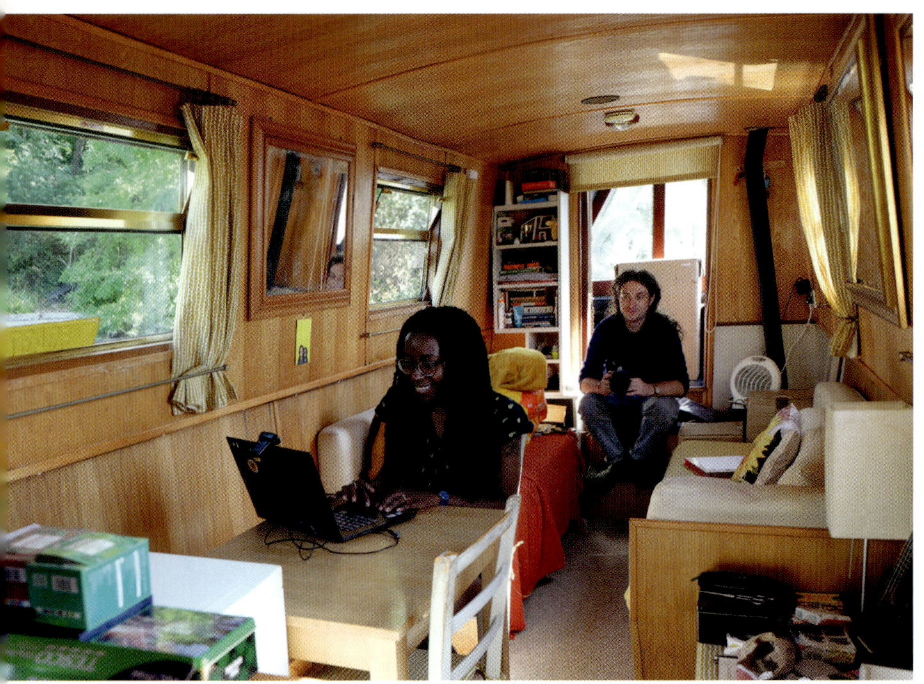

We are Tim and Sam and we have been living on our 53-foot narrowboat, the *Mary L*, since the summer of 2020. During this time, we have travelled on many waterways, including the River Thames and the beautiful Llangollen Canal in North Wales. It's been amazing seeing parts of the country in such a unique way.

A lot has happened since we bought the boat. We may have lived in places far more exotic to us, but this feels like the most adventurous thing we've done yet. It's taken our life in a direction we never thought it would go. We got married in September 2022, so we started our married life as boaters. It all began as a joke but now we really do feel like the new Rosie and Jim.

As a home, we find this boat very comfortable. We love the natural wood interiors and our stove. Moving into a small space wasn't a problem for us. Before the pandemic, we lived in a small studio flat in Chengdu, China.

We are planning to stay on board *Mary L* for a couple more years. After that, who knows?

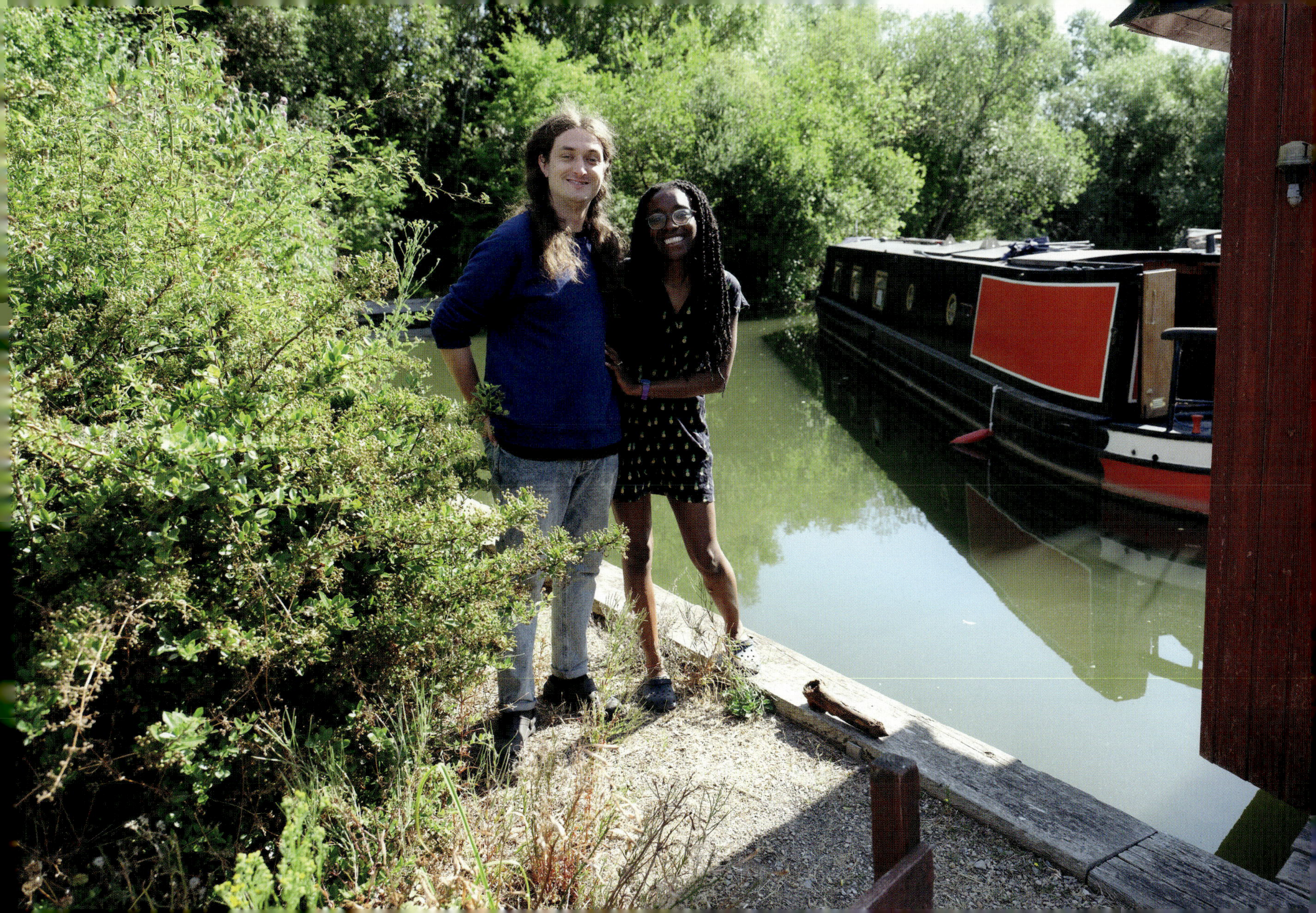

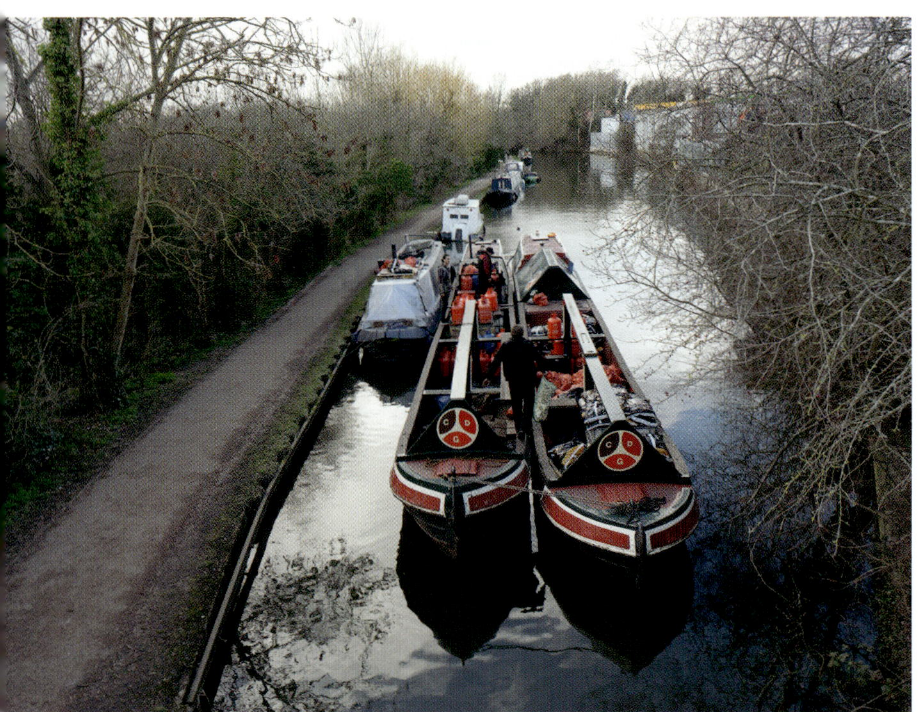

My crew and I are all Polish, and we have been running a delivery service selling coal, diesel, gas and wood on my boats, *Indus* and *Pictor*, for the last seven years. We all have a passion for boats, especially on the canals of London, which has been home to historic coal boats since the Industrial Revolution during the eighteenth century. We deliver along areas of the Grand Union Canal, Regent's Canal, Paddington Arm, Uxbridge to Brentford and Lee and Stort Canals.

We work a pair of traditional working boats. One boat supplies the power and the other is called the 'butty' boat that we pull along – usually breasted up as you can see in the photograph. This gives us more control. Both these boats are full-length narrowboats, which is 72 feet long, the longest that will fit into our locks.

We have a great relationship with our clients, which has built up over time. When clients ring up to order things it can get really hard to find their exact location. They go onto Google maps to send me a 'pin' of their location, but also some of the photographs we get sent bring a smile – neighbours' boats around the vicinity and photographs of trees, flowers, etc., anything to help locate them.

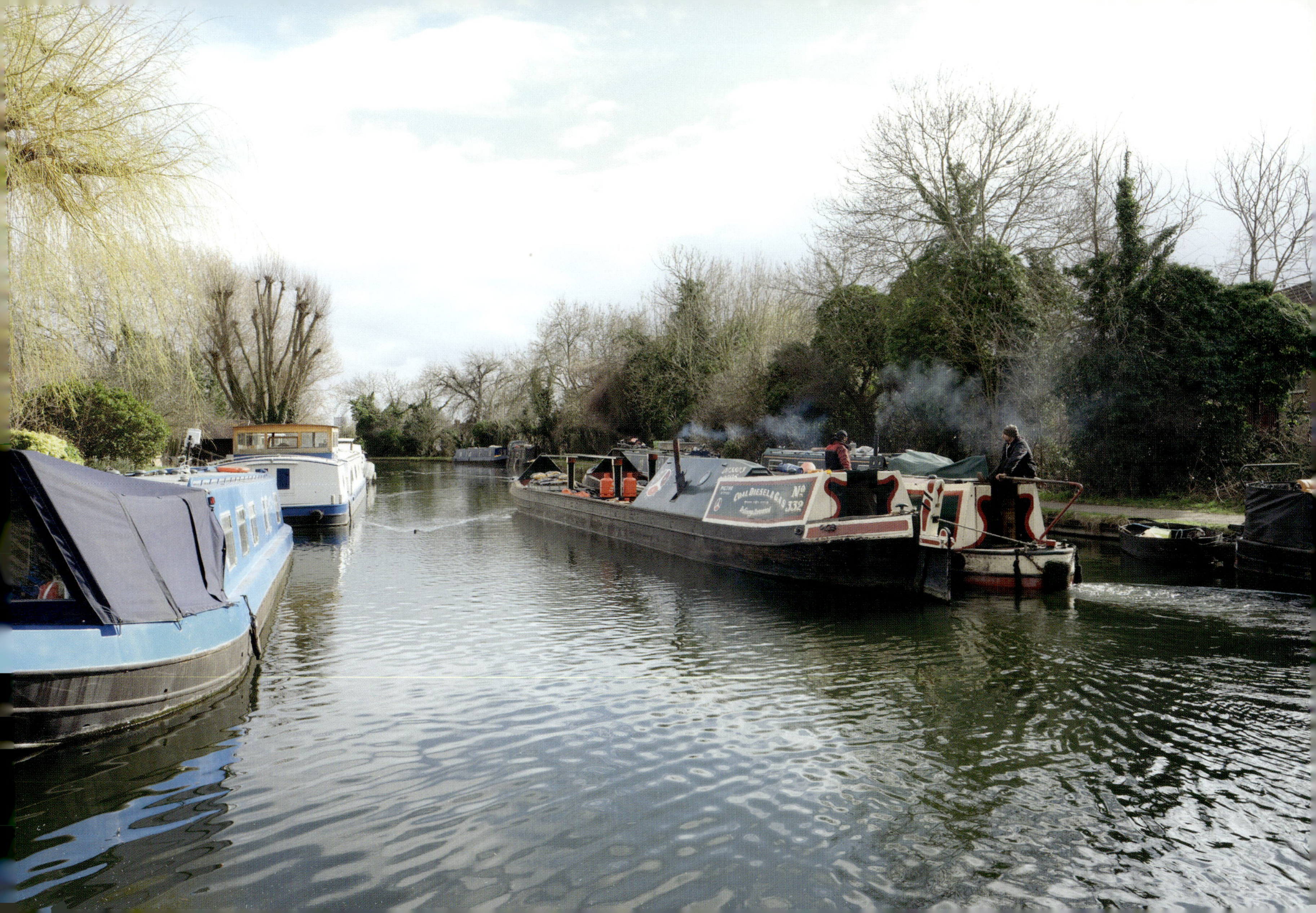

PICTON
COAL DIESEL & GAS No 332

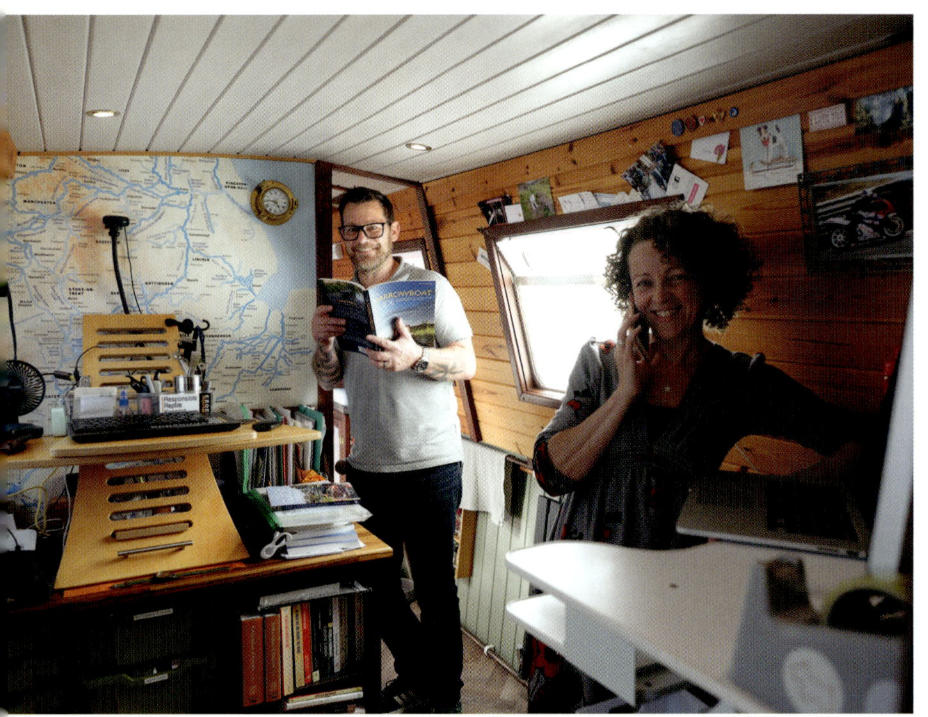

Tony and I met in early 2014. He and his terrier, Puck, had been living aboard *The Watchman* nearly ten years at that point, so they were already seasoned boaters. We lived between his boat and my house for a year or so before deciding to merge our lives fully. I knew that living on a boat is a huge part of what makes Tony the man he is, and, as I'd fallen in love with the freedom and self-sufficiency boat life brings, the decision to make the boat our home was an easy one to make.

We had the boat stretched to make room for me to move aboard. It was originally 50 feet long, but it was cut in half and extended by 11 feet to make it 61 feet. It was quite an expensive process and we could have bought a second 50-foot boat for what it cost, but the stretch option had several advantages. Not only did we get to keep the boat we know and love, but it was also the quickest and most quantifiable way to get what we needed in order to live together full time.

If we'd opted to sell our 50-foot boat we had no way of knowing how long that would take or how much we might get for it. Then we'd face the difficulty of finding a 60–62-foot boat that could accommodate two workstations. I'm a graphic designer and Tony's a writer, and we both work from the office aboard our boat.

Moving aboard was both fun and traumatic. I'd been living in a three-bedroom house with lots of nice furniture and other possessions which would not fit on the boat. This was stuff I'd collected, cared for and owned for decades. And it wasn't just tables and chairs – there were heirlooms and memories too, and now it all had to go. The car boot sales we attended were sometimes heartbreaking.

But I've come to realise that owning lots of stuff is often a hindrance or an inconvenience at least. Possessions are not benign. Each thing you own claims a little piece of your life. You have to spend your hard-earned cash to buy it, then you have to find somewhere to keep it, and you have to care for it, clean it, insure it and possibly replace it when it wears out or gets broken. The things you own somehow end up owning you.

Nowadays I'm pretty much free from such worries, and having nowhere to put the items I might be compelled to buy curtails any urges I have. I look at people I know with attics, garages and storage units full of stuff they never use and I'm glad I don't have that issue in my life now. Living on a boat is very liberating in lots of ways.

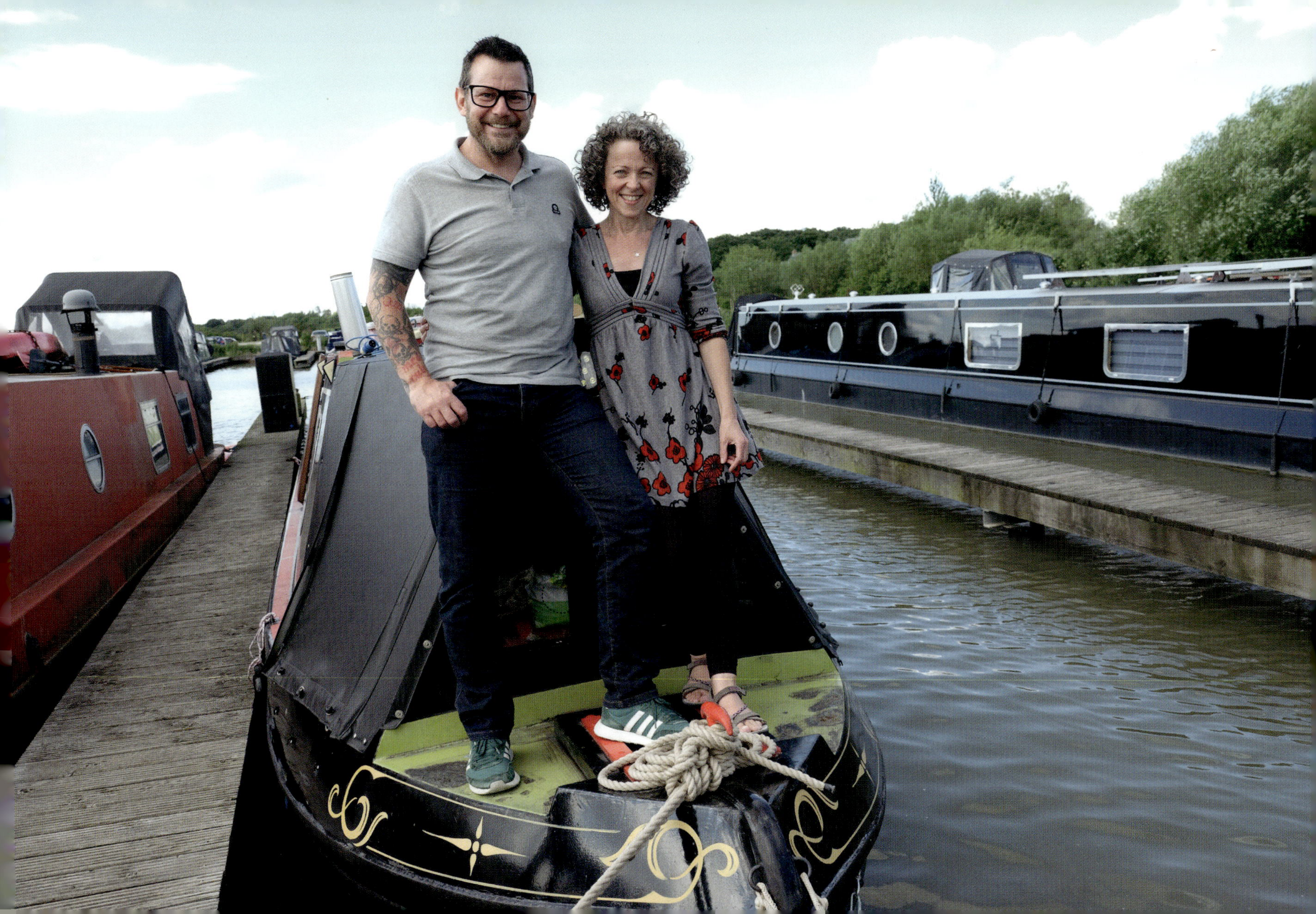

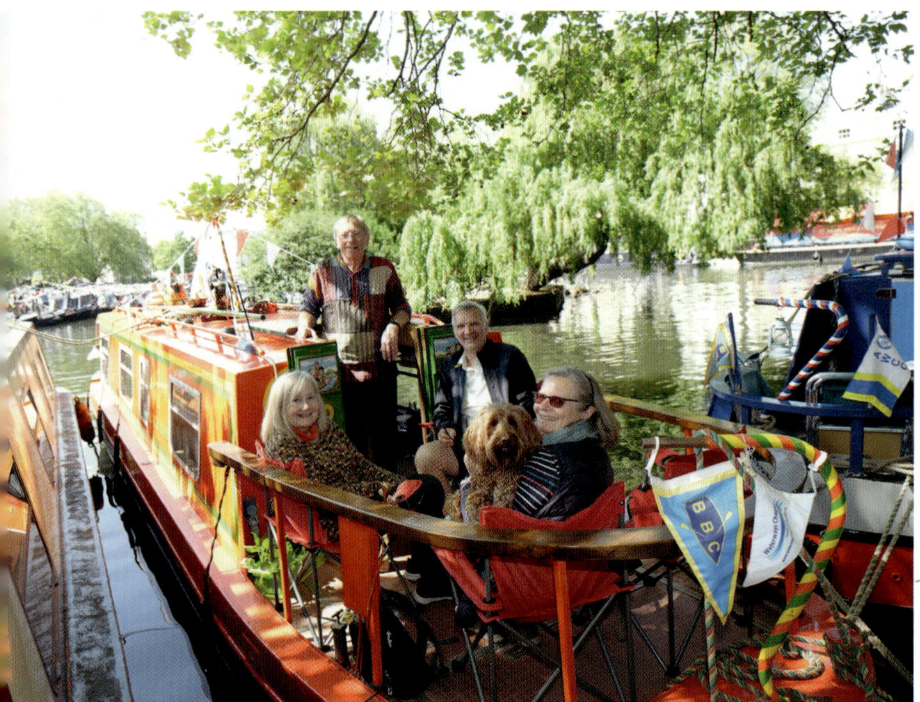

We are Tina and James Osborne – seen here relaxing on our narrowboat at the Little Venice Cavalcade (left and standing in the photo). We were joined by friends Brian Clarke (Commodore of Byfleet Boat Club on the right) and his wife Claire (front centre) with ship's mate, Chilli the dog.

We thoroughly enjoyed travelling up from Surrey and the exhilaration of the tidal Thames. We came to join over 130 colourful decorated narrowboats gathering together from all over the country. By day we meet with friends and enjoy the camaraderie of fellow boaters and watch the entertainment in the evening. We were delighted that another Byfleet Boat Club member won the Illuminated Parade on the Sunday evening – sparkling lights everywhere and wild cheers from the crowd. This is a real family and friends' occasion on the first bank holiday weekend in May each year – not to be missed.